BUSINESS AND LEGAL FORMS

FOR

CRAFTS

TAD CRAWFORD

ALLWORTH PRESS, NEW YORK

Published by Allworth Press, an imprint of Allworth Communications, Inc., 10 East 23rd Street, New York, NY 10010.

Book design by Douglas Design Associates, New York, NY.

Library of Congress Catalog Card Number: 97-72221

ISBN: 1-880559-87-0

Printed in Canada.

Table of Contents

Table of Contents (Continued)

The Success Kit

To create this book of business and legal forms for crafts is a challenge that requires considering the many different types of crafts. Crafts may be produced as a one-of-a-kind work or a limited edition, in which case the legal issues are close to those presented for fine arts such as sculpture and painting, or may be produced in more substantial quantities, in which case the legal issues are like those affecting manufactured goods. The forms in this book should help all artists creating crafts, although some forms will be more relevant than others depending on the type of craft and quantities of work produced. Throughout the text and business forms the creator of craftwork is referred to as an artist. This seems preferable to the outdated "craftsman," cumbersome "craftsperson," archaic sounding "artisan," overly inclusive "home worker," or the awkward amalgams of "crafts artist" or "craftworker."

Attaining the knowledge of good business practices and implementing their use is an important step toward success for any professional, including the professional artist creating craftworks. The forms contained in this book deal with the most important business transactions that an artist is likely to undertake. At the back of the book is an extra copy of each form on 8 1/2-by-11-inch sheets and perforated, so the artist can remove them from the book and make copies for use in his or her own business. In addition, the forms are included on CD-ROM to make customization easier. The fact that the forms are designed for use and that they favor the artist give them a unique value.

Understanding the business concepts behind the forms is as important as using them. By knowing why a certain provision has been included and what it accomplishes, the artist is able to negotiate when faced with someone else's business form. The artist knows what is and is not desirable. The negotiation checklists offer a map for the negotiation of any form.

All forms, whether the artist's or someone else's, can be changed. Before using these forms, the artist should consider reviewing them with his or her attorney. This provides the opportunity to learn whether local or state laws may make it worthwhile to modify any of the provisions. For example, would it be wise to include a provision for arbitration of disputes, or are the local courts speedy and inexpensive, making an arbitration provision unnecessary?

The forms must be filled out, which means that the blanks in each form must be completed. Beyond this, however, the artist can always delete or add provisions on any form. Deletions or additions to a form are usually initialed in the margin by both parties. It is also a good practice to have each party initial each page of the contract, except the page on which the parties sign.

The artist must ascertain that the person signing the contract has authority to do so. If the artist is dealing with a company, the company's name should be included, as well as the name of the individual authorized to sign the contract and the title of that individual. If it isn't clear who will sign or if that person has no title, the words "Authorized Signatory" can be used instead of a title.

If the artist will not be meeting with the other party to sign the contract, it would be wise to have that party sign the forms first. After the artist gets back the two copies of the form, they can be signed and one copy returned to the other party. As discussed in more detail under letter contracts, this has the advantage of not leaving it up to the other party to decide whether to sign and thus make a binding contract.

If additional provisions that won't fit on the contract forms should be added, simply include a provision stating, "This contract is subject to the provisions of the rider attached hereto and made a part hereof." The rider is simply another piece of paper which would be headed, "Rider to the contract between _____ and _____, dated the ____ day of _____, 19____." The additional provisions are put on this sheet and both parties sign it.

Contracts and Negotiation

Most of the forms in this book are contracts. A contract is an agreement that creates legally enforceable obligations between two or more parties. In making a contract, each party gives something of value to the other party. This is called the exchange of consideration. Consideration can take many forms, including the giving of money or an artwork or the promise to create an artwork or pay for an artwork in the future.

Contracts require negotiation. The forms in this book are favorable to the artist. When they are presented to a buyer, store, or even a museum, changes may be requested. This book's explanation of the use of each form should help the artist evaluate changes either party may want to make in any of the forms. The negotiation checklists should also clarify what changes would be desirable in forms presented to the artist.

Keep in mind that negotiation need not be adversarial. Certainly the artist and the other party may disagree on some points, but the basic transaction is something that both want. The buyer wants to own the artwork, the store wants to sell it, and the museum wants to display it. This larger framework of agreement must be kept in mind at all times when negotiating. Of course, the artist must also know which points are nonnegotiable and be prepared to walk away from a deal if satisfaction cannot be had on these points.

When both parties have something valuable to offer each other, it should be possible for each side to come away from the negotiation feeling that they have won. Win-win negotiation requires each side to make certain the basic needs of both are met so that the result is fair. The artist cannot negotiate for the other side, but a wise negotiation strategy must allow the other side to meet their vital needs within a larger context that also allows the artist to obtain what he or she must have.

It is a necessity to evaluate negotiating goals and strategy before conducting any negotiations. The artist should write down what must be achieved and what can be conceded or modified. The artist should try to imagine how the shape of the contract will affect the future business relationship with the other party. Will it probably lead to success for both sides and more business or will it fail to achieve what one side or the other desires?

When negotiating, the artist should keep written notes close at hand concerning goals and strategy. Notes should be kept on the negotiations too, since many conversations may be necessary before final agreement is reached. At certain points the artist should compare what the negotiations are achieving with the original goals. This will help evaluate whether the artist is conducting the negotiations according to plan.

Most negotiations are done over the telephone. This makes the telephone a tool to be used wisely. The artist should decide when to speak with the other party. Before calling, it is important to review the notes and be familiar with the points to be negotiated. If the artist wants the other party to call, the file should be kept close at hand so that there is no question as to where the negotiations stand when the call comes. If the artist is unprepared to negotiate when the other party calls, the best course is to call back. Negotiation demands the fullest attention and readiness.

Oral Contracts

Although all the forms in this book are written, the question of oral contracts should be addressed. There are certain contracts that must be written, such as a contract for services that will take more than one year to perform, a contract to transfer an exclusive right of copyright (an exclusive right means that no one else can do what the person receiving that right of copyright can do), or, in many cases, a contract for the sale of goods worth more than $500. So—without delving into the full complexity of this subject—certain contracts can be oral. If the artist is faced with a breached oral contract, an attorney certainly should be consulted for advice. The artist should not give up simply because the contract was oral.

However, while some oral contracts are valid,

a written contract is always best. Even people with the most scrupulous intentions do not always remember exactly what was said or whether a particular point was covered. Disputes, and litigation, are far more likely when a contract is oral rather than written. That likelihood is another reason to make the use of written forms, like those in this book, an integral part of the business practices of any artist whose work may someday have value.

Letter Contracts

If the artist feels that sending a well-drafted form will be daunting to the other party, the more informal approach of a letter, signed by both parties, may be adopted. In this case, the forms in this book will serve as valuable checklists for the content and negotiation of the letter contract. The last paragraph of the letter would read, "If the foregoing meets with your approval, please sign both copies of this letter beneath the words AGREED TO to make this a binding contract between us." At the bottom of the letter would be the words AGREED TO with the name of the other party so he or she can sign. Again, if the other party is a company, the company name, as well as the name of the authorized signatory and that individual's title, would be placed beneath the words AGREED TO. This would appear as follows:

AGREED TO:

XYZ Corporation

By_____
Alice Hall, Vice President

Two copies of this letter are sent to the other party, who is instructed to sign both copies and return one copy for the artist to keep. To be cautious, the artist can send the letters unsigned and ask the other party to sign and return both copies, at which time the artist will sign and return one copy to the other party. This gives the other party an opportunity to review the final draft, but avoids a situation in which the other party may choose to delay signing, thereby preventing the artist from offering a similar contract to anyone else because the first contract still may be signed.

For example, if a wholesaler wanted to wait and see if it could resell jewelry it was contracting to buy, it might hold the contract and only sign after it knew it could make the resale. If the resale did not come through, the wholesaler might not sign the contract and the deal would be off. The artist can avoid this by being the final signatory, by insisting that both parties meet to sign, or by stating in the letter a deadline by which the other party must sign. If such a situation ever arises, it should be remembered that any offer to enter into a contract can always be revoked up until the time that the contract is actually entered into.

Standard Provisions

The contracts in this book contain a number of standard provisions, called "boilerplate" by lawyers. These provisions are important, although they will not seem as exciting as the provisions that relate more directly to the artist and the artwork. Since these provisions can be used in almost every contract and appear in a number of the contracts in this book, an explanation of each of the provisions is given here.

Amendment. Any amendment of this Agreement must be in writing and signed by both parties.

This guarantees that any changes the parties want will be made in writing. It avoids the possibility of one party relying on oral changes to the agreement. Courts will rarely change a written contract based on testimony that there was an oral amendment of the contract.

Arbitration. All disputes arising under this Agreement shall be submitted to binding arbitration before _____ in the following location _____ and shall be settled in accordance with the rules of the American Arbitration Association. Judgment upon the arbitration award may be entered in any court having jurisdiction thereof. Notwithstanding the foregoing, either party may refuse to arbitrate when the dispute is for a sum of less than $_____.

Arbitration can offer a quicker and less expensive way to settle disputes than litigation. However, the artist would be wise to consult a local attorney and make sure that this is advisable in the jurisdiction where the lawsuit would be likely to take place. The arbitrator could be the American Arbitration Association or some other person or group that both parties trust. The artist would also want the arbitration to take place where he or she is located. If small claims court is easy to use in the jurisdiction where the artist would have to sue, it might be best to have the right not to arbitrate if the disputed amount is small enough to be brought into the small claims court. In this case, the artist would put the maximum amount that can be sued for in small claims court in the space at the end of the paragraph.

Assignment. This Agreement shall not be assigned by either party hereto, provided that the Artist shall have the right to assign monies due to the Artist hereunder.

By not allowing the assignment of a contract, both parties can have greater confidence that the stated transactions will be between the original parties. Of course, a company may be purchased by new owners. If the artist only wanted to do business with the people who owned the company when the contract was entered into, change of ownership might be stated as a ground for termination in the contract. On the other hand, money is impersonal and there is no reason why the artist should not be able to assign the right to receive money.

Bankruptcy or Insolvency. If the Gallery should become insolvent or if a petition in bankruptcy is filed against the Gallery or a Receiver or Trustee is appointed for any of the

Gallery's assets or property, or if a lien or attachment is obtained against any of the Gallery's assets, this Agreement shall immediately terminate and the Gallery shall return to the Artist all of the Artist's work that is in the Gallery's possession.

This provision seeks to protect the artist against creditors of the gallery who might use the artist's work or proceeds from that work to satisfy claims they have against the gallery itself. Because a provision of this kind does not protect the artist completely, many states have enacted special consignment laws protecting artists and their work. However, the definition of "art" in these laws will exclude many types of crafts, so the artist should check the law in his or her own state. The full texts of all of the state consignment laws appear in *The Artist-Gallery Partnership* by Tad Crawford and Susan Mellon (Allworth Press).

Complete Understanding. This Agreement constitutes the entire and complete understanding between the parties hereto, and no obligation, undertaking, warranty, representation, or covenant of any kind or nature has been made by either party to the other to induce the making of this Agreement, except as is expressly set forth herein.

This provision is intended to prevent either party from later claiming that any promises or obligations exist except those shown in the written contract. A shorter way to say this is, "This Agreement constitutes the entire understanding between the parties hereto."

Cumulative Rights. All rights, remedies, obligations, undertakings, warranties, representations, and covenants contained herein shall be cumulative and none of them shall be in limitation of any other right, remedy, obligation, undertaking, warranty, representation, or covenant of either party.

This means that a benefit or obligation under one provision will not be made less because of a different benefit or obligation under another provision.

Death or Disability. In the event of the Artist's death, or an incapacity of the Artist making completion of the Work impossible, this Agreement shall terminate.

A provision of this kind leaves a great deal to be determined. Will payments already made be kept by the artist or the artist's estate? And who will own the work at whatever stage of completion has been reached? Will either the commissioning party or the artist's estate have the right or obligation to complete the work? If the commissioning party completes it, who will own the copyright? These and related issues should be resolved when the contract is negotiated.

Force Majeure. If either party hereto is unable to perform any of its obligations hereunder by reason of fire or other casualty, strike, act or order of a public authority, act of God, or other cause beyond the control of such party, then such party shall be excused from such performance during the pendancy of such cause. In the event such inability to perform shall continue longer than ____ days, either party may terminate this Agreement by giving written notice to the other party.

This provision covers events beyond the control of the parties, such as a tidal wave or a war. Certainly the time to perform the contract should be extended in such an event. There may be an issue as to how long an extension should be allowed. Also, if work has commenced and some payments have been made, the contract should cover what happens in the event of termination. Must the payments be returned? And who owns the partially completed work?

Governing Law. This Agreement shall be governed by the laws of the State of_____.
Usually the artist would want the laws of his

or her own state to govern the agreement. However, laws vary from state to state. A number of states have enacted laws favoring artists, especially in the area of consignments of art to a gallery. If the artist's own state lacks this law, it might be preferable to have a gallery contract governed by the law of a different state that has such a consignment law. Again, *The Artist-Gallery Partnership* can be referred to in order to determine the coverage of the law of a particular state.

Indemnify and Hold Harmless. The Purchaser agrees to indemnify and hold harmless the Artist from any and all claims, demands, payments, expenses, legal fees, or other costs in relation to obligations for materials or services incurred by the Purchaser.

This provision protects one party against damaging actions that may have been taken by the other party. Often, one party will warrant that something is true and then indemnify and hold the other party harmless in the event that it is not true. For example, an artist selling a limited edition to a dealer might warrant the size of the edition and then indemnify the dealer in the event the artist has not given accurate information. If the dealer were sued because of the breach of warranty, the artist would be liable to the dealer.

Liquidated Damages. In the event of the failure of XYZ Corporation to deliver by the due date, the agreed upon damages shall be $ _____ for each day after the due date until delivery takes place, provided the amount of damages shall not exceed $_____.

Liquidated damages are an attempt to anticipate in the contract what damages will be caused by a breach of the contract. Such liquidated damages must be reasonable. If they are not, they will be considered a penalty and held to be unenforceable.

Modification. This Agreement cannot be

changed, modified, or discharged, in whole or in part, except by an instrument in writing, signed by the party against whom enforcement of any change, modification, or discharge is sought.

This requires that a change in the contract must be written and signed by the party against whom the change will be enforced. It should be compared with the provision for amendments that requires any modification to be in writing and signed by both parties. At the least, however, this provision explicitly avoids the claim that an oral modification has been made of a written contract. Almost invariably, courts will give greater weight to a written document than to testimony about oral agreements.

Notices and Changes of Address. All notices shall be sent to the Artist at the following address:_____ and to the Purchaser at the following address: _____. Each party shall be given written notification of any change of address prior to the date of said change.

Contracts often require the giving of notice. This provision facilitates giving notice by providing correct addresses and requiring notification of any change of address.

Privacy. The Purchaser gives to the Artist permission to use the Purchaser's name, picture, portrait, and photograph, in all forms and media and in all manners, including but not limited to exhibition, display, advertising, trade, and editorial uses, without violation of the Purchaser's rights of privacy or any other personal or proprietary rights the Purchaser may possess in connection with the reproduction and sale of the artwork.

This provision would be used if the purchaser were also going to be the subject for a portrait. While the purchaser would own the portrait, the artist might have the right to sell reproductions of it or use it for promotional purposes. A similar release of privacy might be requested by a gallery, store, or manufacturer which planned to use the artist's name or photograph in advertising. In such a situation, the artist would want to be certain that the promotion would be tasteful.

Successors and Assigns. This Agreement shall be binding upon and inure to the benefit of the parties hereto and their respective heirs, executors, administrators, successors, and assigns.

This makes the contract binding on anyone who takes the place of one of the parties, whether due to death or simply to an assignment of the contract. With commissioned works, death or disability of the artist raises complex questions about completion and ownership of the work. The issues must be resolved in the contract. Note that the standard provision on assignment in fact does not allow assignment, but that provision could always be modified in the original contract or by a later written, signed amendment to the contract.

Time. Time is of the essence.

This requires both parties to perform to the exact time commitments they have made or be in breach of the contract. It is not a wise provision for the artist to agree to, since being a few days late in performance could cause the loss of benefits under the contract.

Waivers. No waiver by either party of any of the terms or conditions of this Agreement shall be deemed or construed to be a waiver of such term or condition for the future, or of any subsequent breach thereof.

This means that if one party waives a right under the contract, such as the right to an accounting from a gallery, that party has not waived the right forever and can demand that the other party perform at the next opportunity.

So the artist who allowed a gallery not to account would still have the right to demand an accounting. And if the gallery breached the contract in some other way, such as not paying money due, the fact that the artist allowed this once would not prevent the artist from suing for such a breach in the future.

Warranties. The Artist hereby warrants the following:

A warranty is something the other party can rely on to be true. If the artist states a fact that is a basic reason for the other party's entry into the contract, then that fact is a warranty and must be true. For example, stating that a fine print is in an edition of 60 copies is a warranty, since the print will be worth far less if the edition is actually 120 copies. So a warranty could read, "The Artist warrants this work is one of a limited edition of ____ copies, numbered as follows: _____."

Volunteer Lawyers for the Arts

There are now volunteer lawyers for the arts across the nation. These groups provide free assistance to artists below certain income levels and can be a valuable source of information. If, for example, it is not clear whether a certain law to benefit artists (such as a gallery consignment law) has been enacted in a state, the artist should be able to find out by calling the closest volunteer lawyers for the arts group. To find the location of that group, one of the groups listed here can be contacted:

California: California Lawyers for the Arts, Fort Mason Center, Building C, Room 255, San Francisco, California 94123, (415) 775-7200; and 1549 11th Street, Suite 200, Santa Monica, California 90401, (310) 395-8893.

Illinois: Lawyers for the Creative Arts, 213 West Institute Place, Suite 411, Chicago, Illinois 60610, (312) 944-2787.

New York: Volunteer Lawyers for the Arts, 1 East 53rd Street, New York, New York 10022, (212) 319-2787.

A helpful handbook covering all the legal issues which artists face is *Legal Guide for the Visual Artist* by Tad Crawford (Allworth Press).

Having reviewed the basics of dealing with business and legal forms, the next step is to move on to the forms themselves and the negotiation checklists that will make the forms most useful.

Using the Negotiation Checklists

These checklists focus on the key points for negotiation. When a point is covered in the contract already, the appropriate paragraph is indicated in the checklist. These checklists are also valuable to use when reviewing a form given to the artist by someone else.

If the artist will provide the form, the boxes can be checked to be certain all important points are covered. If the artist is reviewing someone else's form, checking the boxes will show which points are covered and which points may have to be added. By using the paragraph numbers in the checklist, the other party's provision can be quickly compared with a provision that would favor the artist. Each checklist for a contract concludes with the suggestion that the standard provisions be reviewed to see if any should be added to those the form provides.

Of course, the artist does not have to include every point on the checklist in a contract, but being aware of these points will be helpful. After the checklists, the exact wording is provided for some of the more important provisions that might be added to the form. Starting with Form 1, the explanations go through each form in sequence.

Contract of Sale
and Basic Contract of Sale

Form 1 and Form 2 are simple contracts for the sale of a work. Form 3 is also a contract to sell a work, but it has provisions which connect the artist to the work after sale. With either Form 1, Form 2, or Form 3, the artist may wish to use Form 4 or Form 5, invoices for the sale, to make his or her records complete.

Form 1 and Form 3 are most appropriate for sales of one-of-a-kind or limited edition works. If the artist is selling works created in quantity, a far simpler form might be used, such as Form 2, which is titled Basic Contract of Sale. The Basic Contract of Sale allows the entry of information when many items are likely to be ordered or when these items are likely to be ordered in quantity. Provisions from Form 1 or Form 3 could be added to the Basic Contract of Sale as necessary. Form 2 can be used with customers buying directly or with wholesalers who are buying for resale. To avoid confusion, it is also possible to create two versions of Form 2. One would be for consumers and not show discounts, the other would be for trade accounts buying for resale and would show discounts and payment terms (such as 30 days after receipt of merchandise). If the trade accounts are taking inventory on consignment, refer to Forms 9, 10, and 11. The instructions for filling in the forms cover both Form 1 and Form 2. The negotiation checklist is based on the provisions in Form 1, but the same concepts apply to Form 2 which can be modified if necessary.

Filling in the Forms

For Form 1, in the Preamble fill in the date and the names and addresses. In Paragraph 1 describe the work. In Pararaph 3 fill in the price. In Paragraph 5 check the box to indicate who will arrange for delivery, and fill in the location and time for delivery and who will pay the expenses for the delivery. In Paragraph 6 fill in when the risk of loss will pass from the artist to the purhaser. In Paragraph 7 fill in the date for the copyright notice. In Paragraph 8 fill in the state whose laws will govern the sale. Both parties should then sign.

For Form 2 give the purchaser's name and address as well as the ship to address if different from the purchaser's. Fill in the date, the purchaser's account number if a repeat customer, the sales rep if any, the order number, the method of shipment, and the date of shipment. Make certain all the ordering information is correctly included. In the case of trade accounts, such as retailers or wholesalers who receive a discount, indicate the amount of the discount and the unit price. Then total the amounts, add shipping and sales tax, subtract payments received, and show the balance due. If a credit card is being used, fill in the credit card information. Have both the purchaser and artist sign the contract if practicable, although the form will serve as a sale receipt even if unsigned.

Negotiation Checklist

❏ Describe the work. (Paragraph 1)

❏ Make certain title does not pass to the purchaser until the artist has been paid in full. (Paragraph 2)

❏ Agree on the price and the payment of sales tax or any other transfer tax. (Paragraph 3)

❏ Agree on the payment of other charges, such as those for framing or installation. If the artist must travel to install the work, agree on a fee or reimbursement for the travel expenses.

❏ Agree on the time for payment. (Paragraph 4)

❏ If the sale is an installment sale, obtain the right to a security interest in the work (see the discussion under other provisions for Form 1).

❏ Specify the manner of payment, such as by personal check, certified check, cash, credit card, or money order.

❏ Specify the currency for payment. This might be necessary if the purchaser is foreign or if the artist is selling work abroad.

❏ Agree on who arranges and pays for delivery, if the purchaser can't simply take the work when it is purchased. (Paragraph 5)

❏ Specify a time for delivery. (Paragraph 5)

❏ Agree when the risk of loss or damage to the work passes from the artist to the purchaser. This risk usually passes on delivery, but the timing can be altered by contract. Keep in mind that if the purchaser buys the work but leaves it with the artist, the risk of loss will not pass to the purchaser until the purchaser could reasonably have been expected to pick up the work. The artist can avoid the uncertainty of this by providing that the risk of loss passes to the purchaser at the time of purchase, regardless of whether the work has been delivered. (Paragraph 6)

❏ Agree whether the work will be insured and, if so, by whom. (Paragraph 6 partially covers this.)

❏ Reserve all copyrights to the artist. (Paragraph 7)

❏ Require copyright notice in the artist's name for any reproductions approved by the artist. (Paragraph 7)

❏ Review the standard provisions in the introductory pages and compare with Paragraph 8.

Other Provisions that can be added to Form 1:

❏ Installment sale. If the artist wants to sell the work on an installment basis, the following provision could be added:

Installment Sale. The price shall be paid in _____ installments, payable $_____ on _____, 19____, $_____ on _____, 19____, and $_____ on _____, 19_____.

❏ Security interest. If the artist allows the buyer to purchase the work on an installment basis, the artist may want the right to have a security interest in the work until payment is made in full. This means that the artist would have a right to the work ahead of any of the purchaser's creditors. This provision might be used with Form 1 or Form 2 in any situation when payment is not made in full at the time of purchase and is for a significant amount. Such a provision would state:

Security Interest. Purchaser grants to the Artist, and the Artist hereby reserves, a security interest under the Uniform Commercial Code in the Work and any proceeds derived therefrom until payment is made in full to the Artist. Purchaser agrees to execute and deliver to the Artist, in the form requested by the Artist, a financing statement and such other documents which the Artist may require to perfect a security interest in the Work. The Purchaser agrees not to transfer, pledge, or encumber the Work until payment has been made in full, nor to incur any charges or obligations in connection therewith for which the Artist may be liable.

To perfect a security interest, which means the formalities have been completed so the artist can take precedence over the purchaser's creditors, requires the filing of Uniform Commercial Code Form 1 with the secretary of state or local agency for filing such as the county clerk. Since the purchaser will usually have to sign what is filed, the contractual provision requires the purchaser to provide whatever documents the artist may need. If large sums are involved or the purchaser's finances are questionable, these documents might be required at the time of signing the contract of sale.

A number of other provisions can be added to Form 1. In general, these provisions govern the relationship of the artist to the work after the sale. Because these provisions are innovative and the artist may wish to use some and not others, Form 3 adds these provisions to the basic provisions contained in Form 1. Before using Form 1, Form 3 should also be reviewed.

Additional provision for Form 2:

❏ Refunds. While Form 2 can be modified by adding provisions from Form 1 and Form 3, a form like Form 2 would usually be kept quite simple. One typical addition might be the refund policy, since this both reassures the customer and places limitations on the artist's obligation to make refunds. The time and manner of payment of the refund—for example, whether immediately in cash or within a certain time period by check—may depend on whether the sale was from a retail location or by direct mail. Of course, the artist may feel the refund policy shown here is too generous and modify it according to his or her particular business exigencies.

Refunds. The purchaser may return any purchase in its original condition within __ days of purchase for a full refund. Shipping costs can only be refunded if the return is a result of our error. All refund requests must be accompanied by the sales check and the refund will be paid as follows_____.

Contract of Sale

AGREEMENT made as of the _____ day of _____, 19_____, between _____ (hereinafter referred to as the "Artist"), located at _____ _____, and _____ (hereinafter referred to as the "Collector"), located at _____, with respect to the sale of an artwork (hereinafter referred to as the "Work").

WHEREAS, the Artist has created the Work and has full right, title, and interest therein; and

WHEREAS, the Artist wishes to sell the Work; and

WHEREAS, the Collector has viewed the Work and wishes to purchase it;

NOW, THEREFORE, in consideration of the foregoing premises and the mutual covenants hereinafter set forth and other valuable considerations, the parties hereto agree as follows:

1. **Description of Work.** The Artist describes the Work as follows:

   Title _____

   Medium _____

   Size _____

   Framing or mounting _____

   Year of creation _____

   Signed by Artist ❑ Yes   ❑ No

   If the Work is part of a limited edition, indicate the method of production _____; the size of the edition_____; how many multiples are signed_____; how many are unsigned_____; how many are numbered_____; how many are unnumbered_____; how many proofs exist_____; the quantity of any prior editions_____; and whether the master image has been cancelled or destroyed ❑ yes   ❑ no.

2. **Sale.** The Artist hereby agrees to sell the Work to the Collector. Title shall pass to the Collector at such time as full payment is received by the Artist pursuant to Paragraph 4 hereof.

3. **Price.** The Collector agrees to purchase the Work for the agreed upon price of $_____, and shall also pay any applicable sales or transfer taxes.

4. **Payment.** Payment shall be made in full upon the signing of this Agreement.

5. **Delivery.** The ❑ Artist ❑ Collector shall arrange for delivery to the following location: _____ _____ no later than _____, 19 _____. The expenses of delivery (including, but not limited to, insurance and transportation) shall be paid by _____.

6. **Risk of Loss and Insurance.** The risk of loss or damage to the Work and the provision of any insurance to cover such loss or damage shall be the responsibility of the Collector from the time of

   _____.

7. **Copyright and Reproduction.** The Artist reserves all reproduction rights, including the right to claim statutory copyright, in the Work. The Work may not be photographed, sketched, painted, or reproduced in any manner whatsoever without the express, written consent of the Artist. All approved reproductions shall bear the following copyright notice: © by (Artist's name) 19_____.

8. **Miscellany.** This Agreement shall be binding upon the parties hereto, their heirs, successors, assigns, and personal representatives. This Agreement constitutes the entire understanding between the parties. Its terms can be modified only by an instrument in writing signed by both parties. A waiver of any breach of any of the provisions of this Agreement shall not be construed as a continuing waiver of other breaches of the same or other provisions hereof. This Agreement shall be governed by the laws of the State of _____.

IN WITNESS WHEREOF, the parties hereto have signed this Agreement as of the date first set forth above.

Artist _____   Collector _____

Basic Contract of Sale

Artist's Letterhead

Purchaser_____   Date_____

Address_____   Account Number_____

_____   Sales Rep_____

Ship to_____   Order Number_____

Address_____   Ship via_____

_____   Date shipped_____

All customers must pay in full at the time of purchase, except for credit-verified trade accounts. If purchaser is such a trade account, payment in full is due within ___ days of receipt of merchandise.

Item Number	Description	Quantity Ordered	Quantity Shipped	Back Ordered	Retail Price	Discount	Unit Price	Amount

	Subtotal _____
Authorization if paying by credit card	Shipping & Handling _____
Card_____	Sales tax _____
Number_____	Payment received _____
Expiration_____	**Balance due** _____

Purchaser_____   Artist_____

Contract of Sale with Moral Rights and Resale Royalty Rights

This contract provides for the artist to have a continuing relationship to the work after the sale. Copyright, of course, implies a continuing relationship through control of the right to reproduce the work. However, Form 3 seeks to give the artist a continuing relationship to the physical work itself which is now owned by the collector.

Several of the provisions relate to moral rights, which include the right to be acknowledged as the creator of the work and to have the integrity of the work protected against alteration. Unfortunately, the Visual Artists Rights Act, which took effect on June 1, 1991, has narrow coverage. It defines a work of visual art as "a painting, drawing, print or sculpture." It protects only unique work or signed, limited editions of two hundred or fewer copies of a sculpture, print, or photograph. This means that many disciplines of the crafts will not find coverage under the Visual Artists Rights Act. So the artist who wishes to gain such protections must do so by contract, using the types of provisions detailed in Form 3.

The provision for the artist to share in the proceeds if the collector resells at a profit reflects the California art resale proceeds law, which itself was inspired by foreign laws such as the French *droit de suite*.

Other provisions include nondestruction of the work, the right of the artist to borrow the work for exhibition, and the right of the artist to be involved in any restoration of the work. The form is similar to Form 1 and the negotiation checklist includes the issues raised in Form 1.

Filling in the Form

In the Preamble fill in the date and the names and addresses. In Paragraph 1 describe the work. In Pararaph 3 fill in the price. In Paragraph 5 check the box to indicate who will arrange for delivery, and fill in the location and time for delivery and who will pay the expenses for the delivery. In Paragraph 6 fill in when the risk of loss will pass from the artist to the collector. In Paragraph 7 fill in the date for the copyright notice. In Paragraph 11 fill in how many days out of how many years the work may be borrowed by the artist for exhibition purposes. In Paragraph 13 fill in the percentages to be paid to the artist in the event of sale or other transfer. In Paragraph 14 fill in the state whose laws will govern the sale. Both parties should then sign.

Negotiation Checklist

❏ Review the negotiation checklist for Form 1, since Paragraphs 1-7 are the same for Form 1 and Form 3, and Paragraph 8 in Form 1 is Paragraph 14 in Form 3.

❏ Determine which provisions that connect the artist to the physical work after sale should bind not only the collector, but owners after the collector. (See the discussion under other provisions.)

❏ Give the artist a right of access to the work in case he or she wishes to make photographic or other reproductions of the work after sale.

❏ Have the collector agree not to destroy the work.

❏ If the collector must destroy the work, require that it be offered back to the artist or the artist's successors in interest. (Paragraph 8)

❏ Have the collector agree not to alter the work. (Paragraph 9)

❏ If alteration occurs, give the artist the right to withdraw his or her name from the work as the artist who created it. (Paragraph 9)

❏ Provide affirmatively that the artist shall be acknowledged as the creator of the work. (Paragraph 10)

❏ Give the artist the right to borrow the work for purposes of exhibition. (Paragraph 11)

❏ If the work requires restoration, give the artist the opportunity to make that restoration. (Paragraph 12)

❏ If the artist does restore the work, provide that a fee shall be paid for this.

❏ Allow the artist to select the restorer.

❏ Do not allow the display of work which, in the artist's opinion, requires restoration.

❏ Provide for a percentage of resale price or transfer value to be paid to the artist as long as the price or value is greater than what the collector originally paid. (Paragraph 13)

❏ Provide a time within which payment of the percentage of resale proceeds must be made. (Paragraph 13)

❏ Base the resale proceeds on the collector's profit, rather than on the resale price, and adjust the percentage to be paid the artist upward, since profit will be less than resale price.

❏ Require that any exhibition of the work by the collector be in a dignified manner.

❏ Require that any work in multiple parts always be exhibited in its totality. (See the discussion under other provisions.)

❏ Restrict the collector from renting or loaning the work.

❏ Review the standard provisions in the introductory pages and then compare with Paragraph 14.

Other provisions that can be added to Form 3:

❏ Transferees bound. If the artist merely wishes to bind the collector, then Form 3 will suffice as it is. However, the reasons for guaranteeing the artist rights to the physical work after sale remain, even if the collector sells or transfers the work. For that reason, the artist may want to have some or all of the provisions which bind the collector also bind subsequent owners. Collectors may resist this because it

could make the work more difficult to resell. Robert Projansky, who innovated one of the earliest contracts connecting the artist to his or her work after sale, drafted the following provision:

Transferees Bound. If anyone becomes the owner of the Work with notice of this contract, that person shall be bound to all its terms as if he had signed a TAR when he acquired the Work.

The TAR is the Transfer Agreement and Record. Under Projansky's contract, in addition to paying part of any profit to the artist, each seller must obtain a filled-in TAR from the buyer and deliver the TAR to the artist within thirty days after the sale or transfer, along with the money due to the artist. The TAR describes the work, gives the addresses of the artist and the old and new owners, states the agreed value (usually the sale price), and states, "Ownership of the above Work of Art has been transferred between the undersigned persons, and the new owner hereby expressly ratifies, assumes and agrees to be bound by the terms of the contract dated _____," which is the original contract between the artist and collector. Along with the contract and TAR is a notice to be affixed to the work that indicates that the work is subject to the terms of the contract.

❏ Work in multiple parts. One famous moral rights case in France involved a refrigerator with panels painted by Bernard Buffet. A collector tried to sell the panels as separate art works. Buffet intervened and the courts required that the work be sold in its totality as the artist originally intended. This is an example of the moral right of integrity. To reach this result in the United States, where moral rights are limited as to the categories of art covered, it might be wise to add the following provision:

Work in Multiple Parts. Purchaser acknowledges that the Work is a single work consisting of ____ parts, and agrees to exhibit, sell, or otherwise transfer the work only in its entirety as a single work.

Contract of Sale with Moral Rights and Resale Royalty Rights

AGREEMENT made as of the _____ day of _____, 19____, between _____ (hereinafter referred to as the "Artist"), located at _____ _____, and _____ (hereinafter referred to as the "Collector"), located at _____, with respect to the sale of an artwork (hereinafter referred to as the "Work").

WHEREAS, the Artist has created the Work and has full right, title, and interest therein; and

WHEREAS, the Artist wishes to sell the Work; and

WHEREAS, the Collector has viewed the Work and wishes to purchase it; and

WHEREAS, the Artist wishes to have a continuing relationship with the Work after its sale, including the right to borrow the Work periodically for exhibition, restore the Work if necessary, receive a residual payment if the Work is resold at a profit, and be acknowledged as the creator of the Work; and

WHEREAS, both parties wish to maintain the integrity of the Work and prevent its destruction;

NOW, THEREFORE, in consideration of the foregoing premises and the mutual convenants hereinafter set forth and other valuable considerations, the parties hereto agree as follows:

1. **Description of Work.** The Artist describes the Work as follows:

    Title _____

    Medium _____

    Size _____

    Framing or mounting _____

    Year of creation _____

    Signed by Artist ❏ Yes   ❏ No

    If the Work is part of a limited edition, indicate the method of production _____; the size of the edition_____; how many multiples are signed_____; how many are unsigned_____; how many are numbered_____; how many are unnumbered_____; how many proofs exist_____; the quantity of any prior editions_____; and whether the master image has been cancelled or destroyed ❏ yes ❏ no.

2. **Sale.** The Artist hereby agrees to sell the Work to the Collector. Title shall pass to the Collector at such time as full payment is received by the Artist pursuant to Paragraph 4 hereof.

3. **Price.** The Collector agrees to purchase the Work for the agreed upon price of $_____, and shall also pay any applicable sales or transfer taxes.

4. **Payment.** Payment shall be made in full upon the signing of this Agreement.

5. **Delivery.** The ❏ Artist ❏ Collector shall arrange for delivery to the following location: _____ no later than_____,19_____. The expenses of delivery (including, but not limited to, insurance and transportation) shall be paid by _____.

6. **Risk of Loss and Insurance.** The risk of loss or damage to the Work and the provision of any insurance to cover such loss or damage shall be the responsibility of the Collector from the time of_____ _____.

7. **Copyright and Reproduction.** The Artist reserves all reproduction rights, including the right to claim statutory copyright, in the Work. The Work may not be photographed, sketched, painted, or reproduced in any manner whatsoever without the express, written consent of the Artist. All approved reproductions shall bear the following copyright notice: © by (Artist's name) 19____.

8. **Nondestruction.** The Collector shall not destroy the Work or permit the Work to be destroyed without first offering to return ownership of the Work to the Artist or his or her successors in interest.

9. **Integrity.** The Collector shall not distort, mutilate, or otherwise alter the Work. In the event such distortion, mutilation, or other alteration occurs, whether by action of the Collector or otherwise, the Artist shall, in addition to any other rights and remedies, have the right to have his or her name removed from the Work and no longer have it attributed to him or her as its creator.

10. **Attribution.** The Artist shall, at all times, have the right to have his or her name appear with the Work and to be acknowledged as its creator.

11. **Right to Exhibit.** The Artist may borrow the Work for up to ___ days once every ___ years for exhibition at a nonprofit institution. The Artist shall give the Collector written notice no later than ___ days before the opening and shall provide satisfactory proof of insurance and prepaid transportation. All expenses of the loan to the Artist shall be paid for by the Artist.

12. **Restoration.** In the event of damage to the Work requiring restoration or repair, the Collector shall, if practicable, offer the Artist the first opportunity to restore or repair the Work and, in any case, shall consult with the Artist with respect to the restoration or repairs.

13. **Resale Proceeds.** On resale or other transfer of the Work for a price or value in excess of that paid in Paragraph 3, the Collector agrees to pay the Artist ____ percent of the gross sale price received or, if the Work is transferred other than by sale, to pay ____ percent of the fair market value of the Work as of the date of transfer.

14. **Miscellany.** This Agreement shall be binding upon the parties hereto, their heirs, successors, assigns, and personal representatives. This Agreement constitutes the entire understanding between the parties. Its terms can be modified only by an instrument in writing signed by both parties. A waiver of any breach of any of the provisions of this Agreement shall not be construed as a continuing waiver of other breaches of the same or other provisions hereof. This Agreement shall be governed by the laws of the State of _____.

IN WITNESS WHEREOF, the parties hereto have signed this Agreement as of the date first set forth above.

Artist _____   Collector _____

Invoice and Basic Invoice

An invoice can be used by itself or in addition to a contract for the sale of an artwork. The invoice serves as a record of the transaction. It is important for tax purposes and also for maintaining records of the sale prices of work and who the purchasers were, in case the artist later wants to borrow the work for exhibition. Artist and purchaser should each receive a copy of the invoice.

Two invoices are provided here. Form 4, Invoice, is more suitable for work that is one-of-a-kind or part of a limited edition. Form 5, Basic Invoice, is designed for merchandise lines in which a variety of items may be ordered in quantity. Some artists may sell merchandise to consumers on account, but Form 5 would be more likely to be used with retailers and wholesalers who receive a discount and have a certain amount of time to make payment. It might also be used as a sales receipt for consumers who have paid in full.

Filling in the Form

For Form 4, Invoice, fill in the date and, for both artist and purchaser, fill in the name, address, and telephone number. Describe the work, including the additional information for limited editions. Fill in the price, the sales tax (if any), the delivery or other charges (if any), and the total to be paid. Finally, indicate whether payment has been received or is due and sign the invoice.

In filling in Form 5, give the purchaser's name and address as well as the ship to address if different from the purchaser's. Fill in the date, the purchaser's account number if a repeat customer, the sales rep if any, the order number, the method of shipment, the date of shipment, and the payment terms. Make certain all the ordering information is included. In the case of trade accounts such as retailers or wholesalers who receive a discount, indicate the amount of the discount and the unit price. Then total the amounts, add shipping and sales tax, subtract payments received, and show the balance due.

Negotiation Checklist

Form 4 and Form 5 do not have to be negotiated, since an invoice is evidence of a transaction which has already taken place. Presumably, the artist has already negotiated using the checklists for Form 1, Form 2, or Form 3, and has a signed contract of sale. Having concluded that negotiation, the artist would then fill in Form 4 or Form 5. If, for example, the contract of sale provides for installment payments, Form 4 would be modified to reflect this. If the artist wants to use only Form 4 without either Form 1 or Form 3, provisions from Form 1 or Form 3 may be added to Form 4. For example, the artist might wish to assert his or her copyright and put the purchaser on notice not to make any reproductions. If neither Form 1 nor Form 3 are being used, Form 4 can be made into a contract rather than an invoice. This can be done by having the purchaser, as well as the artist, sign Form 4. If this is done, use the negotiation checklist for Form 3 to be certain that all the desired provisions are included. The better practice, however, is to use a contract of sale and an invoice.

Other provisions that can be added to Form 4:

❑ Subject to contract of sale. If there is a contract of sale and Form 4 is simply the invoice for that contract, the invoice could recite that the invoice is subject to the contract of sale. This would be drafted as follows:

Subject to Contract of Sale. The work sold pursuant to this invoice is subject to the provisions of the contract of sale between _____ and _____, dated the ____ day of _____, 19____.

Invoice

Artist's name _____ Date_____

Artist's address _____

_____

Artist's telephone _____

Purchaser's name _____

Purchaser's address _____

_____

Purchaser's telephone _____

This invoice is for the following Artwork created by the Artist and sold to the Purchaser:

Title _____

Medium _____

Size _____

Framing or mounting _____

Year of creation _____

Signed by Artist   ❏ Yes   ❏ No

If the Work is part of a limited edition, indicate the method of production _____;

the size of the edition_____; how many multiples are signed_____; how many are

unsigned_____; how many are numbered_____; how many are unnumbered_____;

how many proofs exist_____; the quantity of any prior editions_____; and whether the

master image has been cancelled or destroyed ❏ yes ❏ no.

Price... $_____

Delivery.. $_____

Other charges.................................... $_____

Sales or Transfer tax (if any)............... $_____

Total... $_____

❏ Please remit the balance due.   ❏ Paid in full. Thank you.

Artist _____

Basic Invoice

Artist's Letterhead

Purchaser_____   Date_____

Address_____   Account Number_____

_____   Sales Rep_____

Ship to_____   Order Number_____

Address_____   Ship via_____

_____   Date shipped_____

Payment in full is due within _____ days of receipt of merchandise.

Item Number	Description	Quantity Ordered	Quantity Shipped	Back Ordered	Retail Price	Discount	Unit Price	Amount

Subtotal _____

Shipping & Handling _____

Sales tax _____

Payment received _____

Balance due _____

Commission Contract

Commission agreements offer a great challenge for the artist. At the same time, the artist must not only work to his or her own satisfaction, but must also satisfy the person who has commissioned the work. This creates a delicate balance between creativity and approval, a balance that must be maintained throughout the design and execution of the work. Who determines whether the finished work is satisfactory is crucial, but the potential for discord can be reduced by close cooperation between the artist and purchaser. Especially if the work is costly and will take a long time to complete, the artist should specify certain points at which the purchaser reviews and approves the work to date and then makes progress payments. Termination is another important issue, since the work may be incomplete. Who owns the work, who can complete it, and how much of the price must be paid?

Commissioned works vary greatly, which adds many variables to the contract for a commission. The contract to create a ring or knit a garment, for example, will not be as complex as the contract to create architectural ornamentation for a public square in a city. However, both contracts evolve from the same conceptual framework. Considerations of public commissions are all the more relevant when one considers the number of states and cities which have percent-for-art laws. This requires that some percentage, usually 1 percent, of public construction funds be spent on art. A similar federal program is the Art-in-Architecture program of the General Services Administration, which spends .5 percent of its construction budgets for federal buildings on art.

Filling in the Form

In the Preamble fill in the date and the names and addresses of the artist and the purchaser. In Paragraph 1 describe what form the preliminary design will take and what fee will be paid for the preliminary design. Fill in the information showing the work which will be created if the design is approved, including the description and price. Indicate how long the artist has to deliver the design to the purchaser, what hourly rate the artist will be paid to make changes, and what the limit is on the number of hours the artist must spend making changes. In Paragraph 2 repeat the price, specify the amounts or percentages of the installment payments, indicate the degree of completion for the second installment payment to be made, show which expenses incurred in creating the work will be paid by the purchaser, and specify an interest rate to be charged for late payments. In Paragraph 3 fill in the number of days the artist has to complete the work after receiving approval to proceed. In Paragraph 4 fill in who shall pay for shipping the work when complete, where it is to be delivered, and how the artist will help with any special installation that is necessary. In Paragraph 11 fill in how many days in how many years the artist may borrow the work and the length of advance notice required. Fill in the addresses for notice in Paragraph 16. In Paragraph 17 fill in which state's laws will govern the agreement. Both parties should then sign.

Negotiation Checklist

❏ State that the artist is a professional and that both parties wish to have the work created in the artist's unique style, since this will help with the issue of satisfaction. (Whereas clauses)

❏ Describe the preliminary design for the work and the fee for that design. (Paragraph 1)

❏ If the purchaser offers creative suggestions or sketches, a provision that the work is not a joint work for purposes of copyright ownership should be included. (See other provisions.)

❏ Provide the artist with a chance to modify the preliminary design if the purchaser isn't satisfied, but also provide for additional payments for changes. (Paragraph 1)

❏ Give the artist the right not to revise the preliminary design, or limit the number of hours the artist must work on changes. (Paragraph 1 takes the latter approach.)

❏ If it is not possible to know the price for the work until completion of the preliminary design, state that the price will be approved along with the preliminary design. The progress payments might then be expressed as percentages of the price.

❏ Require the purchaser to give written approval of the work and make progress payments in installments. (Paragraph 2)

❏ Specify which expenses to create the work will be paid by the purchaser and when payment will be made. (Paragraph 2)

❏ If the purchaser is a city or large institution, specify who is authorized to act on behalf of the purchaser.

❏ Require the purchaser to pay sales tax. (Paragraph 2)

❏ State that the artist determines when the work is finished. (Paragraph 2)

❏ If the purchaser must approve the work before making the final payment, require that the approval or rejection be in writing and be given within a reasonable time (such as 30 days) after notification by the artist that the work is complete.

❏ Agree that the artist may deviate from the preliminary design if he or she in good faith believes that this is necessary. (Paragraph 2)

❏ Especially in the case of large commissions, state that any substantial changes shall be approved by the purchaser. Of course, this will require a definition of substantial.

❏ If necessary, permit the artist to hire subcontractors, since otherwise the purchaser may expect the artist to provide only his or her personal services.

❏ Do not agree to satisfy the purchaser, since this is subjective and leaves the artist at the mercy of the purchaser's whims. If the purchaser will not agree to let the artist in good faith determine when the work is complete, at least provide for an objective standard, such as that the work must reasonably conform to the specifications of the preliminary design.

❏ Decide if interest should be charged on late payments. (Paragraph 2)

❏ If the purchaser might interrupt the artist by frequent studio visits, limit the number and duration of visits permitted and require advance notification. (Paragraph 2 allows the purchaser to inspect the work on reasonable notice to the artist.)

❏ For a public commission, specify that performance bonds not be required of the artist. Such bonds guarantee performance by the artist and payment of subcontractors and suppliers, but are difficult to relate to works with aesthetic qualities.

❏ If appropriate to the commission, define the roles of other professionals such as engineers, architects, and designers, and provide for coordination with the artist.

❏ If appropriate to the commission, specify what contractors and materials are to be provided by the purchasers, exactly what work will be completed, and how the artist's performance will interface with such contractors.

❏ If the artist must do research, perhaps in relation to the community in which a commissioned work will be situated, the cooperation of the purchaser (in this case probably the community itself) will be necessary to supply materials and access for the research.

❏ Provide a date for delivery. (Paragraph 3)

❏ Extend the date for delivery if completion of the work is prevented for reasons beyond the artist's control. (Paragraph 3)

❑ If the work is being created for a particular site, specify the site and that the work is not to be moved from that site. (See other provisions.)

❑ Do not allow a provision making time of the essence. (Paragraph 3 states time is not of the essence, but this does not have to be explicitly stated.)

❑ State whether the work is to be insured and, if so, by whom, and what risks will be covered. In the case of a public commission where site preparation, delivery, and installation may be done by the commissioning governmental agency, it would be especially appropriate to shift this obligation to the purchaser. (Paragraph 4)

❑ State which party shall bear the risk of loss prior to delivery. Again, with a public commission, it would be especially appropriate to shift this risk to the purchaser. (Paragraph 4)

❑ Determine what will be done with insurance proceeds in the event of loss or damage. A problem with simply having the artist recommence work is the artist's lost time. Another alternative would be to share the proceeds and decide whether to start the contract again from the point of approval of the preliminary design, which would require another sequence of progress payments and approvals.

❑ If the work might cause injury due to its size, the manner of its installation, or its materials, determine which party shall be liable and whether liability insurance will be provided.

❑ Determine who pays for delivery. (Paragraph 4)

❑ Provide for reimbursement of any travel expenses incurred by the artist, including travel expenses to review the installation site and to install the work, and consider whether the artist should be paid for the time involved in doing the installation. (This is covered in part by Paragraphs 2 and 4.)

❑ If there is a likelihood that the work may have to be stored prior to installation, determine who will pay for the storage.

❑ Determine the grounds for termination of the agreement. (Paragraph 5)

❑ Give the artist the right to terminate the agreement at any time if payments are more than a specified number of days overdue. (Paragraph 5C)

❑ Give the purchaser the right to terminate if the purchaser does not approve of the preliminary design or of the work itself, but cover the artist's right to payment in such an event. (Paragraph 5A and 5B)

❑ Specify the number of days the artist can go over the original completion date before the purchaser will be able to exercise a right to terminate. (Paragraph 5D)

❑ If the purchaser terminates because of the artist's lateness, state that the artist is not liable for anything other than payments received from the purchaser. (Paragraph 5D)

❑ Cover how long events beyond the artist's control can delay completion before the purchaser will be able to exercise a right to terminate. (Paragraph 5E)

❑ Provide for termination in the event of the artist's death. (Paragraph 5F)

❑ If the work is a portrait of the purchaser, determine what will happen in the event of the purchaser's disability or death.

❑ For each ground for termination, determine whether payments must be returned or additional payments must be made. (Paragraph 5)

❑ If termination is made between progress payments, give the artist the power to determine the additional payment due, based on how much additional work was done. (Paragraph 5B)

❏ For each ground for termination, determine who owns the physical work (and works made in the process of creating the work, such as sketches) and who has the right to complete the work. (Paragraph 6)

❏ If the artist's assistants or subcontractors could complete the work after a certain point in the event of the artist's death or disability, do not make these occurrences grounds for termination and instead require the purchaser to accept the work as completed by the assistants or subcontractors.

❏ Assure that title does not pass from the artist to the purchaser until payment has been made in full. (Paragraph 6)

❏ If requested by the purchaser, decide whether to give warranties that the artist is the sole creator of the work, that the artist has unencumbered title to the work, that the work is unique and has not been sold elsewhere, that the work will be fabricated and installed in a competent manner, that the work will be free of inherent vices due to either materials or the manner of construction, and that the maintenance procedures provided by the artist are valid. Limit the duration of any warranties given by the artist regarding the physical condition of the work, perhaps allowing these warranties to last only one year.

❏ Reserve all copyrights to the artist, including copyrights in the preliminary design and any incidental works. (Paragraph 7)

❏ Decide whether to allow reproductions for promotional or other limited purposes by the purchaser.

❏ Provide for copyright notice. (Paragraph 7)

❏ Specify who will register the work with the Copyright Office.

❏ Provide for the artist to receive authorship credit on the finished work or any reproductions. (Paragraph 7)

❏ Do not agree to any clause restricting the artist from doing similar works, since this offers no guidelines as to what the artist cannot do and may hurt the artist's ability to earn a livelihood.

❏ State that the artist is an independent contractor and not an employee. (See other provisions.)

❏ If the work is being done at a site and does not have to be delivered, state that the artist can give written notification to the purchaser at various stages of progress, and when the work is completed.

❏ If the purchaser is providing materials or the services of contractors, as might be likely to occur in a public commission, require that the purchaser indemnify and hold the artist harmless against any claims from the vendors of the materials or the suppliers of the services. (See other provisions.)

❏ State whether the artist agrees to promote the finished work, and consider requiring that a certain amount of promotion be undertaken by the purchaser.

❏ Should the artist give or be required to give instructions on how to maintain and preserve the work?

❏ If the artist borrows the work for exhibition, specify what credit the purchaser will receive.

❏ Review the negotiation checklist for Form 3 regarding the provisions which give the artist rights in the work after sale. (Paragraphs 9, 10, and 11 are drawn from these provisions, but the artist may wish to add additional rights.)

❏ Review the standard provisions in the introductory pages and compare with Paragraphs 12-17.

❏ If an arbitration clause is taken from the standard provisions, consider specifying that artistic decisions are the sole responsibilty of the artist and cannot be reviewed by the arbitrator.

Other provisions that can be added to Form 6:

❑ Sole authorship. One of the problem areas in the copyright law relates to joint works. If two people work together creatively and intend that their contributions will merge into a single work, they are joint authors. This means that the copyright is owned jointly. Either author can license the copyright without the permission of the other author. Proceeds from these licensings would have to be shared. However, in most cases, the artist does not want someone else to have control over what is done with the copyrights in his or her work. Commissioned works raise the risk that the contribution of the purchaser, however minimal, might create a joint work. If the purchaser is giving artistic suggestions, such as sketches, it would be wise not only to reserve all copyrights to the artist but also to provide the following:

Sole Authorship. The Artist is the sole author of the Work, the preliminary design, and any incidental works made in the course of the creation of the Work. The Purchaser makes no claim of copyright therein and agrees that these are not joint works for purposes of the copyright law.

❑ Site specific. When a work is to be exhibited on a particular site, many artists feel that creating the work also designs the space. Because the work and the space are related, the artist does not want the work moved to another location. This restriction might be expressed as follows:

Site Specific. The Purchaser agrees that the Work is site specific and has been designed for the following site:_____.
The Purchaser further agrees not to change the site or move the Work from the site since these actions would irreparably damage the integrity of the Work.

A provision like this again raises the question of whether to try and bind subsequent owners of the work.

❑ Indemnify and hold harmless. This provision protects one party against damaging acts of the other party. If the artist is dealing with a city for a public commission, this provision could be extended to cover the failure on the part of the city to obtain permits and variances, and to conform to the city's own codes.

Indemnify and Hold Harmless. The Purchaser agrees to indemnify and hold the Artist harmless from any and all claims, demands, payments, expenses, legal fees, or other costs in relation to obligations for materials or services incurred by the Purchaser.

❑ Independent contractor. This provision clarifies the relationship between the artist and the purchaser.

Independent Contractor. The Artist shall perform his or her work under this contract as an independent contractor and not as an employee or agent of the Purchaser.

It could also be stated, "This work is not a work for hire for purposes of the copyright law." In this particular contract the artist's ownership of the copyright has already been resolved by Paragraph 7.

❑ Special government provisions. If the contract is with a government, special provisions may appear. These may provide for nondiscrimination in hiring (including hiring handicapped people), paying of time-and-a-half for overtime work, agreement not to hire people under a sentence of imprisonment (which might include people on parole), a requirement to list job openings with certain government employment agencies, agreement not to let public officials benefit from the contract, a warranty that only bona fide commercial agents were used by the artist and no one else received a percentage of the price, performance bonds, a duty to report offers of bribes, and a provision forbidding participation in international boycotts.

Commission Contract

AGREEMENT made as of the _____ day of _____, 19 ____, between _____
(hereinafter referred to as the "Artist"), located at _____and
_____ (hereinafter referred to as the "Purchaser"), located at _____.

WHEREAS, the Artist is a recognized professional artist; and

WHEREAS, the Purchaser admires the work of the Artist and wishes to commission the Artist to create a work of art ("the Work") in the Artist's own unique style; and

WHEREAS, the parties wish to have the creation of this work of art governed by the mutual obligations, covenants, and conditions herein;

NOW, THEREFORE, in consideration of the foregoing premises and the mutual covenants hereinafter set forth and other valuable considerations, the parties hereto agree as follows:

1. **Preliminary Design.** The Artist hereby agrees to create the preliminary design for the Work in the form of studies, sketches, drawings, or maquettes described as follows: _____ in return for which the Purchaser agrees to pay a fee of $_____ upon the signing of this Agreement. The Artist agrees to develop the preliminary design according to the following description of the Work as interpreted by the Artist:

   Title_____   Medium_____

   Size_____   Price_____

   Description_____

   _____

   The Artist shall deliver the preliminary design to the Purchaser within _____ days of the date hereof. The Purchaser may, within two weeks of receipt of the preliminary design, demand changes, and the Artist shall make such changes for a fee of _____ per hour; provided, however, that the Artist shall not be obligated to work more than _____ hours making changes.

2. **Progress Payments.** Upon the Purchaser's giving written approval of the preliminary design, the Artist agrees to proceed with construction of the Work, and the Purchaser agrees to pay the price of $_____ for the Work as follows:_____% upon the giving of written approval of the preliminary design, _____% upon the completion of _____% of the construction of the Work, and _____% upon the completion of the Work. The Purchaser shall also promptly pay the following expenses to be incurred by the Artist in the course of creating the Work _____

   _____. The Purchaser shall pay the applicable sales tax, if any, with the final progress payment. Completion of the Work is to be determined by the Artist, who shall use the Artist's professional judgment to deviate from the preliminary design as the Artist in good faith believes necessary to create the Work. If, upon the Artist presenting the Purchaser with written notice of any payment being due, the Purchaser fails to make said payment within two weeks of receipt of notice, interest at the rate of _____% shall accrue upon the balance due. The Purchaser shall have a right to inspect the Work in progress upon reasonable notice to the Artist.

3. **Date of Delivery.** The Artist agrees to complete the Work within _____ days of receiving the Purchaser's written approval of the preliminary design. This completion date shall be extended for such period of time as the Artist may be disabled by illness preventing progress of the Work. The completion date shall also be extended in the event of delays caused by events beyond the control of the Artist, including but not limited to fire, theft, strikes, shortages of materials, and acts of God. Time shall not be considered of the essence with respect to the completion of the Work.

4. Insurance, Shipping, and Installation. The Artist agrees to keep the Work fully insured against fire and theft and bear any other risk of loss until delivery to the Purchaser. In the event of loss caused by fire or theft, the Artist shall use the insurance proceeds to recommence the making of the Work. Upon completion of the Work, it shall be shipped at the expense of _____ to the following address specified by the Purchaser: _____. If any special installation is necessary, the Artist shall assist in said installation as follows:_____.

5. Termination. This Agreement may be terminated on the following conditions:

(A) If the Purchaser does not approve the preliminary design pursuant to Paragraph 1, the Artist shall keep all payments made and this Agreement shall terminate.

(B) The Purchaser may, upon payment of any progress payment due pursuant to Paragraph 2 or upon payment of an amount agreed in writing by the Artist to represent the pro rata portion of the price in relation to the degree of completion of Work, terminate this Agreement. The Artist hereby agrees to give promptly a good faith estimate of the degree of completion of the Work if requested by the Purchaser to do so.

(C) The Artist shall have the right to terminate this Agreement in the event the Purchaser is more than sixty days late in making any payment due pursuant to Paragraph 2, provided, however, nothing herein shall prevent the Artist bringing suit based on the Purchaser's breach of contract.

(D) The Purchaser shall have the right to terminate this Agreement if the Artist fails without cause to complete the Work within ninety days of the completion date in Paragraph 3. In the event of termination pursuant to this subparagraph, the Artist shall return to the Purchaser all payments made pursuant to Paragraph 2, but shall not be liable for any additional expenses, damages, or claims of any kind based on the failure to complete the Work.

(E) The Purchaser shall have a right to terminate this Agreement if, pursuant to Paragraph 3, the illness of the Artist causes a delay of more than six months in the completion date or if events beyond the Artist's control cause a delay of more than one year in the completion date, provided, however, that the Artist shall retain all payments made pursuant to Paragraphs 1 and 2.

(F) This Agreement shall automatically terminate on the death of the Artist, provided, however, that the Artist's estate shall retain all payments made pursuant to Paragraphs 1 and 2.

(G) The exercise of a right of termination under this Paragraph shall be written and set forth the grounds for termination.

6. Ownership. Title to the Work shall remain in the Artist until the Artist is paid in full. In the event of termination of this Agreement pursuant to Subparagraphs (A), (B), (C), or (D) of Paragraph 5, the Artist shall retain all rights of ownership in the Work and shall have the right to complete, exhibit, and sell the Work if the Artist so chooses. In the event of termination of this Agreement pursuant to Paragraph 5 (E) or (F), the Purchaser shall own the Work in whatever degree of completion and shall have the right to complete, exhibit, and sell the Work if the Purchaser so chooses. Notwithstanding anything to the contrary herein, the Artist shall retain all rights of ownership and have returned to the Artist the preliminary design, all incidental works made in the creation of the Work, and all copies and reproductions thereof and of the Work itself, provided, however, that in the event of termination pursuant to Paragraph 5 (E) or (F) the Purchaser shall have a right to keep copies of the preliminary design for the sole purpose of completing the Work.

7. Copyright and Reproduction. The Artist reserves all rights of reproduction and all copyrights in the Work, the preliminary design, and any incidental works made in the creation of the Work. Copyright notice in the name of the Artist shall appear on the Work, and the Artist shall also receive authorship credit in connection with the Work or any reproductions of the Work.

8. Privacy. The Purchaser gives to the Artist permission to use the Purchaser's name, picture, portrait, and photograph, in all forms and media and in all manners, including but not limited to exhibition, display, advertising, trade, and editorial uses, without violation of the Purchaser's rights of privacy or any other personal or propriatery rights the Purchaser may possess in connection with reproduction and sale of the Work, the preliminary design, or any incidental works made in the creation of the Work.

9. Nondestruction, Alteration, and Maintenance. The Purchaser agrees that the Purchaser will not intentionally destroy, damage, alter, modify, or change the Work in any way whatsoever. If any alteration of any kind occurs after receipt by the Purchaser, whether intentional or accidental and whether done by the Purchaser or others, the Work shall no longer be represented to be the Work of the Artist without the Artist's written consent. The Purchaser agrees to see that the Work is properly maintained.

10. Repairs. All repairs and restorations which are made during the lifetime of the Artist shall have the Artist's approval. To the extent practical, the Artist shall be given the opportunity to accomplish said repairs and restorations at a reasonable fee.

11. Possession. The Purchaser agrees that the Artist shall have the right to possession of the Work for up to _____ days every _____ years for the purpose of exhibition of the Work to the public, at no expense to the Purchaser. The Artist shall give the Purchaser written notice at least _____ days prior to the opening and provide proof of sufficient insurance and prepaid transportation.

12. Nonassignability. Neither party hereto shall have the right to assign this Agreement without the prior written consent of the other party. The Artist shall, however, retain the right to assign monies due to him or her under the terms of this Agreement.

13. Heirs and Assigns. This Agreement shall be binding upon the parties hereto, their heirs, successors, assigns, and personal representatives, and references to the Artist and the Purchaser shall include their heirs, successors, assigns, and personal representatives.

14. Integration. This Agreement constitutes the entire understanding between the parties. Its terms can be modified only by an instrument in writing signed by both parties.

15. Waivers. A waiver of any breach of any of the provisions of this Agreement shall not be construed as a continuing waiver of other breaches of the same or other provisions hereof. .

16. Notices and Changes of Address. All notices shall be sent by registered or certified mail, return receipt requested, postage prepaid, to the Artist and Exhibitor at the address first given above unless indicated to the contrary here _____. Each party shall give written notification of any change of address prior to the date of said change.

17. Governing Law. This Agreement shall be governed by the laws of the State of _____.

IN WITNESS WHEREOF, the parties hereto have signed this Agreement as of the date first set forth above.

Artist_____   Purchaser_____

Contract to Create a Limited Edition

A limited edition may be an excellent way to make affordable work that can reach a larger audience. It is certainly possible for the artist to create the edition and then seek outlets for sale. However, a safer arrangement is to have a distributor who already wants to sell the edition. This distributor may also be willing to underwrite some or all of the expenses of creating the edition. Form 7 is a contract between an artist and a distributor for the creation of a limited edition. See Form 17, Licensing Contract, with respect to manufacturing items in unlimited quantities.

Unless the artist makes all the copies, he or she will also have to oversee this process. Whether the artist or the distributor is paying for the edition, the copies must achieve the quality desired by the artist. The contract with the fabricator should describe the subject matter of the edition and specify the size of the edition (including signed and unsigned copies, numbered and unnumbered copies, proofs, or samples, and whether the fabricator keeps any of the proofs), the price and terms of payment, a schedule (including trial proofs or samples and delivery of the edition itself), the exact materials and manner of fabrication, whether any master image will be cancelled (and, if so, provision of a cancellation proof), and ownership and right to possession of the fabricator's materials if a master image is not cancelled.

The artist's aesthetic judgment must govern the acceptability of the fabricator's work, and the edition must correspond to the trial proofs or samples which the artist approved. If original art is provided to the fabricator, the standard of care for that art, liability for loss or damage, and responsibility for insuring the art, if it is to be insured, should all be resolved. It is important that the contract with the fabricator be coordinated to meet the terms of the artist's contract with the distributor.

Form 7 assumes that the distributor is con-

tracting with the fabricator. Since the distributor is paying the expenses, this may affect the commission percentage taken by the distributor. Another arrangement, of course, would be for the distributor to purchase the edition outright. This guarantees that the artist will receive money at a particular time, but if the distributor later raises the sale price, the artist may have received less than he or she would have received by waiting and sharing in the proceeds. If both options are available, the artist will have to make a case-by-case decision as to what is best.

In addition, because some states have enacted laws regulating the sale of multiples, the artist should provide the information necessary to allow sellers to comply with these laws. California has extended its law to apply to limited editions of fine art multiples, which include fine prints, photographs, sculpture casts, collages, or similar art objects.

Filling in the Form

In the Preamble fill in the date and the names and addresses of the artist and distributor. In Paragraph 2 fill in the description of the edition. Fill in the date for copyright notice in Paragraph 3. Complete the amount of the advance to the artist in Paragraph 6, as well as the number of artist's proofs or samples that the artist will receive. In Paragraph 7 specify the territory for sales and the duration of the right to sell. In Paragraph 8 set forth the price for each copy and the division of proceeds between the artist and distributor. In Paragraph 11 indicate how much of the edition shall be returned to the artist in the event of termination. In Paragraph 12 show the percentage of the sale price which will be covered by insurance. Specify a promotion budget in Paragraph 13. In Paragraph 18 fill in the state whose laws will govern the contract. Both parties should then sign.

Negotiation Checklist

❏ Agree on all the details of the edition, including who will own each variety of proof or sample. (Paragraphs 2, 6, and 10)

❏ Provide informational details sufficient to allow the sellers of the prints to comply with state laws regulating multiples. (Paragraph 2)

❏ Reserve all copyrights to the artist and require that the distributor register the copyright. (Paragraph 3)

❏ Permit promotional reproductions and use of the artist's name in promotions. (Paragraphs 3 and 13)

❏ Require the distributor to budget for promotion and give the artist the right to require changes in promotion that is harmful to the artist's reputation. (Paragraph 13)

❏ Agree that the artist has artistic control over the edition and need not sign until he or she is satisfied with the edition. (Paragraph 4)

❏ Specify that the artist must sign the trial proofs or samples to indicate approval to print.

❏ Provide for the distributor to contract with the fabricator and pay the fabricator directly. (Paragraph 5)

❏ Determine who shall choose the fabricator. (Paragraph 4)

❏ Provide for the distributor to pay all expenses in relation to the edition, such as the artist's travel expenses.

❏ If the artist is contracting with the fabricator and paying expenses, consider which expenses should be reimbursed, when they should be reimbursed, and whether there should be an advance against such expenses.

❏ Provide for the payment of advances to the artist, which will be subtracted from money due the artist from sales. Always state that advances are nonrefundable, so the artist need not return them. (Paragraphs 6 and 9)

❏ Require the distributor to provide working space, materials, and technical advice, without charge to the artist.

❏ Provide for the distributor to purchase the edition outright.

❏ If the distributor buys the edition, provide for the artist to receive part of the edition, as well as the artist's proofs or samples.

❏ Specify an exclusive territory and time for the distributor to sell the edition. (Paragraph 7)

❏ Agree that the artist shall not be limited in any way with respect to the creation and sale of other works, including other editions. (Paragraph 7)

❏ Do not give the distributor a right of first refusal on other editions that the artist creates during the term of the contract. A right of first refusal would require the artist to submit each work to the distributor to see if the distributor wanted it, perhaps on the same terms as the contract being entered into.

❏ State that the artist owns any master image and any materials used to create the edition. This would be done to prevent unauthorized copies, although the copyright provision is also drafted to prevent such copies. (See other provisions.)

❏ Agree on the retail price and the distributor's commission. (Paragraph 8)

❏ If the distributor wants to sell at higher than normal discounts to museums, designers, or wholesalers, consider whether the additional discount should come from the distributor's share of the proceeds.

❏ Require accountings for sales and specify a time for payment of monies owed to the artist. (Paragraph 9)

❏ Agree that title remains with the artist until the artist has been paid in full and that title shall then pass directly to the purchaser. While the distributor as a merchant has the power to pass title of goods normally sold by the merchant, this provision at least shows that the parties do not intend for title to vest in the distributor. (Paragraph 11)

❏ Forbid the distributor to encumber the edition in any way, such as by pledging it as collateral for a debt.

❏ Agree that the distributor shall not incur any expenses for which the artist may be held responsible.

❏ Provide for the artist to have a security interest in the edition, especially if the artist paid to create the edition and is simply consigning it to the distributor. Security interests are reviewed under other provisions in the discussion of Form 1.

❏ Specify who is responsible for the risk of loss. (Paragraph 12)

❏ Specify the amount of insurance to be carried, who shall carry it, the division of insurance proceeds, and the artist's right to a copy of the policy. (Partially covered by Paragraph 12)

❏ Agree on a division of remaining inventory in the event of termination of the contract. The percentage formulation may be awkward because it may result in fractions of a copy going to each party. Include a provision for rounding off to a whole number in such a case. (Paragraph 11)

❏ Review the negotiation checklist for Form 3 and consider whether the distributor should have to comply with any of these provisions when selling the prints.

❏ Compare the standard provisions in the introductory pages with Paragraphs 14-18.

Other Provisions that can be added to Form 7:

❏ Artist's ownership of materials. As mentioned above, the artist may wish to own the master image and other production materials to prevent later copies being made. If the fabricator agrees to transfer ownership, the artist and distributor will have to negotiate which of them shall own these materials.

Artist's Ownership of Materials. Distributor agrees that the Artist is the owner of the plates and all materials relating to the creation of the edition, and hereby transfers all right, title, and interest which the Distributor may have therein to the Artist.

❏ Fabricator's materials. The distributor may object to the transfer of ownership, since the distributor has paid for the plates and materials. In this case, the parties might agree to destroy the fabricator's materials.

Fabricator's Materials. The parties agree that, after making the edition, the fabricator's materials shall be destroyed and the Artist shall be provided with proof of such destruction.

Contract to Create a Limited Edition

AGREEMENT made as of the _____ day of _____, 19____, between _____ (hereinafter referred to as the "Artist"), located at _____ and _____ (hereinafter referred to as the "Distributor"), located at _____.

WHEREAS, the Artist is a professional artist who creates art, including limited editions, for sale and exhibition; and

WHEREAS, the Distributor is in the business of publishing, promoting, distributing, and marketing limited editions; and

WHEREAS, the Artist and Distributor wish to work together with respect to the Artist's creation of a limited edition which shall be published by the Distributor pursuant to the terms and conditions of this Agreement.

NOW, THEREFORE, in consideration of the foregoing premises and the mutual covenants hereinafter set forth, and other valuable considerations, the parties hereto agree as follows:

1. **Creation and Title.** The Artist hereby agrees to create a limited edition (hereinafter referred to as the "edition") and warrants that the Artist shall be the sole creator of the edition, that the Artist is and shall be the owner of unencumbered title in the copyrights for the edition, and that no copies shall exist other than those specified in Paragraph 2.

2. **Description of the Edition and Artist's Certification.** The edition shall conform to the following description:

   Title _____

   Medium _____

   Colors _____

   Size _____

   Materials _____

   Number of copies _____

   Year fabricated _____

   At the conclusion of the creation of the edition, the Artist shall date, sign, and number the copies. The Artist shall certify to the Distributor that the edition conforms to the descriptive information in this Paragraph 2, and shall also certify the year fabricated; the authorized maximum number of copies to be signed or numbered; the authorized maximum number of unsigned or unnumbered copies; the number of proofs or samples created (including trial proofs, Artist's proofs, right to fabricate proof, other fabricator's proofs, Distributor's proofs, and any other proofs); the total size of the edition; whether or not the plates, stones, blocks, or other master image have been cancelled or altered (or, if not cancelled or altered, the restrictions and safeguarding of any master image); any prior or subsequent editions created from such master image; in the event of other editions, the size of all other editions and the series number of the present edition; and the name of the workshop, if any, where the edition was created.

3. **Copyright and Reproduction.** The Artist reserves all reproduction rights, including the right to claim statutory copyright, in the edition and any work created by the Artist during the process of creating the limited edition. The edition may not be photographed, sketched, painted, or reproduced in any manner whatsoever without the express, written consent of the Artist. The Artist shall have the right to control any further use of the fabricator's materials and the making of any derivative work based on the edition. The Artist does grant to the Distributor the nonexclusive right to include images of the edition in its catalog and other promotional materials, provided

such catalog and promotional materials are not offered for sale. The edition and all approved reproductions shall bear the following copyright notice: © by (Artist's name) 19____. The Distributor shall register the copyright with the Copyright Office within three months of publication.

4. **Artistic Control.** The Artist shall have artistic control over the creation of the edition. All artistic decisions shall be made solely by the Artist. The Artist shall have no obligation to sign the edition until the Artist is satisfied with its quality and deems it to be finished. If the fabricator is to be selected by the Distributor, the Artist shall in the exercise of his or her sole discretion have a right of approval over this selection.

5. **Costs of Creating the Edition.** The Distributor shall be solely responsible for and pay all costs of creating the edition. The Distributor shall contract directly with the fabricator or other party responsible for the mechanical processes of creating the edition. The Distributor shall pay any additional costs deriving from the Artist's exercise of artistic control pursuant to Paragraph 4.

6. **Advances to Artist.** The Artist shall receive nonrefundable advances of $_____, payable one-third on signing of this Agreement, one-third on approval of the fabrication of the edition based on an acceptable sample, and one-third on signing of the edition. In addition, the Artist shall at the time of signing receive ____ Artist's proofs from the edition which the Artist shall be free to sell at any time and in any territory at the price specified in Paragraph 7 and shall not share the proceeds of such sales with the Distributor.

7. **Territory, Term, and Termination.** The Distributor shall have the right to sell the edition in the following territory: _____ for a period of _____ years from the date first set forth above. The term shall automatically renew for additional one-year periods unless notice of termination is given by either party thirty days in advance of the renewal commencement. The Distributor's right shall be exclusive only with respect to the sale of the edition described in Paragraph 2, and the Artist shall remain free to create and sell art work of any kind.

8. **Pricing and Commissions.** The price for each copy shall be $____, which may be reduced up to 10 percent for normal trade discounts. Net receipts, which are monies actually received by the Distributor from the sale of the edition, shall be divided ____ percent to the Artist and ____ percent to the Distributor.

9. **Payments to the Artist and Accountings.** All monies payable to the Artist, after the subtraction of advances, shall be paid to the Artist on the last day of the month following the month of sale with an accounting showing the sale price, the name and address of the purchaser, the number of copies sold, and the inventory of copies remaining.

10. **Distributor's Proofs.** The Distributor shall receive ____ Distributor's proofs from the edition, which the Distributor agrees not to sell until after the date of termination determined pursuant to Paragraph 7. All other proofs shall be the property of the Artist.

11. **Title to Copies** Title in each copy sold shall remain in the Artist until such time as Artist has been paid in full pursuant to Paragraph 9 and title shall then pass directly to the purchaser. In the event of termination pursuant to Paragraph 7, title in ____ percent of the edition shall pass to the Distributor and the balance of the edition shall remain the property of and be returned to the Artist.

12. **Loss or Damage and Insurance.** The Distributor shall be responsible for loss of or damage to the edition from the date of delivery to the Distributor until the date of delivery to any purchaser or, if this Agreement is terminated pursuant to Paragraph 7, until the return of the Artist's portion of the edition to the Artist. Distributor shall maintain insurance for each copy at ____ percent of the sale price agreed to in Paragraph 8 and shall divide any insurance proceeds as if these proceeds were net receipts pursuant to Paragraph 8.

13. Promotion. The Distributor agrees to promote the edition in its catalog, by press releases, by direct mail, and by advertising for which the sum of $ _____ shall be spent. The Distributor agrees that all promotion shall be dignified and in keeping with the Artist's reputation as a respected professional. The Artist consents to the use of Artist's name and Artist's portrait, picture, or photograph in such promotion, provided that Artist shall have the right to review any such promotion and Distributor shall change such promotion if Artist objects on the ground that it is harmful to the Artist's reputation.

14. Nonassignability. Neither party hereto shall have the right to assign this Agreement without the prior written consent of the other party. The Artist shall, however, have the right to assign monies due to him or her under the terms of this Agreement.

15. Heirs and Assigns. This Agreement shall be binding upon the parties hereto, their heirs, successors, assigns, and personal representatives, and references to the Artist and the Distributor shall include their heirs, successors, assigns, and personal representatives.

16. Integration. This Agreement constitutes the entire understanding between the parties. Its terms can be modified only by an instrument in writing signed by both parties.

17. Waivers. A waiver of any breach of any of the provisions of this Agreement shall not be construed as a continuing waiver of other breaches of the same or other provisions hereof.

18. Governing Law. This Agreement shall be governed by the laws of the State of_____.

IN WITNESS WHEREOF, the parties hereto have signed this Agreement as of the date first set forth above.

Artist _____   Distributor _____
                                                              Company Name

                                              By _____
                                                         Authorized Signatory, Title

Contract for Receipt and Holding of Work

The artist frequently faces a dilemma. On the one hand, there is a good reason to leave art with someone else. On the other hand, this other party has not yet made any commitment to the artist. For example, the artist may want to show with a gallery, to convince a dealer to represent him or her, or to have work considered for exhibition by a retail outlet. In all of these cases the artist may want to leave art with the other party.

Once work has left the artist's hands, it is important that it be preserved and kept in good condition. Anyone holding the art as part of his or her regular business dealings has a duty of reasonable care. The artist may want to raise this standard of care. Insurance may be needed to protect the work.

Another problem that may arise when the artist's work is entrusted to someone else is the risk that it may be infringed by unauthorized reproductions or even sold or rented without the artist receiving a fee or exercising the right to control what is done with the work. Form 8 makes explicit the restrictions against any such use of the work by the party holding it.

The artist should also consider using Form 8 when slides or photographs of art are submitted. While these materials are not as valuable as original art, it is important to inform the other party that copying is prohibited.

The holding fee is designed to encourage that the work not be kept for an unreasonable period of time. Of course, a holding fee may be impractical in many situations (such as when the artist is sending the work out for framing or is leaving it with a gallery that has not solicited the work for review). Parties entrusted with art may not be willing to agree to a high standard of care or to the insuring of the work. In such cases, the value of Form 8 is that it alerts the artist to the risks faced in giving the work to the other party.

Of course, the artist's copyright is protection against unauthorized reproductions and displays. Use of Form 8 alerts the other party to the artist's determination to prevent such unauthorized uses.

Filling in the Form

In the Preamble fill in the date and the names and addresses of the parties. In Paragraph 1 give the purpose for which the work has been delivered to the other party. In Paragraph 4 check the boxes to show the duration of recipient's liability and indicate the method of return transportation. In Paragraph 5 check the box regarding insurance. State when the work is to be returned in Paragraph 6 and, if relevant, specify the number of days and holding fee. In Paragraph 7 give the small claims court limit on claims and specify an arbitrator. In Paragraph 8 indicate which state's laws will govern the agreement. Fill in the Schedule of Works with the relevant information. Both parties should then sign.

Negotiation Checklist

❑ State the purpose for leaving the work with the other party. (Paragraph 1)

❑ Specify that the recipient accepts the information provided on the Schedule of Works to show that there is no dispute as to which works were delivered and what their values are. (Paragraph 2)

❑ Require immediate, written notification of any dispute as to the listing of works or their values. (Paragraph 2)

❑ State that if no objection is made within ten days, the terms shall be considered accepted even if the recipient has not signed the form. (Paragraph 2)

❑ Reserve ownership of the physical work to the artist. (Paragraph 3)

❑ Reserve artist's ownership of the copyright and all reproduction rights. (Paragraph 3)

❑ Require that the work be held in confidence. (Paragraph 3)

❏ State that the recipient shall be strictly liable in the event of loss, theft, or damage, and indicate the duration of this responsibility. (Paragraph 4)

❏ Require return of the work to the artist at the expense of the recipient. (Paragraph 4)

❏ Require the recipient to pay for the transportation from the artist to the recipient.

❏ Specify the method of transportation. (Paragraph 4)

❏ Require wall-to-wall all-risks insurance be provided by the recipient. (Paragraph 5)

❏ Make the artist a named beneficiary on any insurance policy protecting the work.

❏ Provide for the payment of a holding fee to the artist if the work is kept beyond a certain period of time. (Paragraph 6)

❏ Give the artist a security interest in the work to protect against claims by creditors of the recipient. Security interests are reviewed under other provisions in the discussion of Form 1.

❏ State that the artist's written permission is required for any reproduction, display, sale, or rental of the work. In essence, this requires another contract which would deal specifically with the relevant issues within each arrangement and provide for fees and appropriate limitations. (Paragraph 3)

❏ Review the standard provisions in the introductory pages and compare with Paragraphs 7-8.

An abbreviated form of the Schedule of Works for Form 8 appears below. The full Schedule is shown with the perforated form.

Schedule of Works

	Title	Medium	Description	Size	Value
1.					
2.					
3.					
4.					
5.					

Contract for Receipt and Holding of Work

AGREEMENT made as of the _____ day of _____, 19____, between _____ (hereinafter referred to as the "Artist"), located at _____, and _____ (hereinafter referred to as the "Recipient"), located at_____.

WHEREAS, the Artist is a professional artist of good standing; and

WHEREAS, the Artist wishes to leave certain works with the Recipient for a limited period of time; and

WHEREAS, the Recipient in the course of its business receives and holds works;

NOW, THEREFORE, in consideration of the foregoing premises and the mutual covenants hereinafter set forth and other valuable considerations, the parties hereto agree as follows:

1. **Purpose.** Artist hereby agrees to entrust the works listed on the Schedule of Works to the Recipient for the purpose of: _____.

2. **Acceptance.** Recipient accepts the listing and values on the Schedule of Works as accurate if not objected to in writing by return mail immediately after receipt of the artworks. If Recipient has not signed this form, any terms on this form not objected to in writing within ten days shall be deemed accepted.

3. **Ownership and Copyright.** Copyright and all reproduction rights in the works, as well as the ownership of the physical works themselves, are the property of and reserved to the Artist. Recipient acknowledges that the works shall be held in confidence and agrees not to display, copy, or modify directly or indirectly any of the works submitted, nor will Recipient permit any third party to do any of the foregoing. Reproduction, display, sale, or rental shall be allowed only upon Artist's written permission specifying usage and fees.

4. **Loss, Theft, or Damage.** Recipient agrees to assume full responsibility and be strictly liable for loss, theft, or damage to the works from the time of ❑ shipment by the Artist ❑ receipt by the Recipient until the time of ❑ shipment by the Recipient ❑ receipt by the Artist. Recipient further agrees to return all of the works at its own expense by the following method of transportation: _____. Reimbursement for loss, theft, or damage to a work shall be in the amount of the value entered for that artwork on the Schedule of Works. Both Recipient and Artist agree that the specified values represent the value of the work.

5. **Insurance.** Recipient ❑ does ❑ does not agree to insure the works for all risks from the time of shipment from the Artist until the time of delivery to the Artist for the values shown on the Schedule of Works.

6. **Holding Fees.** The artworks are to be returned to the Artist within _____ days after delivery to the Recipient. Each work held beyond _____ days from delivery shall incur the following daily holding fee: $_____ which shall be paid to the Artist on a weekly basis.

7. **Arbitration.** Recipient and Artist agree to submit all disputes hereunder in excess of $_____ to arbitration before _____ at the following location _____ under the rules of the American Arbitration Association. The arbitrator's award shall be final and judgment may be entered on it in any court having jurisdiction thereof.

8. **Miscellany.** This Agreement contains the full understanding between the parties hereto and may only be modified by a written instrument signed by both parties. It shall be governed by the laws of the state of _____.

IN WITNESS WHEREOF, the parties hereto have signed this Agreement as of the date first set forth above.

Artist_____   Recipient_____
Company Name

By_____
Authorized Signatory, Title

Consignment Contract with Record of Consignment and Statement of Account

Many artists who sell their work through retailers or wholesalers rely on trust instead of contracts. Trust is fine when everything is going smoothly, but it is of little value after disputes arise and neither party is truly certain which contractual terms originally bound the artist and other party together. Contracts can vary from a simple consignment of one piece of work to an ongoing representation arrangement, under which the other party has certain rights to represent more of the artist's work. Form 9, Consignment Contract, would be likely to be used when crafts are sold more like paintings or sculptures, while Form 10, Distribution Contract, or Form 11, Basic Distribution Contract, would be more applicable when crafts are sold in larger quantities more like manufactured items. The discussion that follows is based on Form 9 and refers to the other party as the gallery, but the points discussed here can apply to any consignment agreement.

A basic rule is: never give the gallery rights to sell work that the gallery has no capacity to sell. This means that the scope of the representation must be carefully scrutinized. Also, since the work will be in the possession of the gallery, the responsibility of the gallery for damage, loss, and repairs must be resolved.

One danger facing the artist is the possibility that the gallery may go bankrupt. If this happens, creditors of the gallery may have a right to seize consigned work. Many states have enacted laws to protect the artist from such seizures. However, the artist must check on a state-by-state basis to determine the status of the law. One way to do this is to contact the nearest group of volunteer lawyers for the arts.

Insofar as possible, the artist must verify that the gallery is stable financially. Of course, it can be difficult to know what goes on behind the scenes at an apparently successful enterprise. But late payments to other artists or suppliers certainly suggest economic difficulty. In any case, one might want to obtain a security interest in the work in order to have a right to the work even if the gallery does go bankrupt.

One other important issue is the identities of the purchasers of the artist's work. If the artist does not know who purchased the works and where the purchasers live, a retrospective exhibition and even access to take photographs are nearly impossible. The gallery may resist giving these names on the theory that the artist will then sell directly to the gallery's clients. One solution might be to have a neutral third party hold the names and contact the purchasers for reasons specified in the contract, such as a retrospective exhibition.

The commission for the gallery varies in the range of 25 to 50 percent of the retail sale price. Reasons for a higher commission would certainly include higher costs to the gallery in making the sales, such as those incurred in extensive promotion or foreign travel. A related issue is: who will bear the various expenses of exhibitions and promotion? While it is a fair assumption that the gallery will usually carry these expenses, it nonetheless bears review. If the gallery pays for frames or similar items, who will own them after the exhibition?

The artist should not be bound for too long a period of time by a contract with a gallery. What was appropriate at one time may no longer serve the artist as he or she grows in terms of both aesthetic and financial success. One way to deal with this is to provide for a right of termination after a certain time period, such as one or two years.

Highly successful artists may receive a stipend each month from the gallery. This is an amount of money that the artist receives regardless of sales. If sales are made, the amounts paid as a stipend are subtracted from the amounts due to the artist. Problems can arise when sales are not made and the gallery takes work to cover the stipend. If the gallery ends up with too many of the artist's works, it is as if the artist has an alter ego. The gallery may be tempted to sell its own works by the artist ahead of works by the artist that are on consignment.

The artist may want to create a network with a number of galleries, setting limitations with each as to the types of work, areas, and exclusivity. The mechanism to do this would be a coherent series of contracts that protect the artist, while giving the galleries the rights and types of work that they need to make representing the artist remunerative.

The artist may also deal with consultants or dealers who do not have galleries. For example, artists' reps who sell to corporate America use sales tools such as slides and portfolios, but do not necessarily have galleries. Nonetheless, the same considerations apply to contracts with such representatives as apply to contracts with galleries. Instead of specifying the nature of the exhibition to be given, such a contract might specify the nature of the efforts to be made on behalf of the artist, or, at least, require best efforts on the part of the representative.

Filling in the Form

In the Preamble give the date and the names and addresses of the parties. In Paragraph 1 specify whether the agreement is exclusive or nonexclusive, and indicate the geographic area covered, as well as which media will be represented. In Paragraph 2 give the term of the agreement and indicate special grounds for termination, such as the death of a particular employee of the gallery or a change of location by the gallery. In Paragraph 3 indicate how long the artist's solo exhibition will be and where the exhibition will take place. Then show how expenses will be shared and who will own any property created from these expenses. In Paragraph 4 give the gallery's commission rate for its own sales as well as the commission rate for the artist's sales, if applicable. In Paragraph 7 fill in how often an accounting will be given and when such accountings will commence. In Paragraph 10 specify

how much insurance will be provided. In Paragraph 14 give the name of an arbitrator or arbitrating body and fill in the maximum small claims court limit so lawsuits can be brought in small claims court for small amounts. In Paragraph 16 specify which state's laws will govern the agreement. Both parties should then sign the agreement. The artist should also fill in the Record of Consignment and have a representative of the gallery sign it. The Record of Consignment can be used each time the artist delivers additional works to the gallery. The Statement of Account will be filled out by the gallery when accountings are due.

Negotiation Checklist

❏ State that the artist is the creator and owner of the consigned works and, if required, warrant this to be true.

❏ Determine whether the gallery should have an exclusive or nonexclusive right to represent the artist. (Paragraph 1)

❏ Whether the representation is exclusive or nonexclusive, limit the area in which the gallery will represent the artist. (Paragraph 1)

❏ Specify the media which the gallery will represent for the artist. (Paragraph 1)

❏ If the representation is exclusive, limit the work subject to the contract to that work produced during the term of the contract, not work created before or after the contract. (Paragraph 1)

❏ Require signed documentation of all work consigned to the gallery. (Paragraph 1 and the Record of Consignment)

❏ Specify a reasonable term, which should not be too long unless there is also a right to terminate the contract. (Paragraph 2)

❑ Give a right of termination on thirty or sixty days notice to either party. (Paragraph 2)

❑ Provide for termination in the event of the gallery's bankruptcy or insolvency. (Paragraph 2)

❑ Provide for termination if a particular person dies or leaves the employment of the gallery. (Paragraph 2)

❑ Provide for termination in the event of a change of ownership of the gallery.

❑ Provide for termination in the event the gallery moves to a new area. (Paragraph 2)

❑ Provide for termination in the event of a change of the form of ownership of the gallery.

❑ Provide for termination if a specified level of sales is not achieved by the gallery over a certain time period.

❑ Decide whether the death of the artist should cause a termination.

❑ In the event of termination, require the gallery to pay the expenses of immediately returning all the consigned works to the artist. (Paragraph 2)

❑ Require that the gallery keep confidential all transactions on behalf of the artist.

❑ Require that the gallery exercise best efforts to sell the artist's work.

❑ Specify the efforts to be exercised by the gallery, such as providing an exhibition for a certain number of days during the exhibition season. (Paragraph 3)

❑ Give artistic control over the exhibition and any reproductions of the work to the artist. (Paragraph 3)

❑ If the gallery will not pay all the expenses of the exhibition, which should be enumerated in any case, determine how the payment of various expenses will be divided between the gallery and the artist. (Paragraph 3)

❑ Consider having the gallery pay for the construction of expensive pieces.

❑ Consider having the gallery advance money to pay for construction of expensive pieces. These advances, which should be nonrefundable, would later be recouped by the gallery from sales of the work or by taking ownership of some of the work.

❑ Consider specifying a budget for certain important items, such as promotion, and even detailing how the money will be spent.

❑ State who will own frames and other property created as an expense of the exhibition. (Paragraph 3)

❑ If the artist is to provide his or her mailing list to help in the promotion of the exhibition, consider requiring that this list be kept confidential and not be used for other promotional purposes.

❑ Give the commission rate on retail price to be paid to the gallery for each piece sold. (Paragraph 4)

❑ Do not agree to a "net price" commission, under which the gallery agrees to pay a fixed amount to the artist when the work is sold, since this will allow the gallery to charge higher prices and, in effect, pay a lower commission rate.

❑ If the gallery is selling works in different media, consider whether the commission should vary from one medium to another.

❑ If sales are substantial, review whether the commission rate should decrease as the volume of sales increases.

❑ If the gallery gives a discount on certain sales,

have the discount deducted from the gallery's commission rather than shared between the gallery and the artist. (Paragraph 4)

❏ If the representation is exclusive as to area or types of work, decide if the artist must pay a commission to the gallery on sales by the artist and, if so, which types of sales will be covered and how much the commission will be. It should certainly be less than what the gallery would receive from sales due to the gallery's own efforts. (Paragraph 4)

❏ If the artist is to pay a commission on certain sales by the artist, exclude transfers by gift or barter from such a requirement.

❏ If the artist is to pay a commission on certain sales by the artist, consider excluding a certain dollar amount of sales from this requirement.

❏ If the gallery will sell through other galleries, resolve the issue of double commissions.

❏ Specify the retail prices and allowable discounts for sales of the work. (Paragraph 5 and the Record of Consignment)

❏ Require that the gallery pay the artist as soon as possible after work is sold. (Paragraph 6)

❏ Require the artist's consent to sales on approval or credit. Sales on approval basically involve loaning the work to a collector who has agreed to purchase the work if he or she approves of it after the loan period. This may also be in the form of a sale with a right to return the work during a specified period of time, in which case payment might not be made in full until that time period has elapsed. (Paragraph 6)

❏ Have the gallery guarantee the proceeds of sales on credit.

❏ Have first proceeds from sales on approval or

credit paid to the artist. (Paragraph 6)

❏ Consider having the gallery purchase work outright, instead of taking it on consignment.

❏ Consider asking for a stipend, an amount paid every month regardless of sales, which would be nonrefundable and paid back by sales of work to the gallery if amounts due the artist from sales were insufficient. (See other provisions.)

❏ If the gallery is buying work outright, or is paying a stipend which may result in the gallery buying work, consider specifying the price at which the work must be sold. State that the artist shall receive a part of the resale proceeds if the work is sold for a higher price.

❏ Require periodic accountings by the gallery which include all the information the artist needs to know that the payment is correct and where the work is. (Paragraph 7 and Statement of Account)

❏ Require a final accounting upon termination of the agreement. (Paragraph 8)

❏ Make the gallery strictly responsible for loss or damage from the receipt of the work until it is returned to the artist. (Paragraph 9)

❏ If possible, have the gallery arrange shipment from the artist to the gallery and make the gallery responsible for loss or damage during that time period.

❏ Provide that in the event of loss or damage that cannot be restored, the artist shall receive the same monies that would be due if the work had been sold. (Paragraph 9)

❏ Give the artist control over any restoration of his or her work. (Paragraph 9)

❏ Require the gallery to insure the work for a

portion of the retail price, presumably enough to pay the artist in full in the event of loss or damage. (Paragraph 10)

❏ Make the artist a named beneficiary of the gallery's insurance policy with respect to the artist's work and provide proof of this insurance to the artist.

❏ Review which risks are covered by any insurance and which risks may be excluded, such as loss by mysterious disappearance or damage due to frequent handling.

❏ Give the artist a security interest to protect the work from creditors of the gallery and require the gallery to execute any documents necessary to perfect the security interest. Security interests are reviewed in other provisions in the discussion of Form 1. (Paragraph 12)

❏ Require the gallery to post a sign stating that the artist's work is on consignment, since this will help to protect the consigned work from seizure by creditors of the gallery.

❏ Provide for title to pass from the artist directly to any purchaser and, if that purchaser is the gallery, only after full payment has been received by the artist. (Paragraph 12)

❏ Have the gallery agree not to encumber the consigned art in any way for which the artist may be liable. (Paragraph 12)

❏ Review the standard provisions in the introductory pages and compare with Paragraphs 13-16.

❏ Keep in mind that state laws vary greatly with respect to artist-gallery relationships, so the choice of which state's law will govern may be far more important than is the case in most contracts. (Paragraph 16)

Other Provisions that can be added to Form 9:

❏ Stipend. The regular flow of income to the artist can be very important. This is what a stipend provides, whether it is paid on a weekly, monthly, or other periodic basis. Such a stipend should always be stated to be nonrefundable. However, the stipend must still be repaid, either by reducing sums payable to the artist from sales, or by having the gallery purchase work from the artist. A somewhat less sophisticated approach would be to have the gallery simply pay one sum as an advance against future sales. Such an advance usually would be paid on signing the contract. If the gallery is purchasing work to pay back an advance or stipend, it will only credit the artist with what the artist would have received had the art been sold (not the full retail price, since the gallery's commission would have been subtracted from that). The following provision is one approach to a contract with a stipend:

Stipend. The Gallery shall pay the Artist the nonrefundable sums of $_____ monthly, commencing with the first payment on the signing of this Agreement and continuing with payments on the first day of each month for the term of this Agreement. All funds paid the Artist hereunder shall be deemed advances which are to be recouped by the Gallery as follows: (1) By subtracting such advances from sums due the Artist for sales of work under this Agreement; or (2) In the event sums due the Artist do not equal or exceed such advances, by purchasing a sufficient number of consigned works that sums due the Artist equal or exceed such advances. If the Gallery is purchasing works hereunder, the Artist shall be credited for the amount which the Artist would have received had the work been sold by the Gallery to an outside purchaser at the retail price specified in the Record of Consignment.

❏ Best Efforts. The requirement that the gallery use best efforts is hard to make into a legal issue, since best efforts is a rather subjective term. It is really better to try and specify exactly what the gallery is required to do. However, there may be some value to include a best efforts provision such as the following:

Best Efforts. The Gallery shall use its best efforts to fulfill its obligations pursuant to this contract.

❏ Payment of Exhibition Expenses. If the gallery is to pay for most of the exhibition expenses, it would be wise to include a provision detailing which expenses. If the gallery is to bear all expenses, this provision should be open-ended, such as the following:

Payment of Exhibition Expenses. The Gallery shall pay all expenses of preparing for the exhibition and the exhibition itself, including but not limited to transporting the work from the Artist's studio to the Gallery (including the cost of insurance and packing), advertising, catalogs, announcements, framing, special installations, photographing the work, the party for the opening, shipping of the work to purchasers, and transporting the work back to the Artist (including the cost of insurance and packing).

Consignment Contract
with Record of Consignment and Statement of Account

AGREEMENT made as of the _____ day of _____, 19_____, between_____ (hereinafter referred to as the "Artist"), located at _____, and _____ (hereinafter referred to as the "Gallery"), located at

_____.

WHEREAS, the Artist is a professional artist of good standing; and

WHEREAS, the Artist wishes to have certain works represented by the Gallery, and

WHEREAS, the Gallery wishes to represent the Artist under the terms and conditions of this Agreement,

NOW, THEREFORE, in consideration of the foregoing premises and the mutual covenants hereinafter set forth and other valuable considerations, the parties hereto agree as follows:

1. **Scope of Agency.** The Artist appoints the Gallery to act as Artist's ❏ exclusive ❏ nonexclusive agent in the following geographic area:_____ for the exhibition and sale of works in the following media: _____. This agency shall cover only work completed by the Artist while this Agreement is in force. The Gallery shall document receipt of all works consigned hereunder by signing and returning to the Artist a Record of Consignment in the form annexed to this contract as Appendix A.

2. **Term and Termination.** This Agreement shall have a term of _____ years and may be terminated by either party giving sixty days written notice to the other party. The Agreement shall automatically terminate with the death of the Artist, the death or termination of employment of _____ with the Gallery, if the Gallery moves outside of the area of _____, or if the Gallery becomes bankrupt or insolvent. On termination, all works consigned hereunder shall immediately be returned to the Artist at the expense of the Gallery.

3. **Exhibitions.** The Gallery shall provide a solo exhibition for the Artist of _____ days between _____ and _____ in the exhibition space located at _____ which shall be exclusively devoted to the Artist's exhibition for the specified time period. The Artist shall have artistic control over the exhibition of his or her work and the quality of reproduction of such work for promotional or advertising purposes. The expenses of the exhibition shall be paid for in the respective percentages shown below:

Exhibition Expenses	Artist	Gallery
Transporting work to Gallery (including insurance and packing)...........	_____	_____
Advertising..	_____	_____
Catalogs...	_____	_____
Announcements..	_____	_____
Frames..	_____	_____
Special installations..	_____	_____
Photographing work..	_____	_____
Party for opening..	_____	_____
Shipping to purchasers..	_____	_____
Transporting work back to artist (including insurance and packing).........	_____	_____
All other expenses arising from the exhibition.....................................	_____	_____

No expense which is to be shared shall be incurred by either party without the prior written consent of the other party as to the amount of the expense. After the exhibition, the frames, photographs, negatives, and any other tangible property created in the course of the exhibition shall be the property of _____.

4. **Commissions.** The Gallery shall receive a commission of ____ percent of the retail price of each work sold. In the case of discount sales, the discount shall be deducted from the Gallery's commission. If the Gallery's agency is exclusive, then the Gallery shall receive a commission of _____ percent of the retail price for each studio sale by the Artist that falls within the scope of the Gallery's exclusivity. Works done on a commissioned basis by the Artist ❏ shall ❏ shall not be considered studio sales on which the Gallery may be entitled to a commission.

5. **Prices.** The Gallery shall sell the works at the retail prices shown on the Record of Consignment, subject to the Gallery's right to make customary trade discounts to such purchasers as museums and designers.

6. **Payments.** The Gallery shall pay the Artist all proceeds due to the Artist within thirty days of sale. No sales on approval or credit shall be made without the written consent of the Artist and, in such cases, the first proceeds received by the Gallery shall be paid to the Artist until the Artist has been paid all proceeds due.

7. **Accounting.** The Gallery shall furnish the Artist with an accounting every _____ months in the form attached hereto as Appendix B, the first such accounting to be given on the first day of _____, 19____. Each accounting shall state for each work sold during the accounting period the following information: the title of the work, the date of sale, the sale price, the name and address of the purchaser, the amounts due the Gallery and the Artist, and the location of all works consigned to the Gallery that have not been sold. An accounting shall be provided in the event of termination of this Agreement.

8. **Inspection of Books.** The Gallery shall maintain accurate books and documentation with respect to all transactions entered into for the Artist. On the Artist's written request, the Gallery will permit the Artist or the Artist's authorized representative to examine these books and documentation during normal business hours of the Gallery.

9. **Loss or Damage.** The Gallery shall be responsible for the safekeeping of all consigned artworks. The Gallery shall be strictly liable for loss or damage to any consigned artwork from the date of delivery to the Gallery until the work is returned to the Artist or delivered to a purchaser. In the event of loss or damage that cannot be restored, the Artist shall receive the same amount as if the work had been sold at the retail price listed in the Record of Consignment. If restoration is undertaken, the Artist shall have a veto power over the choice of the restorer.

10. **Insurance.** The Gallery shall insure the work for ____ percent of the retail price shown in the Record of Consignment.

11. **Copyright.** The Gallery shall take all steps necessary to insure that the Artist's copyright in the consigned works is protected, including but not limited to requiring copyright notices on all reproductions of the works used for any purpose whatsoever.

12. **Security Interest.** Title to and a security interest in any works consigned or proceeds of sale under this Agreement are reserved to the Artist. In the event of any default by the Gallery, the Artist shall have all the rights of a secured party under the Uniform Commercial Code and the works shall not be subject to claims by the Gallery's creditors. The Gallery agrees to execute and deliver to the Artist, in the form requested by the Artist, a financing statement and such other documents which the Artist may require to perfect its security interest in the works. In the event of the purchase of any work by a party other than the Gallery, title shall pass directly from the Artist to the other party. In the event of the purchase of any work by the Gallery, title shall pass only upon full payment to the Artist of all sums due hereunder. The Gallery agrees not to pledge or encumber any works in its possession, nor to incur any charge or obligation in connection therewith for which the Artist may be liable.

13. Assignment. This Agreement shall not be assignable by either party hereto, provided, however, that the Artist shall have the right to assign money due to him or her hereunder.

14. Arbitration. All disputes arising under this Agreement shall be submitted to binding arbitration before _____ in the following location _____ and the arbitration award may be entered for judgment in any court having jurisdiction thereof. Notwithstanding the foregoing, either party may refuse to arbitrate when the dispute is for a sum of less than $_____.

15. Modifications. All modifications of this Agreement must be in writing and signed by both parties. This Agreement constitutes the entire understanding between the parties hereto.

16. Governing Law. This Agreement shall be governed by the laws of the State of _____.

IN WITNESS WHEREOF, the parties hereto have signed this Agreement as of the date first set forth above.

Artist _____   Gallery _____
                                                          Company Name

                                            By_____
                                                    Authorized Signatory, Title

APPENDIX A: Record of Consignment

This is to acknowledge receipt of the following works on consignment:

	Title	Medium	Description	Retail Price
1.				
2.				
3.				
4.				
5.				
6.				
7.				
8.				
9.				

                    Gallery _____
                                        Company Name

                    By_____
                            Authorized Signatory, Title

APPENDIX B: Statement of Account

Date: _____, 19_____

Acounting for period from _____, 19_____, through _____, 19_____.

The following works were sold during this period:

Title	Date Sold	Purchaser's Name and Address	Sale Price	Gallery's Commission	Due Artist
1. _____	____	_____	_____	_____	_____
_____	____	_____	_____	_____	_____
2. _____	____	_____	_____	_____	_____
_____	____	_____	_____	_____	_____
3. _____	____	_____	_____	_____	_____
_____	____	_____	_____	_____	_____
4. _____	____	_____	_____	_____	_____
_____	____	_____	_____	_____	_____

The total due you of $_____ is enclosed with this Statement of Account.

The following works remain on consignment with the Gallery:

Title	Location
1. _____	_____
2. _____	_____
3. _____	_____
4. _____	_____
5. _____	_____
6. _____	_____
7. _____	_____
8. _____	_____
9. _____	_____

Gallery _____
Company Name

By_____
Authorized Signatory, Title

Distribution Contract and Basic Distribution Contract

The artist with inventory from crafts lines may want a larger company to handle its distribution. This larger company may be a distributor or another crafts producer. One of the best ways to find a distributor is to find a company that has successfully sold lines similar to the ones to be created by the artist. If this company is a producer, of course, tension may develop if the lines are so similar as to be competitive. In contacting a distributor, the sales manager is a good person to speak with. The sales manager can give insight into the market which that company can reach effectively and direct the artist to the final decision maker with respect to taking on an item or a line for distribution.

A fundamental issue is whether to sell outright or consign the inventory to the distributor. Each arrangment has advantages. If sold, the artist does not have to worry about how the public will receive the line. The distributor has taken this risk. The number fabricated can be matched to the order from the distributor, so the costs are kept to a minimum. Arrangements for payment might vary, but one approach might be a partial payment made when the contract is signed with the balance due thirty to sixty days after delivery. As the dollar volume of sales increases the artist might seek a higher percentage of the price.

If the goods are consigned, the artist retains title until the distributor sells them on behalf of the artist. Despite the retention of title, consignment has several risks. There is no guarantee the goods will ever be sold, in which case the artist will receive no payment. The distributor, as a merchant, has the right to pass good title even if it sells the inventory in violation of the agreement with the artist. If creditors of the distributor believe the goods belong to the distributor, they may be able to seize them in the event the distributor goes bankrupt. Certainly the capability to sell, integrity, and financial condition of any potential distributor must be reviewed carefully by the artist.

When goods are consigned the artist should expect to receive more than when goods are sold. This is because consignment is more burdensome for the artist, since capital is tied up in the consigned inventory and other expenses and risks also exist. While a sale arrangement can easily be priced as a percentage of retail price, a consignment might be more likely to be a percentage of net receipts. Net receipts are the wholesale prices received by the distributor (reduced by certain items which must be carefully defined, such as sales taxes collected).

Form 10, Distribution Contract, is drafted for a continuing relationship between the artist and distributor. For each product, a memorandum is prepared that begins by stating: "The following is to confirm the distribution for the product listed below pursuant to the Contract dated _____, 19___, between _____ and _____." This would continue by giving a brief description, size, any additional specifications, quantity, retail price, delivery date, and distribution date. Both parties would sign and date the memorandum. If the contract is for one product, then only one such memorandum need be prepared. Or Paragraph 1 can be amended to state that the contract is for one product and the information that would have been given in the memorandum can be given in Paragraph 1.

Whether the goods are sold or consigned, the distributor may want to have a voice in such matters as price and quality. The distributor taking consigned products must sell the products to earn a profit, while the distributor that has purchased products will lose money if it cannot resell the products. Especially if the distributor has purchased the products, it may insist on a right of approval to ensure that quality standards will be maintained.

The rights granted to the distributor to sell the products must be carefully limited. As in any grant of rights, only those rights that can be effectively exploited by the other party should be granted to that party. If the distributor sells in the United States, that should be a limitation of the grant of rights given to the distributor. The artist is free to seek another distributor for the rest of the world, whether that proves to be one distributor (working with subdistributors in each country) or many distributors (perhaps one in each country). The distributor may need nonexclusive direct mail rights as well, although the artist may resist giving this if the direct mail campaigns will compete with one another.

The term of the contract has to be long enough to let the distributor sell the goods, but not so long that the artist cannot get back the rights granted if the distributor is unable to sell effectively. The time for payment, periodic statements of account, and the right to inspect the records of the distributor will be covered in the contract. If the products are consigned, the artist will want the right to perfect a security interest in the products. This means that if certain filings are made with the appropriate government agency, the artist will have priority over unsecured creditors of the distributor with respect to the consigned inventory in the event of the distributor's bankruptcy. The risk of loss or damage to the consigned goods, and insurance coverage, must also be dealt with.

One of the most important issues is the responsibility for and nature of the promotion of the products. What will each party do and who will bear the expenses? Will the distributor do more than place the product in its catalog? For example, will the distributor have booths at the major trade shows and perhaps advertise in appropriate media? Who will supply press releases and review samples and pay the cost of distributing them? It is likely that both the artist and the distributor should actively promote the products, in which case the contract offers the opportunity to divide the responsibilities in a way that will make the promotional campaign most effective.

Form 11, Basic Distribution Contract, is a simplified distribution contract for a nonexclusive consignment. It can be modified by adding additional provisions from Form 10. The negotiation checklist is for Form 10, but it can be used to modify Form 11.

Filling in the Forms

For Form 10, in the Preamble fill in the names and addresses of the parties. Keep in mind that Paragraph 1 requires the signing of a separate memorandum for each product to be distributed. In Paragraph 2 specify the rights granted to the distributor with respect to exclusivity types of markets and territories. Check the appropriate box to select either Paragraph 4 (if the products are being sold) or Paragraph 5 (if the products are being consigned). For Paragraph 4, fill in the amount of the discount from retail price to reach the price to be paid for the products. For Paragraph 5, fill in what percentage of the net receipts will be paid to the artist. In Paragraph 7 specify for products sold to the distributor whether any payment will be made at the time of signing the memorandum for each title and how many days after delivery payment of the balance will be made. In Paragraph 8 specify when the statement of account must be given for each monthly accounting period. In Paragraph 11 fill in the number of months after termination during which the distributor may sell off purchased inventory. In Paragraph 12 specify for consigned inventory the amount of insurance to be maintained. In Paragraph 13 state the promotion to be done by the distributor and any information about the distributor to be placed on or with the products. In Paragraph 14 state when sell offs at distress prices may be commenced for inventory purchased by the distributor. In Paragraph 18 specify the arbitrator and the place of arbitration. In Paragraph 19 indicate the addresses for notice if these addresses are not those shown in the Preamble. In Paragraph 20 specify which state's laws will govern the contract. Both parties should then sign.

For Form 11, fill in the distributor's name and address as well as the ship to address if different from the distributor's. Fill in the date, the distributor's account number if a repeat purchaser, the sales rep (if any), the order number, the method of shipment, and the date of shipment. Make certain all order information is correctly included. Indicate the amount of commission the distributor will retain (which is the equivalent of a discount), and the unit price due to the artist on sale. Fill in which party will pay for shipping. If there are other provisions to be added, perhaps from Form 10 or the concepts in the negotiation checklist, add them under Other Provisions. Both parties should then sign.

Negotiation Checklist

❏ Specify whether the contract will cover one product or many products, in which case the information to appear in the separate memorandum for each product should be listed. (Paragraph 1)

❏ State any requirements that may cause extra expense, such as an unusual packing or shipping requirement. If there are special requirements as to quality, appropriate specifications should be set forth in the memorandum for each product.

❏ Limit the grant of rights to what the artist wants the distributor to sell and what the distributor can effectively sell. For each type of distribution, specify the territory and whether the right is exclusive or nonexclusive. (Paragraph 2)

❏ If the distributor cannot sell effectively in Canada or other foreign countries, these territories should be reserved to the artist. (Paragraph 2)

❏ If the distributor is to sell in foreign countries, have the distributor bear the expense of any freight forwarding, customs duties, or taxes.

❏ Reserve to the artist all rights not granted to the distributor. (Paragraph 2)

❏ Agree that the parties will consult to avoid creating products which are in direct competition.

❏ Specify a term for the contract. Unless termination is permitted on sixty or ninety days written notice, the term should be relatively brief, such as one year after initial distribution. (Paragraph 3)

❏ State whether the products are being sold or consigned. (Paragraphs 4 and 5)

❏ If the products are being sold, seek the highest percent of retail price which might escalate upward as the sales volume increases. (Paragraph 4)

❏ Make all products purchased nonreturnable. (Paragraph 4)

❏ If products are being consigned, be specific as to what net receipts include and what is excluded from the definition. Net receipts should include the gross receipts (all money received by the distributor) from the sale of the products. To arrive at net receipts, gross receipts might be reduced by discounts the distributor gives its customers for early payment, money received to reimburse the distributor for expenses to be incurred (such as shipping and handling charges for direct mail orders), and similar items, each of which should be carefully evaluated. (Paragraph 5)

❏ For a consignment, seek the highest pass-through of net receipts to the artist. This might escalate upward with increasing sales volume. (Paragraph 5)

❏ For consigned products do not allow the distributor to make sales at more than a certain discount from retail price (such as 60 percent discount) without obtaining the artist's consent. (Paragraph 5) In such cases, consider whether the distributor should receive a lower proportion of the net receipts.

❏ If the distributor is also a manufacturer, do not allow the distributor to sell the artist's products at a higher discount than the distributor sells its own products.

❏ Seek to have the distributor pay the freight and insurance charges to deliver the products. (Paragraph 6) Keep in mind that "C.I.F. Dallas, Texas" stands for cost, insurance, and freight, and means that the cost of the merchandise, packing, shipping to the destination (in this case, Dallas), and insuring during shipment are included in the quoted price. On the other hand, "F.O.B. Taos, New Mexico" stands for free on board and means that the goods will be loaded for shipment without charge (in this case, loaded at Taos). If a manufacturer sells products F.O.B. at the location of the plant, this means that the cost of shipping and insurance will have to be paid by either the artist or the distributor.

❏ If products are sold outright, payment should be made as quickly as possible. Thirty days after delivery would be reasonable, but it might be possible to receive a partial payment at the time of signing the contract. (Paragraph 7)

❏ If products are consigned, payment will be made as inventory is sold. If the distributor considers inventory sold when orders are received, the distributor will probably want to pay based on the average amount of time it takes to collect payment after receipt of an order. This may be sixty to ninety days, but the artist should certainly seek payment sooner, such as twenty days after the close of the month for which the accounting is being given. (Paragraphs 7 and 8)

❏ For consigned inventory, negotiate for an advance payment at the time of signing the

memorandum for each product. Such advances are recouped against future payments for each title and help cash flow, especially if payment is to be made sixty to ninety days after the receipt of orders.

❏ State that consigned inventory shall be considered sold when the order is received by the distributor, not when the payment is received by the distributor. (Paragraph 7)

❏ State that for consigned products the distributor shall bear the risk of loss for uncollectible accounts. (Paragraph 7)

❏ Make time of the essence with respect to payment. (Paragraph 7)

❏ Bill interest on late payments, but do not violate state usury laws. (Paragraph 7)

❏ State that sales proceeds due to the artist shall be kept in a trust account segregated from the funds of the distributor. This provides some protection in the event of the distributor's bankruptcy.

❏ Require periodic statements of account, preferably on a monthly basis, providing information as to the sales for each product and, in the case of consigned inventory, showing net receipts and the amount due the artist. (Paragraph 8)

❏ Give the artist the right to inspect the books and records of the distributor. (Paragraph 9)

❏ If an inspection of the books and records reveals an underpayment to the artist of more than 5 percent, require the distributor to pay the cost of the inspection. (Paragraph 9)

❏ State that title in the inventory does not pass to the distributor until payment in full has been received. (Paragraph 10)

❏ Give the artist a right to perfect a security interest, so that the inventory (especially if consigned) can be protected from creditors of the distributor. (Paragraph 10)

❏ Allow termination of the contract by either party on thirty or sixty days written notice. It is especially detrimental to the artist to be locked into a contract when the distributor is not successful in selling the products. To increase flexibility, this termination can be for single products and does not have to terminate the distribution contract itself. (Paragraph 11)

❏ If the distributor resists allowing termination on thirty or sixty days written notice, specify that termination will be allowed if specified minimum sales figures are not met. This could be either a certain number of items sold or a certain dollar amount generated for the artist.

❏ Allow the artist to terminate on written notice if the distributor is in default under the contract. (Paragraph 11)

❏ State that the contract shall automatically terminate if the distributor is bankrupt or insolvent. (Paragraph 11)

❏ For inventory purchased by the distributor, give a six or nine month sell-off period after termination. (Paragraph 11) During the sell-off period, the distributor is allowed to sell inventory that remains on hand. The distributor may demand that the sell-off right include the right to make a distress sale of the inventory. Distress sales are made in bulk at discounts that usually range from 75 to 90 percent off retail price. If the distributor is at fault in failing to sell a product, a distress sale may injure the future potential of the product with a different distributor.

❏ After termination, require that any consigned inventory be returned to the artist at the expense of the distributor. (Paragraph 11)

❏ For consigned inventory, state that the distributor shall bear the risk of loss or damage from any cause from the time of delivery to the distributor until the time of return to the artist. (Paragraph 12)

❏ If the distributor will not agree to bear the risk of loss or damage to the inventory, specify how inventory shrinkage will be documented. For example, such shrinkage could be documented by a written report and photographs. Without documentation, the distributor can claim loss or damage and the artist will have difficulty in verifying the claim and making his or her own insurance claim (if the distributor is not providing insurance and the artist is).

❏ Require the distributor to insure consigned inventory for the benefit of the artist and specify the amount of the insurance. (Paragraph 12) This should be enough to cover the cost of replacing the inventory in the event of loss or damage. If the distributor argues that the cost of insurance, or even the cost of the warehousing, should be paid by the artist, it can be pointed out that the products are in the distributor's warehouse so the distributor can benefit from selling them and that insurance and warehousing should simply be a normal overhead expense of the distributor's operation.

❏ If there is an allowance for inventory shrinkage, limit the allowance to 5 percent of the consigned inventory and require that any additional shrinkage be accounted for as if the inventory had been sold.

❏ Require that consigned inventory be kept separate from the distributor's own stock in an area marked to show that the products belong to the artist. This is to try and protect the inventory from creditors of the distributor. (Paragraph 12)

❏ State that the distributor shall undertake at its

own expense an annual physical inventory of any consigned inventory in accordance with accepted accounting procedures.

❏ Require the distributor to use best efforts to sell the inventory, including placing each product in its catalog. (Paragraph 13)

❏ Specify other kinds of promotional activities that the distributor should pay for, such as the preparation and sending of press releases, display of products at trade shows, and advertising. If the distributor will advertise, the nature of the advertising and a minimum budget might be specified. The distributor may try to have the artist handle and pay for the sending of press releases and advertising, and it may be that these expenses will be shared in some way between the parties. (Paragraph 13)

❏ Require the distributor to warrant that none of its promotional materials shall either infinge any copyright or violate any other rights (such as rights of privacy).

❏ Decide who should pay for other promotional expenses, such as whether the artist should provide extra copies of each product for media reviewers. (Paragraph 13)

❏ Specify the information about the distributor to go on or with each product, including the placement of this information. By letting the public know how to order the product, orders should be increased. However, the artist may want certain types of orders (such as direct mail) to come to him or her rather than going to the distributor. (Paragraph 13)

❏ The distributor should have a right to make distress sales of inventory it has purchased. However, this right should not be exercisable until a reasonable effort has been made to sell through normal trade channels. So the distributor should have to wait for some period

of time, such as eighteen or twenty-four months after initial distribution, before it can sell at distress prices. Also, it should have to offer the inventory back to the artist at the lesser of either the distress price or the original price. Often the artist will have a way to dispose of such inventory and will want it. (Paragraph 14)

❏ Agree that the contract and its terms are confidential and will not be disclosed to any other party.

❏ Do not allow the distributor an option with respect to future products, since each product requires the best distributor for its particular markets. Unless it is clear that the distributor will successfully handle all of the artist's products, it is best to proceed one product at a time.

❏ Compare the standard provisions in the introductory pages with Paragraphs 15-20.

Other provisions that can be added to Form 10:

❏ Review by Distributor. Especially if the distributor is purchasing the inventory, it may demand a right to review each product it moves from prototype to production. The artist must consider whether such review by the distributor is unwanted interference or welcome assistance. A crucial issue will be whether the artist must take the suggestions of the distributor. Certainly the artist should seek to keep the power to make final decisions. On the other hand, it can be helpful to have the distributor approve a work-in-progress at a number of stages, because ultimate satisfaction with the finished product is far more likely. If a distributor is forced to purchase products it feels inferior (and these products are not successful sellers), the long-term relationship with the distributor is jeopardized.

Review by Distributor. Artist shall provide

the Distributor with a prototype of each product and shall make such changes as are reasonably requested. Distributor agrees to review the prototype and any related materials and return the same to Artist with comments for changes within _____ weeks of receipt.

❏ Condition of Inventory. If the distributor is purchasing the inventory, it may demand assurance as to the condition in which the inventory will be delivered. The artist must be careful that any quality standards or requirements for the condition of the inventory on delivery are not made unreasonably difficult. In relation to the quality of the products, the distributor may also seek to cover production specifications in the memorandum for each book under Paragraph 1 of the contract.

Condition of Inventory. The inventory shall be delivered in mint condition and shall be of the same quality as inventory previously supplied by the Distributor. The Distributor shall have no obligation to pay for items that are damaged or produced in a faulty manner.

❏ Referral of Orders. The distributor will want the artist to refer any orders that fall into the scope of the contract's exclusivity to the distributor. For example, a store might try to order from the artist instead of the distributor. The artist should make certain that none of these orders are of the type that the artist has the right to fulfill (such as a direct mail order when both parties have nonexclusive direct-mail rights).

Referral of Orders. The Artist shall refer to the Distributor all orders or inquiries that concern the sale of products in the markets and territory in which the Distributor has exclusive rights.

Distribution Contract

AGREEMENT made as of the _____ day of _____, 19_____, between _____ (hereinafter referred to as the "Artist"), located at _____, and _____ (hereinafter referred to as the "Distributor"), located at _____.

WHEREAS, Artist has developed and created inventory of a product or products and seeks distribution; and

WHEREAS, Distributor is in the business of distribution and wishes to distribute products of the Artist;

NOW, THEREFORE, in consideration of the foregoing premises and the mutual covenants hereinafter set forth and other valuable considerations, the parties hereto agree as follows:

1. **Duties of the Parties and Products Covered.** This Agreement shall provide the terms under which Distributor and Artist shall henceforth do business. The Artist shall perform at its sole expense and be solely responsible for the development and manufacture of products. The Distributor shall perform at its sole expense and be solely responsible for soliciting orders pursuant to the grant of rights in Paragraph 2, order processing and billing, maintaining and collecting accounts receivable, shipping and warehousing of products and processing of returns, and listing Artist's products in its catalog. The expense of and responsibility for promotion shall be determined pursuant to Paragraph 13 hereof. For each product to be distributed a Distribution Memorandum in the form attached hereto as Schedule A shall be completed and signed by the parties.

2. **Grant of Rights.** For each product, Artist grants to Distributor the ❏ exclusive ❏ nonexclusive rights to distribute and sell the products in the following markets:_____ and in the following territories: _____. All rights not granted to Distributor are reserved by Artist.

3. **Term.** For each product, this Agreement shall have a term ending one year after the distribution date, after which it is automatically renewed for periods of one year.

4. **Sale.** ❏ Artist agrees to sell products to Distributor at a discount of _____ percent off the suggested retail price. All products are purchased on a nonreturnable basis.

5. **Consignment.** ❏ Artist agrees to consign products to Distributor which agrees to pay Artist _____ percent of Distributor's net receipts for each product sold. Net receipts are defined as all proceeds received by the Distributor from sales of the product, except for proceeds received to cover shipping costs or sales tax. In no event shall Distributor sell products at a discount of more than _____ percent from retail price without obtaining the prior written consent of the Artist.

6. **Delivery.** Artist agrees to deliver the products by the delivery date set forth in each Distribution Memorandum. Freight and insurance charges for the delivery shall be paid by Distributor.

7. **Payment.** If products are sold pursuant to Paragraph 4, any payment to be made to the Artist at the time of signing for each product shall be specified in the Distribution Memorandum for that product and the remaining balance shall be payable _____ days after receipt of the inventory in Distributor's warehouse. If products are consigned pursuant to Paragraph 5, payment shall be due _____ days after the last day of the month in which the inventory was sold by the Distributor. Any advance for consigned inventory shall be specified in the Distribution Memorandum for each product, paid at the time of signing that Memorandum, and recouped from first proceeds due Artist hereunder. Time is of the essence with respect to payment. Consigned inventory shall be deemed sold in the accounting period in which the order is received. The Distributor shall bear the risk of any accounts which have purchased inventory consigned hereunder and prove to be uncollectible. Without limitation on any other rights or remedies available to Artist, if Distributor does not pay on time Artist may add a late payment charge of _____ percent per month on the unpaid balance.

8. **Statements of Account.** Distributor shall provide Artist with a monthly statement of account including, for each product, sales for the month and sales to date. If the products are consigned pursuant to Paragraph 5, the statement of account shall also show for each product the net receipts for the month and the amount due Artist.

Each statement of account shall be provided within _____ days after the last day of the month for which the accounting is given.

9. **Inspection of Books.** The Distributor shall maintain accurate books and documentation with respect to all transactions entered into for the Artist. Within two weeks of receipt of the Artist's written request, the Distributor shall permit the Artist or the Artist's authorized representative to examine these books and documentation during the normal business hours of the Distributor. If such inspection causes errors to be found which are to the Artist's disadvantage and represent more than 5 percent of the payment due the Artist pursuant to a statement of account, the cost of that inspection shall be paid for by the Distributor.

10. **Title and Security Interest.** Until such time that Distributor shall fully pay for any inventory pursuant to Paragraph 7, Artist retains and is vested with full title and interest to the inventory not paid for. For any inventory not paid for under this Agreement, a security interest in such inventory or any proceeds of sale therefrom is reserved to the Artist. In the event of any default by the Distributor, the Artist shall have the rights of a secured party under the Uniform Commercial Code and the inventory shall not be subject to claims by the Distributor's creditors. The Distributor agrees to execute and deliver to the Artist, in the form requested by the Artist, a financing statement and such other documents which the Artist may require to perfect its security interest in the inventory. Distributor agrees not to pledge or encumber any inventory to which Artist retains title, nor to incur any charge or obligation in connection therewith for which the Artist may be liable.

11. **Termination.** Either party may terminate this Agreement as to any product by giving the other party sixty days written notice prior to the renewal date. In the event the Distributor is in default of any of its obligations hereunder, the Artist may terminate this Agreement at any time by giving written notice to the Distributor. This Agreement shall automatically terminate in the event of the insolvency or bankruptcy of the Distributor. In the event of termination, Distributor shall at its own expense immediately return to the Artist all inventory consigned pursuant to Paragraph 5 and shall have the right to sell off books purchased pursuant to Paragraph 4 for a period of _____ months only. The rights and obligations of the Distributor pursuant to Paragraphs 7, 8, 9, 11, 12, and 14 shall survive termination hereunder.

12. **Risk of Loss or Damage and Insurance.** In the event the inventory is consigned pursuant to Paragraph 5, Distributor agrees that such inventory is the property of the Artist and shall keep it insured in the name of the Artist against all risks for _____ percent of retail value until it is sold or returned to the Artist. Distributor shall be liable to Artist for any damages to the consigned inventory arising from any cause whatsoever from the time Distributor receives possession through the time the inventory is sold or returned to the Artist. Distributor shall keep the consigned inventory in a warehouse area separate from any area containing products owned by the Distributor, and shall mark said area as containing products which are the property of the Artist.

13. **Promotion.** Distributor agrees to use best efforts to sell the products. Distributor shall include all products in its catalog and, in addition, promote each product as follows: _____

_____

Artist shall cooperate in promotional matters, providing samples, photos, and other material whenever possible, including advance information for Distributor's catalogs. Artist agrees to list information regarding the Distributor as follows:_____

_____

_____

14. **Sell-off Rights.** Commencing _____ months after the date of delivery, Distributor shall have the right to sell off inventory purchased pursuant to Paragraph 4 at whatever price Distributor shall determine, except that prior to any such sell off Distributor shall offer to sell the inventory to Artist at either the sell-off price or Distributor's purchase price, whichever is less. Artist shall accept or reject such offer within thirty days of receipt.

15. **Force Majeure.** If either party is unable to perform any of its obligations hereunder by reason of fire or other casualty, strike, act or order of a public authority, act of God, or other cause beyond the control of the party, then such party shall be excused from such performance during the pendency of such cause.

16. Assignment. This Agreement shall not be assignable by either party hereto, provided, however, that the Artist shall have the right to assign monies due to him or her hereunder, and the Distributor shall have the right to employ at its own cost and expense subdistributors or sales representatives to work for the Distributor in the sale and distribution of the Artist's products.

17. Relationship of Parties. The parties hereto are independent entities and nothing contained in this Agreement shall be construed to constitute a partnership, joint venture, or similar relationship between them.

18. Arbitration. All disputes arising under this Agreement shall be submitted to binding arbitration before _____ in the following location _____ and the arbitration award may be entered for judgment in any court having jurisdiction thereof.

19. Notices and Changes of Address. All notices shall be sent by registered or certified mail, return receipt requested, postage prepaid, to the Artist and Distributor at the addresses first given above unless indicated to the contrary here: _____. Each party shall give written notification of any change of address prior to the date of said change.

20. Miscellany. This Agreement shall be binding upon the parties and their respective heirs, successors, assigns, and personal representatives. This Agreement constitutes the entire understanding between the parties hereto and may not be modified, amended, or changed except by an instrument in writing signed by both parties. A waiver of any breach of any of the provisions of this Agreement shall not be construed as a continuing waiver of other breaches of the same or other provisions hereof. This Agreement shall be governed by the laws of the State of _____.

IN WITNESS WHEREOF, the parties hereto have signed this Agreement as of the date first set forth above.

Distributor_____   Artist_____
                    Company Name   Company Name

By_____   By_____
            Authorized Signatory, Title   Authorized Signatory, Title

Schedule A: Distribution Memorandum

This Memorandum is to confirm that the product listed below is to be distributed pursuant to the contract between the parties dated as of the _____ day of _____, 19____.

Description _____

_____

Size _____

Additional specifications _____

_____

_____

_____

_____

Quantity _____

Retail price _____

Delivery date _____

Distribution date _____

If this product is consigned to Distributor, an advance of $_____ shall be paid on signing this Memorandum.

If this product is sold to Distributor, a partial payment of $_____ shall be paid on signing this Memorandum.

AGREED TO:

Distributor_____   Artist_____
          Company Name   Company Name

By_____   By_____
     Authorized Signatory, Title   Authorized Signatory, Title.

Basic Distribution Contract

Artist's Letterhead

Distributor_____   Date_____

Address_____   Account Number_____

_____   Sales Rep_____

Ship to_____   Order Number_____

Address_____   Ship via_____

_____   Date shipped_____

Item Number	Description	Quantity Ordered	Quantity Shipped	Back Ordered	Retail Price	Commission	Unit Price	Amount Due on Sale

The merchandise shown above is consigned to the Distributor. Shipping costs to Distributor shall be paid by _____. At the end of each month, the Distributor shall render full payment with a statement of account detailing for each item the number sold, the amount due to the Artist after deduction of the Distributor's commission, and the remaining items still on consignment. In the event of loss or damage to any items, such items shall be treated as if sold during the month in which the loss or damage is discovered. Upon Artist's written request, Artist shall have the right to inspect the books of the Distributor during regular business hours. The Distributor shall not pledge or encumber any of the items consigned by the Artist. The Artist reserves a security interest in the consigned items pursuant to the Uniform Commercial Code, and the Distributor shall cooperate in the execution and signing of any documents which Artist may require to perfect the security interest. Neither party may assign its interest hereunder, although the Artist may assign monies due. All disputes in excess of $_____ arising under this Agreement shall be submitted to binding arbitration before _____ in the following location _____ and the arbitration award may be entered for judgement in any court having jurisdiction thereof. This agreement may only be modified in writing and shall be governed by the laws of the State of _____.

Other provisions: _____

_____.

IN WITNESS WHEREOF, the parties hereto have signed this Agreement as of the date shown above.

Artist_____   Distributor_____
                                                        Company Name

                                          By_____
                                                        Authorized Signatory, Title

Contract with a Sales Representative

The artist who manufactures substantial inventories may seek help in reaching the vast number of potential retail outlets and, perhaps, wholesalers as well.

One way to reach the stores would be to contract with a distributor, a method elaborated in Forms 10 and 11. The distributor may employ a sales staff or have many independent sales representatives. The artist may wish to emulate this approach.

Form 12, Contract with a Sales Representative, covers the key issues to be resolved when an artist retains a sales representative. The scope of representation is specified, both with respect to the type of accounts (retail, wholesale, or other types) and the territory. Since this is an exclusive sales contract, the sales representative has a right to payment for sales made by others (for example, if a store in the territory simply sends an order directly to the artist). The schedule of house accounts can be used to exclude certain accounts from the sales representative's right to receive a commission. House accounts might be accounts that have a special history, such as accounts handled by the in-house sales manager or accounts that order directly from the artist.

Sales representatives work to earn commissions, usually a percentage of net receipts. Net receipts will require a definition enumerating any items subtracted from the artist's gross receipts to reach net receipts. For a crafts line with good sales potential, the artist should be able to create a network of sales representatives. Each sales representative covers a particular territory, which is why many such sales representatives are necessary to ensure thorough coverage.

The artist must understand what sales representatives do, and what they do not do. A sales representative goes to the accounts in his or her territory, shows catalogs and sales materials to the account buyers, and takes orders. The sales representative does not publish a catalog, advertise, warehouse and ship, bill accounts, or handle collections of delinquent accounts. All of these functions must be handled by the artist.

The term of the agreement is closely tied with the right of termination. If a sales representative does not sell successfully, the artist has to have the right to replace that sales representative immediately. The artist will have to give statements of account and make payments on a regular basis, probably each month. It should be made clear that the representative is an independent contractor, not an employee or agent of the artist. Assignment of rights and obligations under the contract should not be allowed, except that the sales representative can be given the right to employ other sales representatives if that appears necessary.

Filling in the Form

In the Preamble fill in the date and the names and addresses of the parties. In Paragraph 1 fill in the crafts lines to be included, whether the representation is exclusive, whether both retail and wholesale are covered, the geographical territory in which the sales representative will have exclusive rights, and any sales that would not be commissionable. In Paragraph 2 fill in the term. In Paragraph 4 specify any items to be subtracted in reaching net receipts. In Paragraph 6 state when the monthly statement of account must be rendered. In Paragraph 11 specify an arbitrator and a place for arbitration. In Paragraph 12 indicate if notices should be sent to addresses other than those given in the Preamble. In Paragraph 13 specify which state's laws will govern the contract. Fill in Schedule A with a listing of House Accounts. Both parties should then sign.

Negotiation Checklist

❑ Specify whether the sales representative should work on an exclusive or nonexclusive basis. (Paragraph 1)

❑ Indicate whether all or only some of the artist's crafts lines are to be handled by the sale representative. (Paragraph 1)

❑ Determine whether the sales representative is to cover both retail and wholesale accounts and, if necessary, define retail and wholesale. (Paragraph 1)

❑ Specify the territory to be given to the sales representative. (Paragraph 1)

❑ Exclude house accounts. (Paragraph 1)

❑ Exclude from the scope of the representation all types of sales which the representative is unlikely to make. (Paragraph 1)

❑ Decide whether the contract is an exclusive sales agreement, in which case the sale representative will receive commissions on sales within the scope of the contract even if he or she does not make the sale. (Paragraph 1)

❑ Determine which accounts shall be house accounts. (Paragraph 1 and Schedule A)

❑ Specify a term for the contract, preferably a short term unless the contract can be terminated at will. (Paragraph 2)

❑ Require the sales representative to use best efforts to sell products. (Paragraph 3)

❑ State that the artist shall use best efforts to fulfill orders, but do not make the artist liable for commissions on orders which cannot be fulfilled. If an item is never manufactured or has gone out of stock, of course the artist would be unable to fulfill the order and would not want to pay any commission. (Paragraph 3)

❑ Specify the commissions to be received by the sales representative to stores. (Paragraph 4)

❑ Define "net receipts," which is the amount against which commissions will be paid. Net receipts will be amounts received by the artist from wholesalers and retailers, perhaps reduced by certain expenses. (Paragraph 4)

❑ State that commissions shall be reduced for bad debts and any returned merchandise at the time of declaring the bad debt or receiving the returned merchandise. (Paragraph 4)

❑ Specify a time for the payment of commissions. (Paragraph 5)

❑ Create a reserve against bad debts and returned merchandise, which would be a certain percentage of commissions to be held back by the artist until the amount of bad debts and returns can be determined.

❑ State that the artist shall give monthly statements of account and specify what information the accountings will provide. (Paragraph 6)

❑ Indicate that the parties are independent of each other. (Paragraph 7)

❑ Require the sales representative to indemnify the artist for injuries to the sales representative or others while traveling. (Paragraph 7)

❑ Do not allow assignment of the agreement by either party. If there will be a change of sales representatives, the artist will want to choose the new person. (Paragraph 8)

❑ Consider whether to allow the sales representative to employ others to make sales visits. (Paragraph 8)

❑ Allow each party to inspect the other party's books on reasonable notice. (Paragraph 9)

❑ Specify that by giving a short advance notice, such as thirty or sixty days, the contract can be terminated. (Paragraph 10)

❑ State that the contract can be terminated immediately for cause. (Paragraph 10)

❑ If the contract has a longer term and cannot be terminated quickly, provide that certain minimum sales levels must be achieved or the contract will terminate.

❑ State that the contract shall automatically terminate in the event of the bankruptcy or insolvency of either party. (Paragraph 10)

❑ Compare the standard provisions in the introductory pages with Paragraphs 11-13.

Contract with a Sales Representative

AGREEMENT made as of the _____ day of _____, 19_____, between _____ (hereinafter referred to as the "Artist"), located at _____, and _____ (hereinafter referred to as the "Sales Representative"), located at _____.

WHEREAS, Artist has created a crafts line for which he or she seeks sales representation; and

WHEREAS, Sales Representative is in the business of representing such lines;

NOW, THEREFORE, in consideration of the foregoing premises and the mutual covenants hereinafter set forth and other valuable considerations, the parties hereto agree as follows:

1. **Scope of Representation.** The Artist appoints the Sales Representative to act as Artist's ❏ exclusive ❏ nonexclusive sales representative in selling the following crafts lines_____ created by the Artist to ❏ retail ❏ wholesale crafts accounts in the following sales territory: _____ _____. House accounts, which are listed in Schedule A, are excluded from this Agreement and no commissions shall be payable on such accounts. Other accounts excluded from this Agreement include but are not limited to direct mail sales or other sales to individual buyers and_____.

2. **Term.** This Agreement shall have a term of _____ months, which shall be automatically renewed until the date of termination.

3. **Duties of the Parties.** The Sales Representative agrees to use his or her best efforts to promote and sell the Artist's products in the sales territory. The Artist shall use best efforts to have inventory sufficient to meet market demand in the territory handled by the Sales Representative, and shall make deliveries of all products sold by the Sales Representative, but shall have no liability for commissions with respect to orders which are not fulfilled for causes including but not limited to products which were not created, products which are out of stock, or products which are discontinued.

4. **Commissions.** For the services of the Sales Representative, the Artist agrees to pay Sales Representative a commission of ____ percent of the net receipts from all sales made by the Sales Representative to retail accounts and ____ percent of the net receipts from all sales made by the Sales Representative to wholesale accounts. Net receipts shall be all payments due the Artist for the products sold, less any deductions specified here:_____ _____. Commissions paid on sales which result in returns or bad debts shall be deducted from commissions due for the month in which the returns or bad debts are recorded.

5. **Payment.** Commissions shall be paid to the Sales Representative on a monthly basis at the time of rendering the Statement of Account for the month.

6. **Statements of Account.** Statements of account shall be given by the Artist to the Sales Representative on a monthly basis _____ days after the last day of the month accounted for. Each statement shall show for the month the net receipts from sales made by the Sales Representative to eligible accounts, the appropriate commission rates, the commissions due, and any deductions from commissions.

7. **Relationship of the Parties.** The parties hereto are independent entities and nothing contained in this Agreement shall be construed to constitute the Sales Representative an agent, employee, partner, joint venturer, or any similar relationship with or of the Artist. Further, the Sales Representative hereby indemnifies the Artist against any claim by the Sales Representative or others accompanying him or her with respect to injuries or damages sustained or caused while traveling, including but not limited to those caused while traveling by automobile or any other form of transportation.

8. **Assignment.** This Agreement shall not be assignable by either party hereto, provided, however, that the Sales Representative shall have the right to employ or commission at its own cost and expense other sales representatives to sell the Artist's works in the territory of the Sales Representative.

9. **Inspection of Books.** Each party shall maintain accurate books and documentation with respect to all transactions

entered into pursuant to this Agreement. Within two weeks of receipt of a written request by either party, the other party shall permit the requesting party or its authorized representative to examine these books and documentation during normal business hours.

10. **Termination.** Either party may terminate this Agreement by giving the other party sixty days written notice. In the event either party is in default of any of its obligations hereunder, the other party may terminate this Agreement at any time by giving written notice of termination. This Agreement shall automatically terminate in the event of the insolvency or bankruptcy of either party. The rights and obligations of the parties pursuant to Paragraphs 4, 5, and 7 shall survive termination hereunder.

11. **Arbitration.** All disputes arising under this Agreement shall be submitted to binding arbitration before _____ in the following location _____ and the arbitration award may be entered for judgment in any court having jurisdiction thereof.

12. **Notices and Changes of Address.** All notices shall be sent by registered or certified mail, return receipt requested, postage prepaid, to the Artist and Sales Representative at the addresses first given above unless indicated to the contrary here: _____
_____. Each party shall give written notification of any change of address prior to the date of said change.

13. **Miscellany.** This Agreement shall be binding upon the parties and their respective heirs, successors, assigns, and personal representatives. This Agreement constitutes the entire understanding between the parties hereto and may not be modified, amended, or changed except by an instrument in writing signed by both parties. A waiver of any breach of any of the provisions of this Agreement shall not be construed as a continuing waiver of other breaches of the same or other provisions hereof. This Agreement shall be governed by the laws of the State of _____.

IN WITNESS WHEREOF, the parties hereto have signed this Agreement as of the date first set forth above.

Sales Representative_____   Artist_____
                                    Company Name   Company Name

By_____   By_____
                    Authorized Signatory, Title   Authorized Signatory, Title

Schedule A: House Accounts

Account Name	Address
1.	
2.	
3.	
4.	
5.	
6.	
7.	
8.	
9.	

Contract with an Independent Contractor

FORM 13

Artists often hire independent contractors, such as an assistant, set builder, or carpenter. Independent contractors run their own businesses and hire out on a job by job basis. They are not employees, which saves the artist in terms of employee benefits, payroll taxes, and paperwork. By not being an employee, the independent contractor does not have to have taxes withheld and is able to deduct all business expenses directly against income.

A contract with an independent contractor serves two purposes. First, it shows the intention of the parties to have the services performed by an independent contractor. Second, it shows the terms on which the parties will do business.

As to the first purpose of the contract — showing the intention to hire an independent contractor, not an employee, the contract can be helpful if the Internal Revenue Service (IRS) decides to argue that the independent contractor was an employee. The tax law automatically classifies as independent contractors physicians, lawyers, general building contractors, and others who follow an independent trade, business, or profession, in which they offer their services to the public on a regular basis. However, many people don't fall clearly into this group. Since IRS reclassification from independent contractor to employee can have harsh consequences for the hiring party, including payment of back employment taxes, penalties, and jeopardy to qualified pension plans, the IRS has promulgated guidelines for who is an employee.

Basically, an employee is someone who is under the control and direction of the employer to accomplish work. The employee is not only told what to do, but how to do it. On the other hand, an independent contractor is controlled or directed only as to the final result, not as to the means and method to accomplish that result. Some twenty factors enumerated by the IRS dictate the conclusion as to whether someone is an employee or an independent contractor, and no single factor is controlling. Factors suggesting someone is an independent contractor would include that the person supplies his or her own equipment and facilities; that the person works for more than one party (and perhaps employs others at the same time); that the person can choose the location to perform the work; that the person is not supervised during the assignment; that the person receives a fee or commission rather than an hourly or weekly wage; that the person can make a loss or a profit; and that the person can be forced to terminate the job for poor performance but cannot be dismissed like an employee. The artist should consult his or her accountant to resolve any doubts about someone's status.

The second purpose of the contract is to specify the terms agreed to between the parties. What services will the contractor provide and when will the services be performed? On what basis and when will payment be made by the artist? Will there be an advance, perhaps to help defray expenses?

The artist should consult with his or her insurance agent with respect to the insurance the artist should carry when dealing with independent contractors. Certainly the artist should make sure there is adequate coverage for property damage or liability arising from lawsuits for injuries. The contractor should definitely have its own liability policy as well as workers' compensation and any state disability coverage.

Independent contractors can perform large jobs or render a day's services. Form 13 is designed to help artists deal with small independent contractors who are performing a limited amount of work. The negotiation checklist is also directed toward this situation, such as hiring an assistant or carpenter. However, some further discussion is necessary to cover the issues arising when the artist has a larger project to complete, such as a major studio renovation.

If the artist were dealing with a substantial renovation to the studio or other construction, the contract would have to be more complex. First, it's always wise to have references for a contractor who is new to the artist. Keep deposits small, since it can be hard to get a deposit back if the contractor doesn't perform. There should also be clarity as to the quality and perhaps even the brands of any materials to be used.

The contractor can be asked to post a surety bond, which is a bond to guarantee full performance. However, many small contractors may have difficulty obtaining such a bond, since the insurance company may require the posting of collateral. In any event, the artist might explore with his or her own insurance agent the feasibility of demanding this from the contractor. A point to keep in mind is that the contractor's failure to pay subcontractors or suppliers of material can result in a lien against the artist's property for work done to that property. A lien is like a mortgage on a building; it must be satisfied or removed before the property can be sold. A surety bond would avoid problems with liens.

A contractor should be required to give a bid. That bid will be the basis for the terms of the contract. The contractor may want to wait until after completing the work to determine a fee. Obviously this is unacceptable. The contractor may want to charge a fee for labor, but charge cost plus a markup for materials. This is probably also unacceptable, since the artist has a budget and needs to know that budget can be met. Another variation is for the contractor to allow for a 10 percent variation in the bid or the costs of materials based on what actually happens. This should be carefully evaluated by the artist and is less desirable than a firm fee.

The fee and the job description should only be modified by a written amendment to the contract. If this isn't required, disputes are likely to result.

The artist should, if possible, require the contractor to warrant a number of facts, such as the contractor being licensed if necessary, the materials being new and of good quality, the contractor being responsible for any damages arising from its work, and any construction being guaranteed for some period of time. The contractor would agree to protect the artist (by paying losses, damages, and any attorney's fees) in the event any of these warranties were breached.

Keep in mind that Form 13 is designed for day-to-day dealings with freelancers, not the hiring of builders for major renovations.

Filling in the Form

In the preamble fill in the date and the names and addresses of the parties. In Paragraph 1 show in detail what services are to be performed. Attach another sheet of description or a list of procedures, diagram, or a plan to the contract, if needed. In Paragraph 2 give a schedule. In Paragraph 3 deal with the fee and expenses. In Paragraph 4 specify a time for payment. In Paragraph 5 indicate how cancellations will be handled. In Paragraph 6[E] fill in any special criteria that the contractor should warrant as true. In Paragraph 7 fill in any insurance the contractor must carry. In Paragraph 10 specify who will arbitrate, where the arbitration will take place, and, if local small claims court would be better than arbitration, give amounts under the small claims court dollar limit as an exclusion from arbitration. In Paragraph 11 give the state whose laws will govern the contract. Both parties should then sign.

Negotiation Checklist

❏ Carefully detail the services to be performed. If necessary, attach an additional sheet of description, a list of procedures, or a plan or diagram. (Paragraph 1)

❏ Give a schedule for performance. (Paragraph 2)

❏ State the method for computing the fee. (Paragraph 3)

❏ If the contractor is to bill for expenses, limit which expenses may be charged. (Paragraph 3)

❏ Require full documentation of expenses in the form of receipts and invoices. (Paragraph 3)

❏ Place a maximum amount on the expenses that can be incurred. (Paragraph 3)

❏ Pay an advance against expenses, if the amount of the expenses are too much for the contractor to wait to receive back at the time of payment for the entire job. (Paragraph 3)

❏ State a time for payment. (Paragraph 4)

❏ Deal with payment for cancellations. (Paragraph 5)

❏ If expenses are billed for, consider whether any markup should be allowed.

❏ Require warranties that the contractor is legally able to perform the contract, that all services will be done in a professional manner, that any subcontractor or employee hired by the contractor will be professional, that the contractor will pay all taxes for the contractor and his or her employees, and any other criteria for the proper performance of the services. (Paragraph 6)

❏ Review insurance coverage with the artist's insurance agent.

❏ Specify what insurance coverage the contractor must have. (Paragraph 7)

❏ State that the parties are independent contractors and not employer-employee. (Paragraph 8)

❏ Do not allow assignment of rights or obligations under the contract. (Paragraph 9)

❏ The artist should check with his or her attorney as to whether arbitration is better than suing in the local courts, and whether small claims court might be better than arbitration. (Paragraph 10)

❏ Allow for an oral modification of either the fee or expense agreement, if such oral change is necessary to move the project forward quickly. (Paragraph 11)

❏ Compare Paragraph 11 with the standard provisions in the introductory pages.

Contract with an Independent Contractor

AGREEMENT entered into as of the_____day of _____, 19____, between _____
(hereinafter referred to as the "Artist"), located at _____,
and _____(hereinafter referred to as the "Contractor"), located at

_____.

The parties hereto agree as follows:

1. Services to be Rendered. The Contractor agrees to perform the following services for the Artist

_____
_____
_____
_____
_____
_____.

If needed, a list of procedures, diagram, or plan for the services shall be attached to and made part of this Agreement.

2. Schedule. The Contractor shall complete the services pursuant to the following schedule_____
_____
_____.

3. Fee and Expenses.   The Artist shall pay the Contractor as follows:
❑ Project rate $_____
❑ Day rate $_____/ day
❑ Hourly rate $_____/ hour
❑ Other _____ $_____

The Artist shall reimburse the Contractor only for the expenses listed here _____
_____.
Expenses shall not exceed $_____. The Contractor shall provide full documentation for any expenses to be
reimbursed, including receipts and invoices. An advance of $_____ against expenses shall be paid to the
Contractor and recouped when payment is made pursuant to Paragraph 4.

4. Payment. Payment shall be made: ❑ at the end of each day ❑ upon completion of the project ❑ within thirty
days of Artist's receipt of Contractor's invoice.

5. Cancellation. In the event of cancellation, Artist shall pay a cancellation fee under the following circumstances
and in the amount specified _____
_____.

6. Warranties. The Contractor warrants as follows:

(A) Contractor is fully able to enter into and perform its obligations pursuant to this Agreement.
(B) All services shall be performed in a professional manner.
(C) If employees or subcontractors are to be hired by Contractor they shall be competent professionals.
(D) Contractor shall pay all necessary local, state, or federal taxes, including but not limited to withholding taxes,
workers' compensation, F.I.C.A., and unemployment taxes for Contractor and its employees.

(E) Any other criteria for performance are as follows:

_____

_____.

7. **Insurance.** The Contractor shall maintain in force the following insurance _____

_____

_____.

8. **Relationship of Parties.** Both parties agree that the Contractor is an independent contractor. This Agreement is not an employment agreement, nor does it constitute a joint venture or partnership between the Artist and Contractor. Nothing contained herein shall be construed to be inconsistent with this independent contractor relationship.

9. **Assignment.** This Agreement may not be assigned by either party without the written consent of the other party hereto.

10. **Arbitration.** All disputes shall be submitted to binding arbitration before _____ in the following location _____ and settled in accordance with the rules of the American Arbitration Association. Judgment upon the arbitration award may be entered in any court having jurisdiction thereof. Disputes in which the amount at issue is less than $_____ shall not be subject to this arbitration provision.

11. **Miscellany.** This Agreement constitutes the entire agreement between the parties. Its terms can be modified only by an instrument in writing signed by both parties, except that oral authorizations of additional fees and expenses shall be permitted if necessary to speed the progress of work. This Agreement shall be binding on the parties, their heirs, successors, assigns, and personal representatives. A waiver of a breach of any of the provisions of this Agreement shall not be construed as a continuing waiver of other breaches of the same or other provisions hereof. This Agreement shall be governed by the laws of the State of _____.

IN WITNESS WHEREOF, the parties hereto have signed this as of the date first set forth above.

Artist_____   Contractor_____
                                                          Company Name

                                           By_____
                                                          Authorized Signatory, Title

Rental Contract

Rental of work can create a flow of income for the artist rather than a single payment. If the collector renting a work enjoys it over time, the collector may very well want to purchase the work rather than return it to the artist. The artist's retention of ownership of the original art thus creates the possibility of two sources of income, the rental and a later sale whether to the collector who rented the artwork or a different collector.

Because the artist will own work being held by someone else, the contract must provide a standard of care for the work, determine what will happen in the event of loss or damage, handle the question of insurance, deal with maintenance and repairs, restrict where the art is to be located, and specify the manner of and audiences to which the work may be displayed. A risk to guard against is the bankruptcy of the collector, in which case the art may become subject to the claims of the collector's creditors. To prevent this, the artist will want the right to a secured interest in the work and may choose to file Uniform Commercial Code Form 1 to make this right enforceable. A secured interest means that the artist's claim to the work will have priority over unsecured creditors.

Because this contract to rent also gives the collector the option to buy any of the works at the price specified in the schedule of work, all of the considerations involved in selling a work may also be present here.

Filling in the Form

In the Preamble fill in the date and the names and addresses of the parties. In Paragraph 2 specify the amount of the payments and the frequency, such as monthly. In Paragraph 3 state the date of delivery to the renter and who will pay the costs of the delivery. In Paragraph 4 fill in the percentage of the sale price to be insured. State the term of the contract in Paragraph 5. Indicate where the work will be located in Para-

graph 8. In Paragraph 11 specify who will pay for the return of the work. In Paragraph 12 check the box to show if rental fees paid will reduce the price if the work is purchased. Give the addresses for notices in Paragraph 19, and provide which state's laws will govern the contract in Paragraph 20. Both parties should then sign. If the renter is a business, add the business name and show the title of the person signing. Then fill in the Schedule of Works, specifying both the rental price and the sale price for each work.

Negotiation Checklist

❑ State that the artist owns the work. (Paragraph 1)

❑ Specify the rental fee. (Schedule of Works)

❑ Provide for the manner of payment of the rental fee, such as a lump sum for a certain time period or a monthly or quarterly payment. (Paragraph 2)

❑ Require the payment of interest if the rental payments are late.

❑ Specify who is responsible for delivery of the work. (Paragraph 3)

❑ State who will pay the cost of delivery. (Paragraph 3)

❑ Obtain a signed receipt from the renter that acknowledges the receipt of the work, in good condition, on the Schedule of Works.

❑ Require the renter to make an immediate objection if a work is not in good condition when received. (Paragraph 3)

❑ Have the renter agree to return the work in the same good condition as received. (Paragraph 3)

❏ Make the renter responsible for loss or damage to the work from the time of receipt until delivery back to the artist. (Paragraph 4)

❏ If possible, make the renter responsible for loss or damage from the time of shipment from the artist until delivery back to the artist.

❏ Require that the work be insured by the renter for the benefit of the artist and that proof be given that the insurance is in effect. (Paragraph 4)

❏ Review the insurance coverage to be certain of which risks are covered and which are excluded from coverage.

❏ Specify the term of the contract. (Paragraph 5)

❏ Restrict the uses which can be made of the work. (Paragraph 6)

❏ Deal with how any framing, cleaning, and repairs are to be handled. (Paragraph 7)

❏ Limit the locations where the renter may keep the work. (Paragraph 8)

❏ Give the artist access to the work during the rental term. (Paragraph 8)

❏ Reserve all reproduction rights to the artist. (Paragraph 9)

❏ Provide for termination on notice or in the event of the renter's insolvency or bankruptcy. (Paragraph 10)

❏ Specify who is responsible to return the work. (Paragraph 11)

❏ State who will pay the costs of returning the work. (Paragraph 11)

❏ Give the artist a security interest in the work and require that the renter execute any documents necessary to effect the security interest. (Paragraph 13)

❏ Provide for the payment of attorney's fees in the event of litigation, since it is more likely the artist will be the one who has to sue. (Paragraph 14)

❏ If the artist chooses to give the renter an option to purchase the work, review the negotiation checklist for Form 3 and compare with Paragraph 12 in the rental contract.

❏ Specify the sale prices for the work. (Schedule of Works)

❏ In the event of sale, reserve title to the artist until payment has been received in full. (Paragraph 13)

❏ Review the standard provisions in the introductory pages and compare with Paragraphs 15-20.

Rental Contract

AGREEMENT made as of the _____ day of _____, 19 _____, between _____ (hereinafter referred to as the "Artist"), located at _____ , and _____ (hereinafter referred to as the "Renter"), located at

_____.

WHEREAS, the Artist is a recognized professional artist who creates work for rental and sale; and

WHEREAS, the Renter wishes to rent and have the option to purchase certain works by the Artist; and

WHEREAS, the parties wish to have the rentals and any purchases governed by the mutual obligations, covenants, and conditions herein;

NOW, THEREFORE, in consideration of the foregoing premises and the mutual covenants hereinafter set forth and other valuable considerations, the parties hereto agree as follows:

1. **Creation and Title.** The Artist hereby warrants that the Artist created and possesses unencumbered title to the works of art listed and described on the attached Schedule of Works ("the Schedule").

2. **Rental and Payments.** The Artist hereby agrees to rent the works listed on the Schedule at the rental fees shown thereon and the Renter agrees to pay said rental fees as follows: $_____ per_____.

3. **Delivery and Condition.** The Artist shall be responsible for delivery of the works listed on the Schedule to the Renter by the following date: _____. All costs of delivery (including transportation and insurance) shall be paid by _____. The Renter agrees to make an immediate written objection if the works upon delivery are not in good condition or appear in any way in need of repair. Further, the Renter agrees to return the works in the same good condition as received, subject to the provisions of Paragraph 4.

4. **Loss or Damage and Insurance.** The Renter shall be responsible for loss of or damage to the rented works from the date of delivery to the Renter until the date of delivery back to the Artist. The Renter shall insure each work against all risks for the benefit of the Artist up to _____ percent of the sale price shown in the Schedule and shall provide Artist with a Certificate of Insurance showing the Artist as the named beneficiary.

5. **Term.** The term of this Agreement shall be for a period of _____ months, commencing as of the date of the signing of the Agreement.

6. **Use of Work.** The Renter hereby agrees that the rental under this Agreement is solely for personal use and that no other uses shall be made of the work, such other uses including but not being limited to public exhibition, entry into contests, and commercial exploitation.

7. **Framing, Cleaning, Repairs.** The Artist agrees to deliver each work ready for display. The Renter agrees not to remove any work from its frame or other mounting or in any way alter the framing or mounting. The Renter agrees that the Artist shall have sole authority to determine when cleaning or repairs are necessary and to choose who shall perform such cleaning or repairs.

8. **Location and Access.** The Renter hereby agrees to keep the works listed on the Schedule at the following address: _____, which may be changed only with the Artist's written consent, and to permit the Artist to have reasonable access to said works for the purpose of taking photographs of same.

9. **Copyright and Reproduction.** The Artist reserves all reproduction rights, including the right to claim statutory copyright, on all works listed on the Schedule. No work may be photographed, sketched, painted, or reproduced in any manner whatsoever without the express, written consent of the Artist. All approved reproductions shall bear a copyright notice composed of the following elements: the word Copyright or © by (Artist's name) 19____.

10. Termination. Either party may terminate this Agreement upon fifteen days written notice to the other party. This Agreement shall automatically terminate in the event of the Renter's insolvency or bankruptcy. Upon termination, the Artist shall refund to the Renter a pro rata portion of any prepaid rental fees allocable to the unexpired rental term, said refund to be made after the works have been returned to the Artist in good condition.

11. Return of Works. The Renter shall be responsible for the return of all works upon termination of this Agreement. All costs of return (including transportation and insurance) shall be paid by _____.

12. Option to Purchase. The Artist hereby agrees not to sell any works listed on the Schedule during the term of this Agreement. During the term the Renter shall have the option to purchase any work listed on the Schedule at the sale price shown thereon. This option to purchase shall be deemed waived by Renter if he or she fails to make timely payments pursuant to Paragraph 2. If the Renter chooses to purchase any work, all rental fees paid to rent that work ❏ shall ❏shall not be applied to reduce the sale price. Any purchase under this paragraph shall be subject to the following restrictions:

(A) The Artist shall have the right to borrow any work purchased for up to sixty days once every five years for exhibition at a nonprofit institution at no expense to the Renter-Purchaser, provided that the Artist gives 120 days advance notice in writing prior to the opening and offers satisfactory proof of insurance and prepaid transportation.

(B) The Renter-Purchaser agrees not to permit any intentional destruction, damage, or modification of any work.

(C) If any work is damaged, the Renter-Purchaser agrees to consult with the Artist before restoration is undertaken and must give the Artist the first opportunity to restore the work, if practicable.

(D) The Renter-Purchaser agrees to pay the Artist any sales or other transfer tax due on the full sale price.

(E) The Renter agrees to make full payments of all sums due on account of the purchase within fifteen days after notifying the Artist of the Renter's intention to purchase.

13. Security Interest. Title to and a security interest in any works rented or sold under this Agreement is reserved in the Artist. In the event of any default by the Renter, the Artist shall have all the rights of a secured party under the Uniform Commercial Code and the works shall not be subject to claims by the Renter's creditors. Renter agrees to execute and deliver to the Artist, in the form requested by the Artist, a financing statement and such other documents which the Artist may require to perfect its security interest in the works. In the event of purchase of any work pursuant to Paragraph 12, title shall pass to the Renter only upon full payment to the Artist of all sums due hereunder. The Renter agrees not to pledge or encumber any works in his or her possession, nor to incur any charge or obligation in connection therewith for which the Artist may be liable.

14. Attorney's Fees. In any proceeding to enforce any part of this Agreement, the aggrieved party shall be entitled to reasonable attorney's fees in addition to any available remedy.

15. Nonassignability. Neither party hereto shall have the right to assign this Agreement without the prior written consent of the other party. The Artist shall, however, retain the right to assign monies due to him or her under the terms of this Agreement.

16. Heirs and Assigns. This Agreement shall be binding upon the parties hereto, their heirs, successors, assigns, and personal representatives, and references to the Artist and the Renter shall include their heirs, successors, assigns, and personal representatives.

17. Integration. This Agreement constitutes the entire understanding between the parties. Its terms can be modified only by an instrument in writing signed by both parties.

18. Waivers. A waiver of any breach of any of the provisions of this Agreement shall not be construed as a continuing waiver of other breaches of the same or other provisions hereof.

19. Notices and Changes of Address. All notices shall be sent to the Artist at the following address: _____ and to the Renter at the following address: _____ Each party shall give written notification of any change of address prior to the date of said change.

20. Governing Law. This Agreement shall be governed by the laws of the State of _____.

IN WITNESS WHEREOF, the parties have signed this Agreement as of the date first set forth above.

Artist _____   Renter _____

Schedule of Works

	Title	Medium	Size	Rental Fee	Sale Price
1.					
2.					
3.					
4.					
5.					
6.					
7.					
8.					
9.					
10.					
11.					
12.					
13.					
14.					
15.					

Contract for an Exhibition Loan

The invitation to loan work for exhibition can be a milestone in an artist's career. If the institution borrowing the work is prestigious, it lends weight to the artist's resume and helps form the foundation for future successes. The exhibition itself may provide an opportunity to make contacts and perhaps even sell work.

While the loaning of work for exhibition is likely to be beneficial for the artist, safeguards must be put in place to insure that the work is protected and exhibited properly. Careless handling of the work by employees of the institution, vandalism, theft, damage, or loss in shipping are some of the concerns facing the artist. In addition, even the most highly regarded museums have sometimes exhibited art in a manner which the artist considered a mutilation of the work. In one case, the artist withdrew a loaned work that he felt was improperly exhibited, only to have the museum exhibit a work by him from its own collection in a manner which he also felt violated the integrity of the work.

The standard of care is an especially important factor, since the artist retains ownership of the work and the work is being exhibited to the public. Unless the contract specifies the standard of care, it will be assumed that the borrower has only a duty of reasonable care. The borrower may try to lower this standard to make it have no liability regardless of how it treats the work; the artist may seek to raise this standard to make the borrower absolutely liable in the event of damage or loss even if the borrower exercised the highest level of care.

Filling in the Form

In the Preamble fill in the date and the names and addresses of the parties. In Paragraph 2 fill in the dates on which the loan begins and ends as well as the requirement as to how many days the exhibitor must display the work. Include the name of the exhibition, whether the work of other artists can be displayed with the work being loaned, and any other restrictions on the treatment of the work. If the artist is to be paid a fee, specify the amount and time of payment. In Paragraph 3 specify the method of transportation to and from the exhibitor. In Paragraph 5 indicate where the work will be located. In Paragraph 6 state who will bear certain expenses to ready the work for exhibition. In Paragraph 7 specify the fee, if any, for reproduction of the work in the exhibitor's catalog. In Paragraphs 7 and 8, give dates for the copyright notice. Specify the addresses for notices in Paragraph 14. Give the state whose laws will govern the contract in Paragraph 15. Both parties should then sign the contract and fill in the Schedule of Works.

Negotiation Checklist

❏ State that the artist owns the work. (Paragraph 1)

❏ If required, warrant other facts which are true, such as the fact that the artist created the works and has the right to loan them for display. (Paragraph 1)

❏ If possible, the artist should not agree to indemnify the other party for costs or damages arising from a breach of any warranties given by the artist.

❏ Specify the term of the exhibition loan. (Paragraph 2)

❏ Require that the art be exhibited for a certain amount of time during the term of the loan. (Paragraph 2)

❏ Indicate the name of the exhibition in which the works are to be displayed at the institution. (Paragraph 2)

❏ Provide any desired restrictions with respect to the manner of display, such as that the works will not be displayed with the works of other artists. (Paragraph 2)

❏ If a fee is to be paid for the exhibition loan, specify the amount of the fee. (Paragraph 2)

❏ Specify who is responsible for the delivery of the works. (Paragraph 3)

❏ Identify the party who will pay the cost of the delivery. (Paragraph 3)

❏ As soon as possible after delivery, have the exhibitor give a signed receipt describing the condition of the works and stating whether they need repairs. (Paragraph 3)

❏ Require the exhibitor to use the same care with the works as it uses for its own collection. (Paragraph 3)

❏ Make the exhibitor liable for damage to or loss of the works regardless of how high a standard of care the exhibitor may have exercised.

❏ Do not agree to any standard of care that is less than reasonable care, such as a provision which would simply switch the risk of loss or damage to the artist.

❏ Require return of the works in the same condition as received. (Paragraph 3)

❏ State that the exhibitor shall be responsible for returning the works to the artist, and specify the method of transportation. (Paragraph 3)

❏ Indicate who will pay for the cost of returning the works; in this contract the costs are to be paid by the exhibitor. (Paragraph 3)

❏ Make the exhibitor responsible for loss of or damage to the works from the time of shipment until delivery back to the artist. (Paragraph 4)

❏ Require that the exhibitor insure the works for the benefit of the artist and provide proof that the insurance is in effect. (Paragraph 4)

❏ Require that the insurance be for the values specified by the artist in the Schedule of Works. (Paragraph 4)

❏ Be certain as to which risks are covered and which are excluded from coverage under the insurance policy. Even an all-risks, wall-to-wall policy — which sounds as if it should give coverage against all risks from the time of shipment from the artist until the return to the artist (wall-to-wall) — will have exclusions for loss or damage caused by events such as war or confiscation by a government.

❏ Provide that the artist may maintain his or her own insurance policies in addition to those provided by the exhibitor.

❏ Specify that the purpose of the loan is solely for exhibition and not for other kinds of commercial exploitation, such as the sale of postcards or posters. (Paragraph 5)

❏ If the exhibitor is to have the right to sell the works on behalf of the artist, review Form 9.

❏ Require that the works be displayed at a particular location and not be moved or displayed elsewhere without the written consent of the artist. (Paragraph 5)

❏ Specify the manner in which any framing, installation, cleaning, and repairs are to be handled in terms of expense and which party will exercise control. (Paragraph 6)

❏ Reserve the copyright and all reproduction rights to the artist. (Paragraph 7)

❏ Specify and limit any right being given to the exhibitor to reproduce work for its catalog and for publicity. (Paragraph 7)

❏ If any fee is to be paid for reproducing the work in the catalog and for publicity, specify the fee. (Paragraph 7)

❏ If the exhibitor is to be given rights of commercial exploitation with respect to the work, review Form 17 which covers licensing.

❏ Require that the exhibitor credit the collection of the artist and give appropriate copyright notice in the artist's name while exhibiting the work. (Paragraph 8)

❏ Give the artist access to the work during the term of the contract.

❏ Give the artist the right to terminate if the exhibitor does not exhibit the works or otherwise comply with the contract. (Paragraph 9)

❏ Provide for termination in the event of the exhibitor's bankruptcy or insolvency. (Paragraph 9)

❏ In the event of termination, require the immediate return of the works. (Paragraph 9)

❏ If there is a chance of bankruptcy or insolvency, give the artist a security interest in the works and require the exhibitor to execute any documents necessary to effect the security interest.

❏ Compare the standard provisions in the introductory pages with Paragraphs 10-15.

An abbreviated form of the Schedule of Works for Form 15 appears below. The full Schedule is shown with the perforated forms.

Schedule of Works

Title	Date Created	Medium	Size	Insurance Value	Framing, Mounting, or Installation	Condition
1.						
2.						
3.						
4.						
5.						
6.						
7.						
8.						
9.						

Contract for an Exhibition Loan

AGREEMENT made as of the _____ day of _____, 19 ___, between _____ (hereinafter referred to as the "Artist"), located at_____ and _____ (hereinafter referred to as the "Exhibitor"), located at

_____.

WHEREAS, the Artist is a recognized professional artist who creates work for sale and exhibition; and

WHEREAS, the Exhibitor admires and wishes to exhibit the work of the Artist; and

WHEREAS, the parties wish to have the exhibition governed by the mutual obligations, covenants, and conditions herein,

NOW THEREFORE, in consideration of the foregoing premises and the mutual covenants hereinafter set forth and other valuable considerations, the parties hereto agree as follows:

1. **Creation and Title.** The Artist hereby warrants that the Artist created and possesses unencumbered title to the works of art listed and described on the attached Schedule of Works ("the Schedule") and has the right to loan these works for purposes of exhibition.

2. **Duration of Loan, Manner of Exhibition, and Fee.** The Artist hereby agrees to loan to the Exhibitor the works listed on the Schedule for the time period commencing _____, 19___, and concluding _____, 19___. The Exhibitor agrees to exhibit these works for no less than ____ days during this time period as part of the exhibition titled: _____. These works ❑ shall ❑ shall not be exhibited with the works of other artists. Other restrictions on the treatment of the works include:_____ _____. Upon signing of this Agreement, the Exhibitor shall pay the Artist a fee of $_____ for the right to exhibit the works.

3. **Delivery, Condition, and Care.** The Exhibitor shall be responsible for arranging to have the works listed on the Schedule shipped from the Artist's studio to the Exhibitor by the following method of transport: _____. All costs of delivery (including transportation and insurance) shall be paid by the Exhibitor. The Exhibitor agrees to transmit a written report to the Artist within five working days of the delivery of the works, specifying their condition and whether they appear in any way in need of repair. Further, the Exhibitor agrees to use the same standard of care for the works as it uses for comparable works in its own collection. The Exhibitor agrees to return the works in the same condition as received, subject to the provisions of Paragraph 4. The Exhibitor shall return the works by the date specified in Paragraph 2 for the conclusion of the loan and shall use the following method of transport: _____. The Exhibitor shall pay for the costs of delivery (including transportation and insurance) of the works back to the Artist.

4. **Loss or Damage and Insurance.** The Exhibitor shall be responsible for loss of or damage to the works from the time of shipment from the Artist through the time of delivery back to the Artist. The Exhibitor shall insure each work for the benefit of the Artist for the full value listed on the Schedule. This insurance shall be pursuant to a policy providing wall-to-wall all-risks coverage maintained in force by the Exhibitor. The Exhibitor shall provide a Certificate of Insurance for the works if the Artist so requests.

5. **Use of Work.** The Exhibitor hereby agrees that the loan of the works under this Agreement is solely for purposes of exhibition and that no other uses shall be made of the work, such other uses including but not being limited to commercial exploitation, broadcasts, or other reproduction. The Exhibitor further agrees that the works shall be kept at the following location: _____, and shall not be moved or displayed elsewhere without the express, written consent of the Artist.

6. **Framing, Installation, Cleaning, Repairs.** The Artist agrees to deliver each work ready for display unless framing, mounting, or a special installation is required. The Exhibitor agrees not to remove any work from its frame

or other mounting or in any way alter the framing or mounting. In the event framing, mounting, or a special installation is required for the display of any work, it shall be described on the Schedule of Works and paid for by _____. Exhibitor agrees that the Artist shall have sole authority to determine when cleaning or repairs are necessary and to choose who shall perform such cleaning or repairs.

7. **Copyright and Reproduction.** The Artist reserves all reproduction rights, including the right to claim statutory copyright, on all works listed on the Schedule. No work may be photographed, sketched, painted, or reproduced in any manner whatsoever without the express, written consent of the Artist. The Exhibitor may reproduce the works for its catalog of the exhibition and promotion related thereto for a fee of $_____. All approved reproductions shall bear the following copyright notice: © by (Artist's name) 19____.

8. **Collection of the Artist.** When displayed, each work shall be accompanied by a label or plaque identifying the work as a loan from the collection of the Artist. This label or plaque shall also include the following copyright notice: © by (Artist's name) 19____.

9. **Termination of Right to Exhibit.** The right to exhibit pursuant to this Agreement shall terminate as of the date specified in Paragraph 2. In the event of the failure of the Exhibitor to exhibit the works or in the event of an exhibition or other act in violation of the terms of this Agreement, the Artist shall have the right to terminate the right to exhibit under this Agreement by written notice to the Exhibitor. The right to exhibit pursuant to this Agreement shall automatically terminate in the event of the Exhibitor's insolvency or bankruptcy. In the event of termination of the right to exhibit pursuant to this Paragraph 9, the works shall be returned forthwith to the Artist pursuant to the provisions of Paragraph 4.

10. **Nonassignability.** Neither party hereto shall have the right to assign this Agreement without the prior written consent of the other party. The Artist shall, however, retain the right to assign monies due to him or her under the terms of this Agreement.

11. **Heirs and Assigns.** This Agreement shall be binding upon the parties hereto, their heirs, successors, assigns, and personal representatives, and references to the Artist and the Exhibitor shall include their heirs, successors, assigns, and personal representatives.

12. **Integration.** This Agreement constitutes the entire understanding between the parties. Its terms can be modified only by an instrument in writing signed by both parties.

13. **Waivers.** A waiver of any breach of any of the provisions of this Agreement shall not be construed as a continuing waiver of other breaches of the same or other provisions hereof.

14. **Notices and Changes of Address.** All notices shall be sent by registered or certified mail, return receipt requested, postage prepaid, to the Artist and Exhibitor at the addresses first given above unless indicated to the contrary here:_____ . Each party shall give written notification of any change of address prior to the date of said change.

15. **Governing Law.** This Agreement shall be governed by the laws of the State of _____.

IN WITNESS WHEREOF, the parties have signed this Agreement as of the date first set forth above.

Artist_____   Exhibitor_____
                                                                   Company   Name

                                                     By_____
                                                              Authorized Signatory, Title

Lecture Contract

Many artists find lecturing to be an important source of income as well as a rewarding opportunity to express their feelings about their work and being an artist. High schools, colleges, museums, art societies, and other institutions often invite artists to lecture. Slides of the work may be used during these lectures and, in some cases, an exhibition may be mounted at the institution during the artist's visit.

A contract ensures that everything goes smoothly. For example, who should pay for slides that the artist has to make for that particular lecture? Who will pay for transportation to and from the lecture? Who will supply materials for a demonstration of technique? Will the artist have to give one lecture in a day or, as the institution might prefer, many more? Will the artist have to review portfolios of students? Resolving these kinds of questions, as well as the amount of and time to pay the fee, will make any lecture a more rewarding experience.

Filling in the Form

In the Preamble give the date and the names and addresses of the parties. In Paragraph 1 give the dates when the artist will lecture, the nature and extent of the services the artist will perform, and the form in which the artist is to bring examples of his or her work. In Paragraph 2 specify the fee to be paid to the artist and when it will be paid during the artist's visit. In Paragraph 3 give the amounts of expenses to be paid (or state that none or all of these expenses are to be paid), specify which expenses other than travel and food and lodging are covered, and show what will be provided by the sponsor, such as food or lodging. In Paragraph 5 state the interest rate for late payments. In Paragraph 10 give which state's law will govern the contract. Then both parties should sign. In the Schedule of Works list the works to be brought to the lecture and their insurance value.

Negotiation Checklist

❏ How long will the artist be required to stay at the sponsoring institution? (Paragraph 1)

❏ What are the nature and extent of the services the artist will have to perform? (Paragraph 1)

❏ What slides, original art, or other materials must the artist bring? (Paragraph 1)

❏ Specify the work facilities which the sponsor will provide the artist.

❏ Specify the fee to be paid to the artist. (Paragraph 2)

❏ Give a time for payment of the fee. (Paragraph 2)

❏ Consider having part of the fee paid in advance.

❏ Specify the expenses which will be paid by the sponsor, including the time for payment of these expenses. (Paragraph 3)

❏ Indicate what the sponsor may provide in place of paying expenses, such as lodging, meals, or a car. (Paragraph 3)

❏ If illness prevents the artist from coming to lecture, state that an effort will be made to find another date. (Paragraph 4)

❏ If the sponsor must cancel for a reason beyond its control, indicate that the expenses incurred by the artist must be paid and that an attempt will be made to reschedule. (Paragraph 4)

❏ If the sponsor cancels within 48 hours of the time the artist is to arrive, consider requiring the full fee as well as expenses be paid.

❑ Provide for the payment of interest on late payments by the sponsor. (Paragraph 5)

❑ Retain for the artist all rights, including copyrights, in any recordings of any kind which may be made of the artist's visit. (Paragraph 6)

❑ If the sponsor wishes to use a recording of the artist's visit, such as a video, require that the sponsor obtain the artist's written permission and that, if appropriate, a fee be negotiated for this use. (Paragraph 6)

❑ State that the sponsor is strictly responsible for loss or damage to any works from the time they leave the artist's studio until they are returned there. (Paragraph 7)

❑ Require the sponsor to insure the works and specify the values for insurance. (Paragraph 7)

❑ Consider which risks may be excluded from the insurance coverage.

❑ Consider whether the artist should be the beneficiary of the insurance coverage of his or her works.

❑ State who will pay the cost of packing and shipping the works to and from the sponsor. (Paragraph 8)

❑ Indicate who will take the responsibility to pack and ship the works to and from the sponsor.

❑ Review the standard provisions in the introductory pages and compare with Paragraphs 9-10.

Lecture Contract

AGREEMENT made as of the _____ day of _____, 19 ____, between_____
(hereinafter referred to as the "Artist"), located at _____and
_____(hereinafter referred to as the "Sponsor"),
located at _____.

WHEREAS, the Sponsor is familiar with and admires the work of the Artist; and

WHEREAS, the Sponsor wishes the Artist to visit the Sponsor to enhance the opportunities for its students to have contact with working professional artists; and

WHEREAS, the Artist wishes to lecture with respect to his or her work and perform such other services as this contract may call for;

NOW, THEREFORE, in consideration of the foregoing premises and the mutual covenants hereinafter set forth and other valuable considerations, the parties hereto agree as follows:

1. **Artist to Lecture.** The Artist hereby agrees to come to the Sponsor on the following date(s): _____ and perform the following services: _____. The Artist shall use best efforts to make his or her services as productive as possible to the Sponsor. The Artist further agrees to bring examples of his or her own work in the form of _____.

2. **Payment.** The Sponsor agrees to pay as full compensation for the Artist's services rendered under Paragraph 1 the sum of $_____. This sum shall be payable to the Artist on completion of the _____ day of the Artist's residence with the Sponsor.

3. **Expenses.** In addition to the payments provided under Paragraph 2, the Sponsor agrees to reimburse the Artist for the following expenses:

   (A) Travel expenses in the amount of $_____.

   (B) Food and lodging expenses in the amount of $_____.

   (C) Other expenses listed here:_____in the amount of $_____.

   The reimbursement for travel expenses shall be made fourteen days prior to the earliest date specified in Paragraph 1. The reimbursement for food, lodging, and other expenses shall be made at the date of payment specified in Paragraph 2, unless a contrary date is specified here:_____.

   In addition, the Sponsor shall provide the Artist with the following:

   (A) Tickets for travel, rental car, or other modes of transportation as follows: _____
   _____

   (B) Food and lodging as follows: _____
   _____

   (C) Other hospitality as follows: _____
   _____

4. **Inability to Perform.** If the Artist is unable to appear on the dates scheduled in Paragraph 1 due to illness, the Sponsor shall have no obligation to make any payments under Paragraphs 2 and 3, but shall attempt to reschedule the Artist's appearance at a mutually acceptable future date. If the Sponsor is prevented from having the Artist appear by acts of God, hurricane, flood, governmental order, or other cause beyond its control,

the Sponsor shall be responsible only for the payment of such expenses under Paragraph 3 as the Artist shall have actually incurred. The Sponsor agrees in such a case to attempt to reschedule the Artist's appearance at a mutually acceptable future date.

5. **Late Payment.** The Sponsor agrees that, in the event it is late in making payment of amounts due to the Artist under Paragraphs 2, 3, or 8, it will pay as additional liquidated damages _____ percent in interest on the amounts it is owing to the Artist, and said interest is to run from the date stipulated for payment in Paragraphs 2, 3, or 8 until such time as payment is made.

6. **Copyrights and Recordings.** Both parties agree that the Artist shall retain all rights, including copyrights, in relation to recordings of any kind made of the appearance or any works shown in the course thereof. The term "recording" as used herein shall include any recording made by electrical transcription, tape recording, wire recording, film, videotape, or other similar or dissimilar method of recording, whether now known or hereinafter developed. No use of any such recording shall be made by the Sponsor without the written consent of the Artist and, if stipulated therein, additional compensation for such use.

7. **Insurance and Loss or Damage.** The Sponsor agrees that it shall provide wall-to-wall insurance for the works listed on the Schedule of Works for the values specified therein. The Sponsor agrees that it shall be fully responsible and have strict liability for any loss or damage to the works from the time said works leave the Artist's residence or studio until they are returned.

8. **Packing and Shipping.** The Sponsor agrees that it shall fully bear any costs of packing and shipping necessary to deliver the works specified in Paragraph 7 to the Sponsor and return them to the Artist's residence or studio.

9. **Modification.** This Agreement constitutes the entire understanding between the parties. Its terms can be modified only by an instrument in writing signed by both parties.

10. **Governing Law.** This contract shall be governed by the laws of the State of _____.

IN WITNESS WHEREOF, the parties hereto have signed this Agreement as of the date first set forth above.

Artist _____   Sponsor _____
                                                                                     Company Name

                                                                     By _____
                                                                                     Authorized Signatory, Title

Schedule of Works

	Title	Medium	Size	Value
1.				
2.				
3.				
4.				
5.				
6.				
7.				
8.				

Licensing Contract

Licensing is the granting of rights to use images or designs created by the artist on posters, calendars, greeting cards and stationery, apparel, wallpaper, mugs and other household items, or any of innumerable other applications. Needless to say, this can be lucrative for the artist. So many of the products used in everyday life depend on visual qualities to make them attractive to purchasers. These qualities may reside in the design of the product itself or in the use of images on the product. For the artist to enter the world of manufactured, mass-produced goods is certainly a departure from the sale of unique works or limited editions. The world of the consumer is not the world of the collector, nor are manufacturers the same as art dealers. New audiences and new modes of production and distribution necessitate different business arrangements.

The best guide for artists on the subject of licensing is *Licensing Art & Design* by Caryn Leland (Allworth Press). The potentially large sums of money involved, as well as the possible complexity of licensing agreements, make *Licensing Art & Design* a valuable resource for artists who either are licensing images or would like to enter the field of licensing.

Form 17, Licensing Contract, is adapted from a short-form licensing agreement which is contained in *Licensing Art & Design*. A long-form licensing agreement also appears in that resource.

Filling in the Form

In the Preamble fill in the date and the names and addresses of the parties. In Paragraph 1 indicate whether the rights are exclusive or nonexclusive, give the name and description of the image or design, state what types of merchandise the image or design can be used for, specify the geographical area for distribution, and limit the term of the distribution. In Paragraph 3 specify the advance, if any, and the royalty percentage. State the date on which payments and statements of account are to begin in Paragraph 4. Indicate the number of samples to be given to the artist in Paragraph 6. In Paragraph 13 specify which state's laws will govern the contract. Give addresses for correspondence relating to the contract in Paragraph 14. Have both parties sign the contract.

Negotiation Checklist

❑ Carefully describe the image or design to be licensed. (Paragraph 1)

❑ State whether the rights given to the licensee are exclusive or nonexclusive. (Paragraph 1)

❑ Indicate which kinds of merchandise the image or design is being licensed for. (Paragraph 1)

❑ State the area in which the licensee may sell the licensed products. (Paragraph 1)

❑ Give a term for the licensing contract. (Paragraph 1)

❑ Reserve all copyrights and trademarks in the image or design to the artist. (Paragraph 2)

❑ Require that credit and copyright notice in the artist's name appear on all licensed products. (Paragraph 2)

❑ Require that credit and copyright notice in the artist's name appear on packaging, advertising, displays, and all publicity.

❑ Have the right to approve packaging, advertising, displays, and publicity.

❑ Give the licensee the right to use the artist's name and, in an appropriate case, picture, provided that any use must be to promote the product using the image or design and must be dignified. The artist may want the right to provide the biographical materials and pictures and approve the manner of their use.

❏ Determine whether the royalty should be based on retail price or, as is more commonly the case, on net price (which is what the manufacturer actually receives). (Paragraph 3)

❏ If any expenses are to reduce the amount upon which royalties are calculated, these expenses must be specified. (Paragraph 3)

❏ Specify the royalty percentage. (Paragraph 3)

❏ Require the licensee to pay an advance against royalties to be earned. (Paragraph 3)

❏ Indicate that any advance is nonrefundable. (Paragraph 3)

❏ Require minimum royalty payments for the term of the contract, regardless of sales.

❏ Require monthly or quarterly statements of account, accompanied by any payments which are due. (Paragraph 4)

❏ Specify the information to be contained in the statement of account, such as units sold, total revenues received, special discounts, and the like. (Paragraph 4)

❏ Give the artist a right to inspect the books and records of the licensee. (Paragraph 5)

❏ If an inspection of the books and records uncovers an error to the disadvantage of the artist, and that error is more than 5 percent of the amount owed the artist, then require the licensee to pay for the cost of the inspection and any related costs.

❏ Provide for a certain number of samples to be given to the artist by the manufacturer. (Paragraph 6)

❏ Give the artist a right to purchase additional samples at manufacturing cost or, at least, at no more than the price paid by wholesalers. (Paragraph 6)

❏ Consider whether the artist will want the right to sell the products at retail price, rather than being restricted to using the samples and other units purchased for personal use.

❏ Give the artist a right of approval over the quality of the reproductions in order to protect the artist's reputation. (Paragraph 7)

❏ Require the licensee's best efforts to promote the licensed products. (Paragraph 8)

❏ Specify the amount of money that the licensee must spend on promotion and the type of promotion that the licensee will provide .

❏ If the licensee's usage may create trademark or other rights in the product, it is important that these rights be owned by the artist after termination of the license. (Paragraph 9)

❏ Reserve all rights to the artist which are not expressly transferred to the licensee. (Paragraph 10)

❏ Require the licensee to indemnify the artist for any costs arising out of the use of the image on the licensed products. (Paragraph 11)

❏ Have the licensee provide liability insurance, with the artist as a named beneficiary, to protect against defects in the licensed products.

❏ Forbid assignment by the licensee, but allow the artist to assign royalties. (Paragraph 12)

❏ Specify the grounds for terminating the contract, such as the bankruptcy or insolvency of the licensee, failure of the licensee to obey the terms of the contract, cessation of manufacture of the product, or insufficient sales of the licensed products. (This is partially covered in Paragraph 4.)

❏ Review the standard provisions in the introductory pages and compare with Paragraphs 13-16.

Licensing Contract

AGREEMENT made as of the _____ day of _____, 19_____, between _____ (hereinafter referred to as the "Artist"), located at _____ and _____ (hereinafter referred to as the "Licensee"), located at _____

with respect to the use of a certain image or design created by the Artist (hereinafter referred to as the "Image") for manufactured products (hereinafter referred to as the "Licensed Products").

WHEREAS, the Artist is a professional artist of good standing; and

WHEREAS, the Artist has created the Image which the Artist wishes to license for purposes of manufacture and sale; and

WHEREAS, the Licensee wishes to use the Image to create a certain product or products for manufacture and sale; and

WHEREAS, both parties want to achieve the best possible quality to generate maximum sales;

NOW, THEREFORE, in consideration of the foregoing premises and the mutual covenants hereinafter set forth and other valuable considerations, the parties hereto agree as follows:

1. **Grant of Merchandising Rights.** The Artist grants to the Licensee the ❑ exclusive ❑ nonexclusive right to use the Image, titled _____ and described as _____ _____, which was created and is owned by the Artist, as or as part of the following type(s) of merchandise: _____ _____ for manufacture, distribution, and sale by the Licensee in the following geographical area: _____ and for the following period of time: _____.

2. **Ownership of Copyright.** The Artist shall retain all copyrights in and to the Image. The Licensee shall identify the Artist as the creator of the Image on the Licensed Products and shall reproduce thereon a copyright notice for the Artist which shall include the word "Copyright" or the © by (Artist's name) 19____.

3. **Advance and Royalties.** Licensee agrees to pay Artist a nonrefundable advance in the amount of $_____ upon signing this Agreement, which advance shall be recouped from first royalties due hereunder. Licensee further agrees to pay Artist a royalty of _____ percent of the net sales of the Licensed Products. "Net Sales" as used herein shall mean sales to customers less prepaid freight and credits for lawful and customary volume rebates, actual returns, and allowances. Royalties shall be deemed to accrue when the Licensed Products are sold, shipped, or invoiced, whichever first occurs.

4. **Payments and Statements of Account.** Royalty payments shall be paid monthly on the first day of each month commencing _____, 19 _____, and Licensee shall with each payment furnish Artist with a monthly statement of account showing the kinds and quantities of all Licensed Products sold, the prices received therefor, and all deductions for freight, volume rebates, returns, and allowances. The Artist shall have the right to terminate this Agreement upon thirty days notice if Licensee fails to make any payment required of it and does not cure this default within said thirty days, whereupon all rights granted herein shall revert immediately to the Artist.

5. **Inspection of Books and Records.** Artist shall have the right to inspect Licensee's books and records concerning sales of the Licensed Products upon prior written notice.

6. Samples. Licensee shall give the Artist _____ samples of the Licensed Products for the Artist's personal use. The Artist shall have the right to purchase additional samples of the Licensed Products at the Licensee's manufacturing cost.

7. Quality of Reproductions. The Artist shall have the right to approve the quality of the reproduction of the Image for the Licensed Products, and the Artist agrees not to withhold approval unreasonably.

8. Promotion. Licensee shall use its best efforts to promote, distribute, and sell the Licensed Products.

9. Trademarks and Other Rights. The Licensee's use of the Image shall inure to the benefit of the Artist if the Licensee acquires any trademarks, trade rights, equities, titles, or other rights in and to the Image whether by operation of law, usage, or otherwise during the term of this Agreement or any extension thereof. Upon the expiration of this Agreement or any extension thereof or sooner termination, Licensee shall assign and transfer the said trademarks, trade rights, equities, titles, or other rights to the Artist without any consideration other than the consideration of this Agreement.

10. Reservation of Rights. All rights not specifically transferred by this Agreement are reserved to the Artist.

11. Indemnification. The Licensee shall hold the Artist harmless from and against any loss, expense, or damage occasioned by any claim, demand, suit, or recovery against the Artist arising out of the use of the Image for the Licensed Products.

12. Assignment. Neither party shall assign rights or obligations under this Agreement, except that the Artist may assign the right to receive money due hereunder.

13. Nature of Contract. Nothing herein shall be construed to constitute the parties hereto joint venturers, nor shall any similar relationship be deemed to exist between them.

14. Governing Law. This Agreement shall be construed in accordance with the laws of _____; Licensee consents to the jurisdiction of the courts of _____.

15. Addresses. All notices, demands, payments, royalty payments, and statements shall be sent to the Artist at the following address: _____ and to the Licensee at: _____.

16. Modifications in Writing. This Agreement constitutes the entire agreement between the parties hereto and shall not be modified, amended, or changed in any way except by a written agreement signed by both parties hereto.

IN WITNESS WHEREOF, the parties have signed this Agreement as of the date first set forth above.

Artist_____   Licensee_____
                                                                        Company Name

                                                        By_____
                                                                        Authorized Signatory, Title

Release Form for Models

Artists often portray people in their art. Because of this, artists must be aware of individual's rights to privacy and publicity. While the intricacies of these laws can be reviewed in *Legal Guide for the Visual Artist*, this summary will help alert the artist to potential dangers.

The right to privacy can take a number of forms. For example, state laws and court decisions forbid the use of a person's name, portrait, or picture for purposes of advertising or trade. This raises the question of the definitions for the terms "advertising" and "trade." Public display of an image which showed or implied something embarrassing and untrue about someone would also constitute a violation of the right to privacy. And physically intruding into a private space such as a home or office, perhaps to take a photograph for use as a reference, could be an invasion of privacy.

The right of publicity is the right which a celebrity creates in his or her name, image, and voice. To use the celebrity's image for commercial gain violates this right of publicity. And, while the right of privacy generally protects only living people, a number of states have enacted laws to protect the publicity rights of celebrities even after death. These state laws supplement court decisions which held that celebrities who exploited the commercial value of their names and images while alive had publicity rights after their death.

On the other hand, use of people's images for newsworthy and editorial purposes is protected by the First Amendment. No releases need be obtained for such uses, which serve the public interest.

What should the artist do about all of this? The wisest course is to obtain a model release from anyone who will be recognizable in work, including people who can be recognized from parts of their body other than the face. Even if showing unique art in a museum might not create a privacy issue, there is always the possibility that an image or design will be reproduced in other ways. For example, an image can be used for posters, postcards, T-shirts, and apparel, all of which are clearly trade uses. Or that image can be used in an advertisement. Only by having a model release can the artist ensure the right to exploit the commercial value of the image in the future.

Form 18 allows the artist (and others who obtain the artist's permission) to use the model's image for advertising and trade. While some states may not require written releases or the payment of money for a release, it is always wise to use a written release and make at least a small payment as consideration. By the way, Form 18 is intended for use with friends and acquaintances who pose, as well as with professional models who are hired.

It is also important to be aware that if the release is intended to cover one use, and the image is then used in a distorted and embarrassing way for a different purpose, the release may not protect the artist, regardless of what it says. For example: a model signed a model release for a bookstore's advertisement in which she was to appear in bed reading a book. This advertisement was later changed and used by a bedsheet manufacturer known for its salacious advertisements. The title on the book became pornographic and a leering old man was placed next to the bed looking at the model. This invaded the model's privacy despite her having signed a release form.

In general, a minor must have a parent or guardian give consent. While the artist should check the law in his or her state, the age of majority in most states is eighteen.

The artist should be certain to have the release signed during the session, since it is easy to forget if left for signing later. Also, releases should be kept systematically so that each one can be related to the work in which its signatory appears. A simple numbering system can be used to connect the releases to the works. While a witness isn't a necessity, having one can help if a question is later raised about the validity of the release.

If the artist is asked to use a release form supplied by someone else, the artist must make certain that the form protects the artist. The negotiation checklist will be helpful in reviewing the provided form and suggesting changes to strengthen the form.

Filling in the Form

Fill in the dollar amount being paid as consideration for the release. Then fill in the name of the model and the name of the artist. Have the model and a witness sign the form. Obtain the addresses for both the model and the witness and date the form. If the model is a minor, have the parent or guardian sign. Have the witness sign and give the addresses of the witness and the parent or guardian as well as the date.

Negotiation Checklist

❏ Be certain that some amount of money, even a token amount, is actually paid as consideration for the release.

❏ Have the release given not only to the artist, but also to the artist's estate and anyone else the artist might want to assign rights to (such as a manufacturer of posters or T-shirts).

❏ State that the grant is irrevocable.

❏ Cover the use of the name as well as the image of the person.

❏ Include the right to use the image in all forms, media, and manners of use.

❏ Include the right to make distorted or changed versions of the image as well as composite images.

❏ Allow advertising and trade uses.

❏ Allow any other lawful use.

❏ Have the model waive any right to review the finished work, including written copy to accompany the work.

❏ Have the model recite that he or she is of full age.

❏ If the model is a minor, have a parent or guardian sign the release.

Release Form for Models

In consideration of _____ dollars ($_____), receipt of which is acknowledged, I, _____, do hereby give _____,

his or her assigns, licensees, and legal representatives the irrevocable right to use my name (or any fictional name), picture, portrait, or photograph in all forms and media and in all manners, including composite or distorted representations, for advertising, trade, or any other lawful purposes, and I waive any right to inspect or approve the finished version(s), including written copy that may be created in connection therewith. I am of full age.* I have read this release and am fully familiar with its contents.

Witness_____   Model_____

Address_____   Address_____

Date _____, 19 ___

──────────────── **Consent (if applicable)** ────────────────

I am the parent or guardian of the minor named above and have the legal authority to execute the above release. I approve the foregoing and waive any rights in the premises.

Witness_____   Parent or Guardian_____

Address_____   Address_____

Date _____, 19 ___

* Delete this sentence if the subject is a minor. The parent or guardian must then sign the consent.

Property Release

Property does not have rights of privacy or publicity. A public building, a horse running in a field, and a bowl of fruit are all freely available to be portrayed in art.

Nonetheless, there may be times when the artist will want to obtain a release for the use of property belonging to others. This might include personal property, such as jewelry or clothing, or the interiors of private buildings (especially if admission is charged). The most important reason for the release is to have a contract that details the terms of use of the property.

If the artist is lent property to use in a commissioned work, and has any intention of using that work in some way other than the commission, a release should be obtained. For example, if an artist were hired to do a portrait of a pet, selling that portrait to a manufacturer of dog food for use as product packaging would be a breach of an implied provision of the contract. Such a use would require the owner's permission, which could be obtained by using Form 19.

If the owner could be identified from the property, especially if the owner might be embarrassed in some way by the association with the work, it is wise to have a property release.

As with releases for models, property releases should be signed at the time the property is used, and payment, even if only a token payment, should be made to the owner of the property.

Filling in the Form

Fill in the amount being paid for use of the property, as well as the name and address of the owner and the name of the artist. Then specify the property which will be used. Finally, have both parties sign the release, obtain a witness to each signature (if possible), and give the date.

Negotiation Checklist

❑ Make some payment, however small, as consideration for the release.

❑ Be certain the release runs in favor of the artist's assigns and estate as well as the artist.

❑ State that the release is irrevocable.

❑ Include the right to copyright and publish the image made from the property.

❑ Include the right to use the image in all forms, media, and manners of use.

❑ Permit advertising and trade uses.

❑ Allow any other lawful use.

❑ State that the owner has full and sole authority to give the release.

❑ Retain the right to make distorted or changed versions of the image as well as composite images.

❑ Allow use of the owner's name or a fictional name in connection with the image of the property.

❑ Permit color or black and white images, as well as any type of derivative work.

❑ Have the owner waive any right to review the finished work, including written copy to accompany the work.

❑ Make certain the owner is of full age and has the capacity to give the release.

Property Release

In consideration of the sum of _____dollars ($_____),

receipt of which is hereby acknowledged, I, _____,

located at _____, do irrevocably authorize

_____, his or her assigns, licensees, heirs and legal representatives, to copyright, publish, and use in all forms and media and in all manners for advertising, trade, or any other lawful purpose, images of the following property which I own and have full and sole authority to license for such uses: _____ , regardless of whether said use is composite or distorted in character or form, whether said use is made in conjunction with my own name or with a fictitious name, or whether said use is made in color or otherwise or other derivative works are made through any medium.

I waive any right that I may have to inspect or approve the finished version(s), including written copy that may be used in connection therewith.

I am of full age and have every right to contract in my own name with respect to the foregoing matters. I have read the above authorization and release prior to its execution and I am fully cognizant of its contents.

Witness_____   Owner_____

Address_____   Date _____, 19_____

Copyright Applications: Form VA and Short Form VA

To register a work, the artist must send a completed Form VA (or Short Form VA, if appropriate), a nonrefundable filing fee, and a nonreturnable deposit portraying the work to be registered. These three items should be sent together to the Register of Copyrights, Copyright Office, Library of Congress, Washington, D.C. 20559. The instructions for filling in Form VA and Short Form VA are provided by the Copyright Office and are reproduced here with the forms.

The Copyright Office has an information number—(202) 707-3000—and also makes available a free Copyright Information Kit. This includes copies of Form VA and other Copyright Office circulars. To expedite receiving forms or circulars, the Forms and Circulars Hotline number can be used: (202) 707-9100. Forms can also be downloaded from the Copyright Office home page at http://lcweb.loc.gov/copyright.

Because of budget constraints, the Copyright Office will accept reproductions of Form VA such as the tear-out form in this book. If the artist wishes to make copies, however, the copies must be clear, legible, on a good grade of white paper, and printed on a single sheet of paper so that when the sheet is turned over the top of page 2 is directly behind the top of page 1.

It is wise to register any work that the artist feels may be infringed. Registration has a number of values, the most important of which is to establish proof that a particular work was created by the artist as of a certain date. Both published and unpublished artworks can be registered. In fact, unpublished artworks can be registered in groups for a single application fee.

For published (i.e., publicly distributed) works, the proper deposit is usually two complete copies of the work. For unpublished works, one complete copy would be correct. Since the purpose of registering is to protect what the artist has created, it is important that the material deposited fully show what is copyrightable.

Obviously, unique works cannot be sent along with the application for purposes of identifying themselves, so the Copyright Office accepts other identifying materials. These are usually photographs, photostats, slides, drawings, or other two-dimensional representations of the work. The artist should provide as much identifying material as is necessary to show the copyrightable content of the artwork, including any copyright notice which has been used. The proper form for presenting notice of copyright is © or Copyright or Copr., followed by the artist's name, and the year of first publication. Since there is some disagreement about whether one-of-a-kind works can ever be published, according to the definition of that term in the copyright law, the year of creation can also be placed on such works.

The preferable size for identifying materials (other than transparencies) is 8-by-10 inches, but anything from 3-by-3 inches to 9-by-12 inches will be acceptable. Also, at least one piece of the identifying material must give an exact measurement of one or more dimensions of the artwork and give the title on its front, back, or mount.

For a full review of registration and its requirements, the artist can consult Copyright Office Circular 40, *Copyright Registration for Works of the Visual Arts,* and Circular 40a, *Deposit Requirements of Claims to Copyright in Visual Arts Material.*

A copyright registration is effective as of the date that the Copyright Office receives the application, fee, and deposit materials in an acceptable form, regardless of how long it takes to send back the certificate of registration. It may take 120 days before the certificate of registration is sent to the artist. To ensure that the Copyright Office receives the materials, the artist should send them by registered or certified mail with a return receipt requested from the post office.

An artist can request information as to the status of an application. However, a fee will be charged by the Copyright Office if such a status report must be given within 120 days of the submission of the application.

For a more extensive discussion of the legal aspects of copyright, the artist can consult *Legal Guide for the Visual Artist* by Tad Crawford or *The Copyright Guide* by Lee Wilson (Allworth Press).

Filling Out Application Form VA

Detach and read these instructions before completing this form.
Make sure all applicable spaces have been filled in before you return this form.

BASIC INFORMATION

When to Use This Form: Use Form VA for copyright registration of published or unpublished works of the visual arts. This category consists of "pictorial, graphic, or sculptural works," including two-dimensional and three-dimensional works of fine, graphic, and applied art, photographs, prints and art reproductions, maps, globes, charts, technical drawings, diagrams, and models.

What Does Copyright Protect? Copyright in a work of the visual arts protects those pictorial, graphic, or sculptural elements that, either alone or in combination, represent an "original work of authorship." The statute declares: "In no case does copyright protection for an original work of authorship extend to any idea, procedure, process, system, method of operation, concept, principle, or discovery, regardless of the form in which it is described, explained, illustrated, or embodied in such work."

Works of Artistic Craftsmanship and Designs: "Works of artistic craftsmanship" are registrable on Form VA, but the statute makes clear that protection extends to "their form" and not to "their mechanical or utilitarian aspects." The "design of a useful article" is considered copyrightable "only if, and only to the extent that, such design incorporates pictorial, graphic, or sculptural features that can be identified separately from, and are capable of existing independently of, the utilitarian aspects of the article."

Labels and Advertisements: Works prepared for use in connection with the sale or advertisement of goods and services are registrable if they contain "original work of authorship." Use Form VA if the copyrightable material in the work you are registering is mainly pictorial or graphic; use Form TX if it consists mainly of text. **NOTE:** Words and short phrases such as names, titles, and slogans cannot be protected by copyright, and the same is true of standard symbols, emblems, and other commonly used graphic designs that are in the public domain. When used commercially, material of that sort can sometimes be protected under state laws of unfair competition or under the Federal trademark laws. For information about trademark registration, write to the Commissioner of Patents and Trademarks, Washington, D.C. 20231.

Architectural Works: Copyright protection extends to the design of buildings created for the use of human beings. Architectural works created on or after December 1, 1990, or that on December 1, 1990, were unconstructed and embodied only in unpublished plans or drawings are eligible. Request Circular 41 for more information.

Deposit to Accompany Application: An application for copyright registration must be accompanied by a deposit consisting of copies representing the entire work for which registration is to be made.

Unpublished Work: Deposit one complete copy.

Published Work: Deposit two complete copies of the best edition.

Work First Published Outside the United States: Deposit one complete copy of the first foreign edition.

Contribution to a Collective Work: Deposit one complete copy of the best edition of the collective work.

The Copyright Notice: For works first published on or after March 1, 1989, the law provides that a copyright notice in a specified form "may be placed on all publicly distributed copies from which the work can be visually perceived." Use of the copyright notice is the responsibility of the copyright owner and does not require advance permission from the Copyright Office. The required form of the notice for copies generally consists of three elements: (1) the symbol "©", or the word "Copyright," or the abbreviation "Copr."; (2) the year of first publication; and (3) the name of the owner of copyright. For example: "© 1995 Jane Cole." The notice is to be affixed to the copies "in such manner and location as to give reasonable notice of the claim of copyright." Works first published prior to March 1, 1989, **must** carry the notice or risk loss of copyright protection.

For information about notice requirements for works published before March 1, 1989, or other copyright information, write: Information Section, LM-401, Copyright Office, Library of Congress, Washington, D.C. 20559-6000.

LINE-BY-LINE INSTRUCTIONS

Please type or print using black ink.

1 SPACE 1: Title

Title of This Work: Every work submitted for copyright registration must be given a title to identify that particular work. If the copies of the work bear a title (or an identifying phrase that could serve as a title), transcribe that wording *completely* and *exactly* on the application. Indexing of the registration and future identification of the work will depend on the information you give here. For an architectural work that has been constructed, add the date of construction after the title; if unconstructed at this time, add "not yet constructed."

Previous or Alternative Titles: Complete this space if there are any additional titles for the work under which someone searching for the registration might be likely to look, or under which a document pertaining to the work might be recorded.

Publication as a Contribution: If the work being registered is a contribution to a periodical, serial, or collection, give the title of the contribution in the "Title of This Work" space. Then, in the line headed "Publication as a Contribution," give information about the collective work in which the contribution appeared.

Nature of This Work: Briefly describe the general nature or character of the pictorial, graphic, or sculptural work being registered for copyright. Examples: "Oil Painting"; "Charcoal Drawing"; "Etching"; "Sculpture"; "Map"; "Photograph"; "Scale Model"; "Lithographic Print"; "Jewelry Design"; "Fabric Design."

2 SPACE 2: Author(s)

General Instruction: After reading these instructions, decide who are the "authors" of this work for copyright purposes. Then, unless the work is a "collective work," give the requested information about every "author" who contributed any appreciable amount of copyrightable matter to this version of the work. If you need further space, request Continuation Sheets. In the case of a collective work, such as a catalog of paintings or collection of cartoons by various authors, give information about the author of the collective work as a whole.

Name of Author: The fullest form of the author's name should be given. Unless the work was "made for hire," the individual who actually created the work is its "author." In the case of a work made for hire, the statute provides that "the employer or other person for whom the work was prepared is considered the author."

What is a "Work Made for Hire"? A "work made for hire" is defined as: (1) "a work prepared by an employee within the scope of his or her employment"; or (2) " a work specially ordered or commissioned for use as a contribution to a collective work, as a part of a motion picture or other audiovisual work, as a translation, as a supplementary work, as a compilation, as an instructional text, as a test, as answer material for a test, or as an atlas, if the parties expressly agree in a written instrument signed by them that the work shall be considered a work made for hire." If you have checked "Yes" to indicate that the work was "made for hire," you must give the full legal name of the employer (or other person for whom the work was prepared). You may also include the name of the employee along with the name of the employer (for example: "Elster Publishing Co., employer for hire of John Ferguson").

"Anonymous" or "Pseudonymous" Work: An author's contribution to a work is "anonymous" if that author is not identified on the copies or phonorecords of the work. An author's contribution to a work is "pseudonymous" if that author is identified on the copies or phonorecords under a fictitious name. If the work is "anonymous" you may: (1) leave the line blank; or (2) state "anonymous" on the line; or (3) reveal the author's identity. If the work is "pseudonymous" you may: (1) leave the line blank; or (2) give the pseudonym and identify it as such (for example: "Huntley Haverstock, pseudonym"); or (3) reveal the author's name, making clear which is the real name and which is the pseudonym (for example: "Henry Leek, whose pseudonym is Priam Farrel"). However, the citizenship or domicile of the author **must** be given in all cases.

Dates of Birth and Death: If the author is dead, the statute requires that the year of death be included in the application unless the work is anonymous or pseudonymous. The author's birth date is optional but is useful as a form of identification. Leave this space blank if the author's contribution was a "work made for hire."

Author's Nationality or Domicile: Give the country of which the author is a citizen or the country in which the author is domiciled. Nationality or domicile **must** be given in all cases.

Nature of Authorship: Catagories of pictorial, graphic, and sculptural authorship are listed below. Check the box(es) that best describe(s) each author's contribution to the work.

3-Dimensional sculptures: fine art sculptures, toys, dolls, scale models, and sculptural designs applied to useful articles.

2-Dimensional artwork: watercolor and oil paintings; pen and ink drawings; logo illustrations; greeting cards; collages; stencils; patterns; computer graphics; graphics appearing in screen displays; artwork appearing on posters, calendars, games, commercial prints and labels, and packaging, as well as 2-dimensional artwork applied to useful articles.

Reproductions of works of art: reproductions of preexisting artwork made by, for example, lithography, photoengraving, or etching.

Maps: cartographic representations of an area such as state and county maps, atlases, marine charts, relief maps, and globes.

Photographs: pictorial photographic prints and slides and holograms.

Jewelry designs: 3-dimensional designs applied to rings, pendants, earrings, necklaces, and the like.

Designs on sheetlike materials: designs reproduced on textiles, lace, and other fabrics; wallpaper; carpeting; floor tile; wrapping paper; and clothing.

Technical drawings: diagrams illustrating scientific or technical information in linear form such as architectural blueprints or mechanical drawings.

Text: textual material that accompanies pictorial, graphic, or sculptural works such as comic strips, greeting cards, games rules, commercial prints or labels, and maps.

Architectural works: designs of buildings, including the overall form as well as the arrangement and composition of spaces and elements of the design. NOTE: Any registration for the underlying architectural plans must be applied for on a separate Form VA, checking the box "Technical drawing."

3 SPACE 3: Creation and Publication

General Instructions: Do not confuse "creation" with "publication." Every application for copyright registration must state "the year in which creation of the work was completed." Give the date and nation of first publication only if the work has been published.

Creation: Under the statute, a work is "created" when it is fixed in a copy or phonorecord for the first time. Where a work has been prepared over a period of time, the part of the work existing in fixed form on a particular date constitutes the created work on that date. The date you give here should be the year in which the author completed the particular version for which registration is now being sought, even if other versions exist or if further changes or additions are planned.

Publication: The statute defines "publication" as "the distribution of copies or phonorecords of a work to the public by sale or other transfer of ownership, or by rental, lease, or lending"; a work is also "published" if there has been an "offering to distribute copies or phonorecords to a group of persons for purposes of further distribution, public performance, or public display." Give the full date (month, day, year) when, and the country where, publication first occurred. If first publication took place simultaneously in the United States and other countries, it is sufficient to state "U.S.A."

4 SPACE 4: Claimant(s)

Name(s) and Address(es) of Copyright Claimant(s): Give the name(s) and address(es) of the copyright claimant(s) in this work even if the claimant is the same as the author. Copyright in a work belongs initially to the author of the work (including, in the case of a work made for hire, the employer or other person for whom the work was prepared). The copyright claimant is either the author of the work or a person or organization to whom the copyright initially belonging to the author has been transferred.

Transfer: The statute provides that, if the copyright claimant is not the author, the application for registration must contain "a brief statement of how the claimant obtained ownership of the copyright." If any copyright claimant named in space 4 is not an author named in space 2, give a brief statement explaining how the claimant(s) obtained ownership of the copyright. Examples: "By written contract"; "Transfer of all rights by author"; "Assignment"; "By will." Do not attach transfer documents or other attachments or riders.

5 SPACE 5: Previous Registration

General Instructions: The questions in space 5 are intended to find out whether an earlier registration has been made for this work and, if so, whether

there is any basis for a new registration. As a rule, only one basic copyright registration can be made for the same version of a particular work.

Same Version: If this version is substantially the same as the work covered by a previous registration, a second registration is not generally possible unless: (1) the work has been registered in unpublished form and a second registration is now being sought to cover this first published edition; or (2) someone other than the author is identified as a copyright claimant in the earlier registration, and the author is now seeking registration in his or her own name. If either of these two exceptions apply, check the appropriate box and give the earlier registration number and date. Otherwise, do not submit Form VA; instead, write the Copyright Office for information about supplementary registration or recordation of transfers of copyright ownership.

Changed Version: If the work has been changed and you are now seeking registration to cover the additions or revisions, check the last box in space 5, give the earlier registration number and date, and complete both parts of space 6 in accordance with the instruction below.

Previous Registration Number and Date: If more than one previous registration has been made for the work, give the number and date of the latest registration.

6 SPACE 6: Derivative Work or Compilation

General Instructions: Complete space 6 if this work is a "changed version," "compilation," or "derivative work," and if it incorporates one or more earlier works that have already been published or registered for copyright, or that have fallen into the public domain. A "compilation" is defined as "a work formed by the collection and assembling of preexisting materials or of data that are selected, coordinated, or arranged in such a way that the resulting work as a whole constitutes an original work of authorship." A "derivative work" is " a work based on one or more preexisting works." Examples of derivative works include reproductions of works of art, sculptures based on drawings, lithographs based on paintings, maps based on previously published sources, or "any other form in which a work may be recast, transformed, or adapted." Derivative works also include works "consisting of editorial revisions, annotations, or other modifications" if these changes, as a whole, represent an original work of authorship.

Preexisting Material (space 6a): Complete this space **and** space 6b for derivative works. In this space identify the preexisting work that has been recast, transformed, or adapted. Examples of preexisting material might be "Grunewald Altarpiece" or "19th century quilt design." Do not complete this space for compilations.

Material Added to This Work (space 6b): Give a brief, general statement of the **additional** new material covered by the copyright claim for which registration is sought. In the case of a derivative work, identify this new material. Examples: "Adaptation of design and additional artistic work"; "Reproduction of painting by photolithography"; "Additional cartographic material"; "Compilation of photographs." If the work is a compilation, give a brief, general statement describing both the material that has been compiled **and** the compilation itself. Example: "Compilation of 19th century political cartoons."

7,8,9 SPACE 7,8,9: Fee, Correspondence, Certification, Return Address

Deposit Account: If you maintain a Deposit Account in the Copyright Office, identify it in space 7. Otherwise leave the space blank and send the fee of $20 with your application and deposit.

Correspondence (space 7): This space should contain the name, address, area code, and telephone number of the person to be consulted if correspondence about this application becomes necessary.

Certification (space 8): The application cannot be accepted unless it bears the date and the **handwritten signature** of the author or other copyright claimant, or of the owner of exclusive right(s), or of the duly authorized agent of the author, claimant, or owner of exclusive right(s).

Address for Return of Certificate (space 9): The address box must be completed legibly since the certificate will be returned in a window envelope.

FORM VA

For a Work of the Visual Arts
UNITED STATES COPYRIGHT OFFICE

REGISTRATION NUMBER

	VA	VAU

EFFECTIVE DATE OF REGISTRATION

Month	Day	Year

DO NOT WRITE ABOVE THIS LINE. IF YOU NEED MORE SPACE, USE A SEPARATE CONTINUATION SHEET.

1

TITLE OF THIS WORK ▼

NATURE OF THIS WORK ▼ See instructions

PREVIOUS OR ALTERNATIVE TITLES ▼

PUBLICATION AS A CONTRIBUTION If this work was published as a contribution to a periodical, serial, or collection, give information about the collective work in which the contribution appeared.   **Title of Collective Work ▼**

If published in a periodical or serial give: **Volume ▼**   **Number ▼**   **Issue Date ▼**   **On Pages ▼**

2 a

NAME OF AUTHOR ▼

DATES OF BIRTH AND DEATH
Year Born ▼   Year Died ▼

Was this contribution to the work a "work made for hire"?
☐ Yes
☐ No

OR { **AUTHOR'S NATIONALITY OR DOMICILE**
Name of Country
Citizen of ▶ _____
Domiciled in ▶ _____

WAS THIS AUTHOR'S CONTRIBUTION TO THE WORK
Anonymous? ☐ Yes ☐ No
Pseudonymous? ☐ Yes ☐ No

If the answer to either of these questions is "Yes," see detailed instructions.

NATURE OF AUTHORSHIP Check appropriate box(es). **See instructions**
☐ 3-Dimensional sculpture   ☐ Map   ☐ Technical drawing
☐ 2-Dimensional artwork   ☐ Photograph   ☐ Text
☐ Reproduction of work of art ☐ Jewelry design   ☐ Architectural work
☐ Design on sheetlike material

NOTE

Under the law, the "author" of a "work made for hire" is generally the employer, not the employee (see instructions). For any part of this work that was "made for hire" check "Yes" in the space provided, give the employer (or other person for whom the work was prepared) as "Author" of that part, and leave the space for dates of birth and death blank.

b

NAME OF AUTHOR ▼

DATES OF BIRTH AND DEATH
Year Born ▼   Year Died ▼

Was this contribution to the work a "work made for hire"?
☐ Yes
☐ No

OR { **AUTHOR'S NATIONALITY OR DOMICILE**
Name of Country
Citizen of ▶ _____
Domiciled in ▶ _____

WAS THIS AUTHOR'S CONTRIBUTION TO THE WORK
Anonymous? ☐ Yes ☐ No
Pseudonymous? ☐ Yes ☐ No

If the answer to either of these questions is "Yes," see detailed instructions.

NATURE OF AUTHORSHIP Check appropriate box(es). **See instructions**
☐ 3-Dimensional sculpture   ☐ Map   ☐ Technical drawing
☐ 2-Dimensional artwork   ☐ Photograph   ☐ Text
☐ Reproduction of work of art ☐ Jewelry design   ☐ Architectural work
☐ Design on sheetlike material

3 a

YEAR IN WHICH CREATION OF THIS WORK WAS COMPLETED This information must be given in all cases. ◀Year

b **DATE AND NATION OF FIRST PUBLICATION OF THIS PARTICULAR WORK**
Complete this information ONLY if this work has been published.
Month ▶ _____ Day ▶ _____ Year ▶ _____
◀ Nation

4

See instructions before completing this space.

COPYRIGHT CLAIMANT(S) Name and address must be given even if the claimant is the same as the author given in space 2. ▼

TRANSFER If the claimant(s) named here in space 4 is (are) different from the author(s) named in space 2, give a brief statement of how the claimant(s) obtained ownership of the copyright. ▼

APPLICATION RECEIVED

ONE DEPOSIT RECEIVED

TWO DEPOSITS RECEIVED

FUNDS RECEIVED

DO NOT WRITE HERE OFFICE USE ONLY

MORE ON BACK ▶ • Complete all applicable spaces (numbers 5-9) on the reverse side of this page.
• See detailed instructions.   • Sign the form at line 8.

DO NOT WRITE HERE
Page 1 of _____ pages

EXAMINED BY	FORM VA
CHECKED BY	

☐ CORRESPONDENCE
Yes

FOR
COPYRIGHT
OFFICE
USE
ONLY

DO NOT WRITE ABOVE THIS LINE. IF YOU NEED MORE SPACE, USE A SEPARATE CONTINUATION SHEET.

PREVIOUS REGISTRATION Has registration for this work, or for an earlier version of this work, already been made in the Copyright Office?

☐ Yes ☐ No If your answer is "Yes," why is another registration being sought? (Check appropriate box) ▼

a. ☐ This is the first published edition of a work previously registered in unpublished form.

b. ☐ This is the first application submitted by this author as copyright claimant.

c. ☐ This is a changed version of the work, as shown by space 6 on this application.

If your answer is "Yes," give: **Previous Registration Number** ▼   **Year of Registration** ▼

5

DERIVATIVE WORK OR COMPILATION Complete both space 6a and 6b for a derivative work; complete only 6b for a compilation.

a. **Preexisting Material** Identify any preexisting work or works that this work is based on or incorporates. ▼

b. **Material Added to This Work** Give a brief, general statement of the material that has been added to this work and in which copyright is claimed. ▼

6

See instructions
before completing
this space.

DEPOSIT ACCOUNT If the registration fee is to be charged to a Deposit Account established in the Copyright Office, give name and number of Account.

Name ▼   **Account Number** ▼

7

CORRESPONDENCE Give name and address to which correspondence about this application should be sent.   Name/Address/Apt/City/State/ZIP ▼

Area Code and Telephone Number ▶

Be sure to
give your
daytime phone
◀ number

CERTIFICATION* I, the undersigned, hereby certify that I am the

check only one ▼

☐ author

☐ other copyright claimant

☐ owner of exclusive right(s)

☐ authorized agent of ─────────────────────────

Name of author or other copyright claimant, or owner of exclusive right(s) ▲

8

of the work identified in this application and that the statements made
by me in this application are correct to the best of my knowledge.

Typed or printed name and date ▼ If this application gives a date of publication in space 3, do not sign and submit it before that date.

_____ Date▶ _____

☞   Handwritten signature (X) ▼

Mail certificate to:	Name ▼	**YOU MUST:** • Complete all necessary spaces • Sign your application in space 8	**9**
Certificate will be mailed in window envelope	Number/Street/Apt ▼	**SEND ALL 3 ELEMENTS IN THE SAME PACKAGE:** 1. Application form 2. Nonrefundable $20 filing fee in check or money order payable to *Register of Copyrights* 3. Deposit material	
	City/State/ZIP ▼	**MAIL TO:** Register of Copyrights Library of Congress Washington, D.C. 20559-6000	

*17 U.S.C. § 506(e): Any person who knowingly makes a false representation of a material fact in the application for copyright registration provided for by section 409, or in any written statement filed in connection with the application, shall be fined not more than $2,500.

March 1995—300,000   ☆U.S. COPYRIGHT OFFICE WWW FORM: 1995

✐INSTRUCTIONS FOR SHORT FORM VA

For pictorial, graphic, and sculptural works

USE THIS FORM IF—
1. you are the **only** author and copyright owner of this work; *and*
2. the work was **not** made for hire, *and*
3. the work is completely new (does not contain a substantial amount of material that has been previously published or registered or is in the public domain).
If any of the above does not apply, you must use standard Form VA.
NOTE: Short Form VA is not appropriate for an anonymous author who does not wish to reveal his or her identity.

HOW TO COMPLETE SHORT FORM VA
- Type or print in black ink.
- Be clear and legible. (Your certificate of registration will be copied from your form.)
- Give only the information requested.
- Do **not** use continuation sheets or any other attachments.

1 Title of This Work

You must give a title. If there is no title, state "UNTITLED." If you are registering an unpublished collection, give the collection title you want to appear in our records (for example: "Jewelry by Josephine, 1995 Volume"). Alternative title: If the work is known by two titles, you also may give the second title. If the work has been published as part of a larger work (including a periodical), give the title of that larger work instead of an alternative title.

2 Name and Address of Author/Owner of the Copyright

Give your name and mailing address. (You may include your pseudonym followed by "pseud.") Also, give the nation of which you are a citizen or where you have your domicile (i.e., permanent residence).
Please give daytime phone and fax numbers, if available.

3 Year of Creation

Give the year in which you completed the work you are registering at this time. (A work is "created" when it is "fixed" in a tangible form. Examples: drawn on paper, molded in clay, stored in a computer.)

4 Publication

If the work has been published (i.e., if copies have been distributed to the public), give the complete date of publication (month, day, and year) and the nation where the publication first took place.

5 Type of Authorship in This Work

Check the box or boxes that describe the kind of material you are registering. Check *only* the authorship included in the copy you are sending with the application. For example, if you are registering illustrations but have not written the story yet, check only the box for "2-dimensional artwork".

6 Signature of Author

Sign the application in black ink.

7 Person to Contact for Rights and Permissions

This space is optional. You may give the name and address of the person or organization to contact for permission to use the work. You may also provide phone, fax, or e-mail information.

8 Mail Certificate to

This space must be completed. Your certificate of registration will be mailed in a window envelope to this address. Also, if the Copyright Office needs to contact you, we will write to this address.

9 Deposit Account

Complete this space only if you currently maintain a deposit account in the Copyright Office.

MAIL WITH THE FORM—
- a $20.00 filing fee in the form of a check or money order (*no cash*) payable to "Register of Copyrights," **and**
- one or two copies of the work or identifying material consisting of photographs or drawings showing the work. See table below for the requirements for most works. **Note:** Inquire about the requirements for other works or for any work first published before 1978. Copies submitted become the property of the U.S. Government.

If you are registering	And the work is *unpublished*, send	And the work is *published*, send
2-dimensional artwork in a book, map, poster, or print	one complete copy or identifying material	two copies of the best published edition
3-dimensional sculpture, T-shirt design	identifying material	identifying material
a greeting card, pattern, commercial print or label, fabric, wallpaper	one complete copy or identifying material	one copy of the best published edition

Mail everything (**application form, copy or copies, and fee**) *in one package* to: Register of Copyrights
Library of Congress
Washington, D.C. 20559-6000

Questions? Call (202) 707-3000 between 8:30 a.m. and 5:00 p.m. Eastern Time, Monday through Friday. For forms, call (202) 707-9100 24 hours a day, 7 days a week.

SHORT FORM VA ■

For a Work of the Visual Arts
UNITED STATES COPYRIGHT OFFICE

REGISTRATION NUMBER

VA	VAU

Effective Date of Registration

Month	Day	Year

Application Received

Examined By

Deposit Received One	Two

Correspondence ☐

Fee Received

TYPE OR PRINT IN BLACK INK. DO NOT WRITE ABOVE THIS LINE.

Title of This Work: **1**

Alternative title or title of larger work in which this work was published:

Name and Address of Author/Owner of the Copyright: **2**

Nationality or domicile:

Phone and Fax numbers:

Phone (   )   Fax (   )

Year of Creation: **3**

If work has been published, Date and Nation of Publication: **4**

a. Date _____ (Month) _____ (Day) _____ (Year)   *(Month, day, and year all required)*

b. Nation

Type of Authorship in This Work: (Check all that apply.) **5**

☐ 3-Dimensional sculpture
☐ 2-Dimensional artwork
☐ Technical drawing

☐ Photograph
☐ Jewelry design
☐ Architectural work

☐ Map
☐ Text

Signature of Author: **6**

*I certify that the statements made by me in this application are correct to the best of my knowledge.**

Name and Address of Person to Contact for Rights and Permissions: **7**

☐ Check here if same as #2 above

Phone and Fax numbers:
E-mail address:

Phone (   )   Fax (   )
E-mail

OPTIONAL

8

MAIL CERTIFICATE TO

Certificate will be mailed in window envelope

Name ▼

Number/Street/Apartment Number ▼

City/State/ZIP ▼

9

Deposit Account #_____

Name _____

_____

_____

_____

*17 U.S.C. § 506(e): Any person who knowingly makes a false representation of a material fact in the application for copyright registration provided for by section 409, or in any written statement filed in connection with the application, shall be fined not more than $2,500.
September 1995—100,000

☆U.S. COPYRIGHT OFFICE WWW FORM: 1995

Permission Form

Some projects require obtaining permission from the owners of copyrighted materials such as graphics, photographs, paintings, articles, or excerpts from books. The artist ignores obtaining such permissions at great peril. Not only is it unethical to use someone else's work without permission, it can also lead to liability for copyright infringement.

Of course, some copyrighted works have entered the public domain, which means that they can be freely copied by anyone. For works published by United States authors on or before December 31, 1977, the maximum term of copyright protection was seventy five years. If such a work is more than seventy five years old, it should be in the public domain in the United States (but may have a different term of protection in other countries). Works published before December 31, 1977, also had an initial term of twenty eight years and then a renewal term. If the copyright was not renewed, the work would also have gone into the public domain. The Copyright Office can review its records to determine whether a copyright was renewed.

For works published on or after January 1, 1978, the term of protection is usually the life of the author plus fifty years, so these works would only be in the public domain if copyright notice had been omitted or improper. This complicated topic is discussed fully in *Legal Guide for the Visual Artist*. The absence of a copyright notice on works published between January 1, 1978, and February 28, 1989, (when the United States joined the Berne Copyright Union) does not necessarily mean the work is in the public domain. On or after March 1, 1989, copyright notice is no longer required to preserve copyright protection, although such notice does confer some benefits under the copyright law. A basic rule is to obtain permission for using any work, unless the artist is certain the work is in the public domain or determines that the planned use would be a fair use.

Fair use offers another way in which the artist may avoid having to obtain a permission, even though the work is protected by a valid copyright. The copyright law states that copying "for purposes such as criticism, comment, news reporting, teaching (including multiple copies for classroom use), scholarship, or research, is not an infringement of copyright." To evaluate whether a use is a fair use depends on four factors set forth in the law: "(1) the purpose and character of the use, including whether such use is of a commercial nature or is for nonprofit educational purposes; (2) the nature of the copyrighted work; (3) the amount and substantiality of the portion used . . . ; and (4) the effect of the use upon the potential market for or value of the copyrighted work." These guidelines have to be applied on a case-by-case basis. If there is any doubt, it is best to seek permission to use the work.

One obstacle to obtaining permissions is locating the person who owns the rights. A good starting point, of course, is to contact the publisher of the material, since the publisher may have the right to grant permissions. If the creator's address is available, the creator can be contacted directly. In some cases, permissions may have to be obtained from more than one party. Creator's societies and agents may be helpful in tracking down the owners of rights.

For an hourly fee, the Copyright Office will search its records to aid in establishing the copyright status of a work. Copyright Office Circular R22, *How to Investigate the Copyright Status of a Work*, explains more fully what the Copyright Office can and cannot do. Circulars and forms can be ordered from the Copyright Office by calling (202) 707-9100.

Permissions can be time-consuming to obtain, so starting early in a project is wise. A log should be kept of each request for a permission. In the log, each request is given a number. The log describes the material to be used, lists the name and address of the owner of the rights, shows when the request was made and when any reply was received, indicates if a fee must be paid, and includes any special conditions required by the owner.

Fees may have to be paid for certain permissions. If the client is to pay these fees, the artist should certainly specify this in the contract with the client. If the client (such as a collector) has an agreement making the artist liable if lawsuits arise over permissions which should have been obtained by the artist, the artist should resist such a provision or at least limit the amount of liability. For example, the artist might limit his or her liability to the amount of the fee paid for a commission (but this will not stop the artist being named as a defendant by the owner of the work which was infringed). In any case, the artist should keep in mind that permission fees are negotiable and vary widely in amount. For a project that will require many permissions, advance research as to the amount of the fees is a necessity.

Filling in the Form

The form should be accompanied by a cover letter requesting that two copies of the form be signed and one copy returned. The name and address of the artist and the type of use should be filled in. Then the nature of the material should be specified, such as painting, text, photograph, illustration, poem, and so on. The source should be described along with an exact description of the material. If available, fill in the date of publication, the publisher, and the author or artist. Any copyright notice or credit line to accompany the material should be shown. State after Other Provisions any special limitations on the rights granted and also indicate the amount of any fee to be paid. If all the rights are not controlled by the person giving the permission, then that person will have to indicate who else to contact. If more than one person must approve the permission, make certain there are enough signature lines. If the rights are owned by a corporation, add the company name and the title of the authorized signatory. A stamped, self-addressed envelope and a photocopy of the material to be used might make a speedy response more likely.

Negotiation Checklist

❏ State that the permission extends not only to the artist, but also to the artist's successors and assigns. Certainly the permission must extend to the artist's client.

❏ Describe the material to be used carefully, including a photocopy if that would be helpful.

❏ Obtain the right to use the material in future editions, derivations, or revisions of the artwork, book, or other project, as well as in the present version.

❏ State that nonexclusive world rights in all languages are being granted.

❏ In an unusual situation, seek exclusivity for certain uses of the material. This form does not seek exclusivity.

❏ Negotiate a fee, if requested. Whether a fee is appropriate, and its amount, will depend on whether the project is likely to earn a substantial return.

❏ If a fee is paid, add a provision requiring the party giving the permission to warrant that the material does not violate any copyright or other rights and to indemnify the artist against any losses caused if the warranty is incorrect.

❏ Cover electronic rights if the work may be digitized for use on the Web or a CD-ROM.

❏ Keep a log on all correspondence relating to permission forms and be certain one copy of each signed permission has been returned for the artist's files.

Permission Form

The Undersigned hereby grants permission to _____ (hereinafter

referred to as the "Artist"), located at _____, and

to the Artist's successors and assigns, to use the material specified in this Permission Form for the following art-

work, design, book or other project _____

This permission is for the following material:

Nature of material _____

Source _____

Exact description of material, including page numbers_____

                                  If published, date of publication _____

                                  Publisher _____

                                  Author(s) _____

This material may be used for the artwork, book, design, or other project named above and in any future revisions, derivations, editions, or electronic versions thereof, including nonexclusive world rights in all languages.

It is understood that the grant of this permission shall in no way restrict republication of the material by the Under-signed or others authorized by the Undersigned.

If specified here, the material shall be accompanied on publication by a copyright notice as follows_____

_____

and a credit line as follows _____.

Other provisions, if any: _____

If specified here, the requested rights are not controlled in their entirety by the Undersigned and the following own-ers must be contacted: _____

_____

One copy of this Permission Form shall be returned to the Artist and one copy shall be retained by the Undersigned.

_____   _____

            Authorized Signatory   Date

_____   _____

            Authorized Signatory   Date

Trademark Application

A trademark is a distinctive word, phrase, symbol, design, emblem, or combination of these which a manufacturer places on a product to identify and distinguish in the public mind that product from the products of rival manufacturers. A service mark is like a trademark except that it identifies services instead of products. Trademarks (including service marks) can be registered with the U. S. Patent and Trademark Office for federal protection and with the appropriate state office for state protection, although even an unregistered mark can have protection under the common law simply because the mark is used in commerce. An artist who is exploiting work commercially—for example, posters, jewelry, or apparel—might wish to seek trademark protection for a distinctive logo or motto.

Form 23 is the trademark (and service mark) application with the instructions issued by the U. S. Patent and Trademark Office. That office makes available not only forms, but also an excellent pamphlet , *Basic Facts about Registering a Trademark,* that can be requested by calling the Assistant Commissioner for Trademarks, Box New App/Fee, 2900 Crystal Drive, Arlington, VA 22202-3513 or by calling (703) 308-HELP. This pamphlet, the application form, and the instructions to register a trademark (or service mark) can also be downloaded from the home page of the U. S. Patent and Trademark Office at http://www.uspto.gov.

The artist who believes that a certain product should be trademarked will want to be certain that any chosen trademark does not infringe an already registered trademark in commercial use. This can be accomplished by conducting a trademark search prior to filling out the trademark registration application. If other names in use are too similar to that selected by the artist, a decision can be made to select a different name. To conduct a search, the artist can either go to the public search library at the U. S. Patent and Trademark Office located on the second floor of the South Tower Building, 2900 Crystal Drive, Arlington, VA or use the CD-ROMs containing the trademark database at the patent and trademark depository libraries listed on pages 14-15 of *Basic Facts about Registering a Trademark.* While the trademark can be filed without such a search and without the help of an attorney or search service, the search and evaluation of the search may require such expert assistance.

An important revision of the trademark law took effect on November 16, 1989. Trademarks may now be registered before use, whereas previously they could only be registered after use. The application must include a bona fide "intent to use" statement. Every six months an "intent to use" statement must be filed again and additional fees paid, and in no event can such a pre-registration period exceed three years. Trademarks can last forever if the artist keeps using the mark to identify goods or services. The federal trademark has a term of ten years, but can then be renewed for additional ten years terms. The artist should note that to avoid having the trademark registration cancelled, an affidavit must be filed between the fifth and sixth year after the initial registration. Trademarks can be licensed (see Form 17), as long as the artist giving the license ensures that the quality of goods created by the licensee will be of the same quality that the public associates with the trademark. Trademarks are entitled to protection in foreign countries under treaties executed by the United States.

It is important to understand when the symbols TM, SM, and ® can and should be used. The symbols TM (for trademark) and SM (for service mark) can be used at any time, without or prior to the issuance of registration, to inform the public of the artist's claim to trademark protection for a mark. The symbol ® (for registration) should be used only when the mark has in fact been registered with the U. S. Patent and Trademark Office.

Occasionally artists wish to include a trademark in an artwork. For example, an artist may create an image of a street scene which includes a sign with a company logo. Use of the trademark in this way should not be a problem for the artist, except in the unlikely case in which the public might be confused by the painting and imagine it was created by or was a product of the company depicted in the painting.

Closely related to trademarks is the area of trade dress, which has special relevance for designers and other artists who create the look of products for sale to consumers. Trade dress claims arise under section 43(a) of the Lanham Act, a federal statute. A plaintiff must prove three elements to win a trade dress claim: (1) that the features of the trade dress are primarily nonfunctional (i.e., that these features primarily identify the source of the particular goods or services); (2) that the trade dress has secondary meaning (i.e., that the public has come to identify the source of goods or services due to the associations created by the trade dress); and (3) that the competing products' respective trade dresses are confusingly similar, thus giving rise to a likelihood of confusion among consumers as to their sources.

Returning to the subject of trademark registration, the application requires the following: (1) the filled in application form, such as Form 23; (2) a drawing of the trademark; (3) three specimens of the mark; and (4) the filing fee (currently $245) for each class of goods/services listed in the application.

With respect to the drawing of the trademark, *Basic Facts about Registering a Trademark* advises as follows:

> Every application must include a single drawing page. . . .
>
> The drawing must be on pure white, durable, non-shiny paper that is 8 1\2 (21.59 cm) inches wide by 11 (27.94 cm) inches long. There must be at least a one-inch (2.54 cm) margin on the sides, top and bottom of the page, and at least one inch between the heading and the display of the mark.
>
> At the top of the drawing there must be a heading, listing on separate lines, the applicant's complete name, address, the goods and services specified in the application, and in applications based on use in commerce, the date of first use of the mark and the date of first use of the mark in commerce. This heading should be typewritten. If the drawing is in special form, the heading should include a description of the essential elements of the mark.
>
> The drawing of the mark should appear at the center of the page. . . .
>
> If the mark includes words, numbers or letters, the applicant can usually elect to submit either a typewritten or a special-form drawing. To register a mark consisting of only words, letters or numbers, without indicating any particular style or design, provide a typewritten drawing. In a typewritten drawing the mark must be typed entirely in CAPITAL LETTERS, even if the mark, as used, includes lower-case letters. Use a standard typewriter or type of the same size and style as that on a standard typewriter.
>
> To indicate color, use the color linings shown below . . . A plain black-and-white drawing is acceptable even if the mark is used in color. Most drawings do not indicate specific colors.
>
> Be careful in preparing the drawing. While it may be possible to make some minor changes, the rules prohibit any material change to the drawing of the mark after filing. To register a word mark in the form in which it is actually used or intended to be used in commerce, or any mark including a design, submit a special-form drawing. In a special-form drawing, the mark must not be larger than 4 inches by 4 inches (10.16 cm by 10.16 cm). If the drawing of the mark is larger than 4 inches by 4 inches, the application will be denied a filing date and returned to the applicant. In addition, the drawing must appear only in black and white, with every line and letter black and clear. No color or gray is allowed. Do not combine typed matter and special form in the same drawing.

The drawing in special form must be a substantially exact representation of the mark as it appears on the specimens. . . . Do not include non trademark matter in the drawing, such as informational matter which may appear on a label. In the end, the applicant must decide exactly what to register and in what form. The PTO considers the drawing controlling in determining exactly what mark the application covers.

While it is not mandatory to fill in the class of goods/services, some classes that would be especially relevant to the crafts are:

Class 14. Paper, cardboard, articles of paper or of cardboard (not included in other classes); printed matter, newspapers and periodicals, books; book-binding material; photographs; stationery; . . .

Class 18. Leather and imitations of leather, and articles made from these materials and not included in other classes. . .

Class 20. Furniture, mirrors, pictures frames; articles (not included in others classes) of wood, cork, reeds, cane, wicker, horn, bone, ivory, whalebone, shell, amber, mother-of-pearl, meerschaum, celluloid, plastic or substitutes for all these materials.

Class 21. Small domestic utensils and contains (neither made of precious metals nor coated therewith); . . . unworked or semi-worked glass (excluding glass used in building); glassware, porcelain, and earthenware, not included in other classes.

Class 24. Tissues (piece goods); bed and table covers; textile articles not included in other classes.

Class 25. Clothing, including boots, shoes and slippers, headgear.

Class 26. Lace and embroidery, ribbons and braid; buttons, press buttons, hooks and eyes, pins and needles; artificial flowers.

Class 27. Carpets, rugs, mats and matting; linoleums and other materials for covering existing floors; wall hangings (nontextile).

Class 28. Games and playthings; gymnastic and sporting articles (except clothing); ornaments and decorations for Christmas trees.

The Mark

Indicate the mark (for example. "THEORYTEC" or "PINSTRIPES and DESIGN"). This should agree with the mark shown on the mark drawing page.

Classification

It is not necessary to fill in this box. The PTO will determine the proper International Classification based upon the identification of the goods and services in the application. However if the applicant knows the International Class number(s) for the goods and services, the applicant may place the number(s) in this box. The International Classes are listed inside of the back cover of this booklet. If the PTO determines that the goods and services listed are in more than one class, the PTO will notify the applicant during examination of the application, and the applicant will have the opportunity to pay the fees for any additional classes or to limit the goods and services to one or more classes.

Owner of the Mark

The name of the owner of the mark must be entered in this box. The applicant must be filed in the name of the owner of the mark or the application will be void, and the applicant will forfeit the filing fee. Thus it is very important to determine who owns the mark before applying. The owner of the mark is the party who controls the nature and quality of the goods sold, or services rendered, under the mark. The owner may be an individual, a partnership, a corporation, or an association or similar firm. If the applicant is a corporation, the applicant's name is the name under which it is incorporated. If the applicant is a partnership, the applicant's name is the name under which it is organized.

The Owner's Address

Enter the applicant's business address. If the applicant is an individual, enter either the applicant's business or home address.

Entity Type and Citizenship/Domicile

The applicant must check the box which indicates the type of entity that is being applied for. In addition, in the blank following the box, the applicant must specify the following information:

> Space 3(a) -- for an **individual**, the applicant's national citizenship;
> Space 3(b) -- for a **partnership**, the names and national citizenship of the general partners and the state where the
> > partnership is organized (if a U.S. partnership) or country (if a foreign partnership);
> Space3 (c) -- for a **corporation**, the state of incorporation (if a U.S. corporation) , or country (if a foreign corporation); or
> Space 3(d) -- for another type of entity, specify the nature of the entity and the state where it is organized (if in the U.S.) or
> > country where it is organized (if a foreign entity).

Identification of Goods and/or Services

Applicant requests registration of the trademark/service mark shown in the accompanying drawing in the U.S. Patent and Trademark Office on the Principal Register established by the Act of July 1946(15 U.S.C> 1051 et seq., as amended) for the goods/services in this blank.

In this blank the applicant must state the goods and services for which registration is sought and with which the applicant the applicant has actually used the mark in commerce, or in the case of an "intent to use" application, has a bona fide intention to use the mark in commerce. Use clear and concise terms specifying the actual goods and services by their common commercial names. A mark can only be registered for specific goods and services. The goods and services listed will establish the scope of the applicant's rights in the relevant mark. The goods and services listed must be the applicant's actual "goods in trade" or the actual services the applicant renders for the benefit of others. Use language readily understandable to the general public. For example, if the applicant uses or intends to use the mark to identify "candy," "word processors," "baseballs and baseball bats," the identification should clearly and concisely list each such item. If the applicant uses indefinite terms such as "accessories," "components," "devices," "equipment," "food," "parts" or like, then those words must be followed by the word "namely" and the goods or services listed by their common name(s).

The applicant must be very careful when identifying the goods and services. Because the filing of an application establishes certain presumptions of rights as of the filing date, the application may not be amended later to add product or services not within scope of the identification. For example, the identification of "clothing" could be amended to "shirts and jackets,": which narrows the cope, but could not be amended to "retail clothing store services," which would change the scope. Similarly, "physical therapy services" could not be changed to "medical services" because this would broaden the scope of the identification.

The **identification of goods and services** must not describe **the mode** of use of the mark, such as on labels, sign, menus, stationary, containers or in advertising.

If nothing appears in the this blank, or if the identification does not identify any recognizable goods or services, the applicant will be denied a filing date and the application will be returned to applicant.

Basis for Filing

The applicant must check at least one of the four boxes to specify a basis for filing the application the applicant should also fill in blanks which follow the checked box(es). Usually an application is based upon either (1) prior use of the mark in commerce (the first box), or (2) a bona fide intention to use the mark in commerce (the second box). **You may** *not* **check the first and second box. If both the first and second boxes are checked, the PTO will** *not* **accept the application and will return it to the applicant without processing.** If an applicant wishes to apply to register a mark for certain goods and services for which use in commerce has begun and other goods and services based on future use, separate applications must be filed to separate the relevant goods and services from each other.

TRADEMARK/SERVICE MARK APPLICATION, PRINCIPAL REGISTER, WITH DECLARATION	MARK (Word(s) and/or Design)	CLASS NO. (If known)

TO THE ASSISTANT COMMISSIONER FOR TRADEMARKS:

APPLICANT'S NAME:

APPLICANT'S MAILING ADDRESS:

(Display address exactly as it should appear on registration)

APPLICANT'S ENTITY TYPE: (**Check one** and supply requested information)

Individual - Citizen of (Country):

Partnership - State where organized (Country, if appropriate): _____
Names and Citizenship (Country) of General Partners: _____

Corporation - State (Country, if appropriate) of Incorporation:

Other (Specify Nature of Entity and Domicile):

GOODS AND/OR SERVICES:

Applicant requests registration of the trademark/service mark shown in the accompanying drawing in the United States Patent and Trademark Office on the Principal Register established by the Act of July 5, 1946 (15 U.S.C. 1051 et. seq., as amended) for the following goods/services **(SPECIFIC GOODS AND/OR SERVICES MUST BE INSERTED HERE)**:

BASIS FOR APPLICATION: (Check boxes which apply, **but never both the first AND second boxes**, and supply requested information related to each box checked.)

[ ] Applicant is using the mark in commerce on or in connection with the above identified goods/services. (15 U.S.C. 1051(a), as amended.) Three specimens showing the mark as used in commerce are submitted with this application.
- Date of first use of the mark in commerce which the U.S. Congress may regulate (for example, interstate or between the U.S. and a foreign country): _____
- Specify the type of commerce: _____
  (for example, interstate or between the U.S. and a specified foreign country)
- Date of first use anywhere (the same as or before use in commerce date): _____
- Specify intended manner or mode of use of mark on or in connection with the goods/services: _____
  (for example, trademark is applied to labels, service mark is used in advertisements)

[ ] Applicant has a bona fide intention to use the mark in commerce on or in connection with the above identified goods/services. (15 U.S.C. 1051(b), as amended.)
- Specify manner or mode of use of mark on or in connection with the goods/services: _____
  (for example, trademark will be applied to labels, service mark will be used in advertisements)

[ ] Applicant has a bona fide intention to use the mark in commerce on or in connection with the above identified goods/services, and asserts a claim of priority based upon a foreign application in accordance with 15 U.S.C. 1126(d), as amended.
- Country of foreign filing: _____   - Date of foreign filing: _____

[ ] Applicant has a bona fide intention to use the mark in commerce on or in connection with the above identified goods/services and, accompanying this application, submits a certification or certified copy of a foreign registration in accordance with 15 U.S.C 1126(e), as amended.
- Country of registration: _____   - Registration number: _____

NOTE: Declaration, on Reverse Side, MUST be Signed

PTO Form 1478 (REV 6/96)   U.S. DEPARTMENT OF COMMERCE/Patent and Trademark Office
OMB No. 0651-0009 (Exp. 06/30/98) There is no requirement to respond to this collection of information unless a currently valid OMB Number is displayed.

110

DECLARATION

The undersigned being hereby warned that willful false statements and the like so made are punishable by fine or imprisonment, or both, under 18 U.S.C. 1001, and that such willful false statements may jeopardize the validity of the application or any resulting registration, declares that he/she is properly authorized to execute this application on behalf of the applicant; he/she believes the applicant to be the owner of the trademark/service mark sought to be registered, or if the application is being filed under 15 U.S.C. 1051(b), he/she believes the applicant to be entitled to use such mark in commerce; to the best of his/her knowledge and belief no other person, firm, corporation, or association has the right to use the above identified mark in commerce, either in the identical form thereof or in such near resemblance thereto as to be likely, when used on or in connection with the goods/services of such other person, to cause confusion, or to cause mistake, or to deceive; and that all statements made of his/her own knowledge are true and that all statements made on information and belief are believed to be true.

_____   _____
DATE   SIGNATURE

_____   _____
TELEPHONE NUMBER   PRINT OR TYPE NAME AND POSITION

INSTRUCTIONS AND INFORMATION FOR APPLICANT

TO RECEIVE A FILING DATE, THE APPLICATION <u>MUST</u> BE COMPLETED AND SIGNED BY THE APPLICANT AND SUBMITTED ALONG WITH:

1. The prescribed **FEE ($245.00)** for each class of goods/services listed in the application;
2. A **DRAWING PAGE** displaying the mark in conformance with 37 CFR 2.52;
3. If the application is based on use of the mark in commerce, **THREE (3) SPECIMENS** (evidence) of the mark as used in commerce for each class of goods/services listed in the application. All three specimens may be the same. Examples of good specimens include: (a) labels showing the mark which are placed on the goods; (b) photographs of the mark as it appears on the goods, (c) brochures or advertisements showing the mark as used in connection with the services.
4. An **APPLICATION WITH DECLARATION** (this form) - The application must be signed in order for the application to receive a filing date. Only the following persons may sign the declaration, depending on the applicant's legal entity: (a) the individual applicant; (b) an officer of the corporate applicant; (c) one general partner of a partnership applicant; (d) all joint applicants.

SEND APPLICATION FORM, DRAWING PAGE, FEE, AND SPECIMENS (IF APPROPRIATE) TO:

Assistant Commissioner for Trademarks
Box New App/Fee
2900 Crystal Drive
Arlington, VA 22202-3513

Additional information concerning the requirements for filing an application is available in a booklet entitled **Basic Facts About Registering a Trademark,** which may be obtained by writing to the above address or by calling: (703) 308-HELP.

THE FORMS

TEAR-OUT SECTION

The Forms on CD-ROM

In addition to the forms in this tear-out section which are intended for use or photocopying, the forms are also provided on a CD-ROM found at the back of this book. The CD-ROM is compatible with both Windows and Macintosh operating systems. The Adobe Acrobat Reader is also included on the CD-ROM so that you can view, copy, and paste the forms into your word processing program. For more details, open the ReadMe.First file on the CD-ROM.

Contract of Sale

AGREEMENT made as of the _____ day of _____, 19_____, between _____ (hereinafter referred to as the "Artist"), located at _____ _____, and _____ (hereinafter referred to as the "Collector"), located at _____, with respect to the sale of an artwork (hereinafter referred to as the "Work").

WHEREAS, the Artist has created the Work and has full right, title, and interest therein; and

WHEREAS, the Artist wishes to sell the Work; and

WHEREAS, the Collector has viewed the Work and wishes to purchase it;

NOW, THEREFORE, in consideration of the foregoing premises and the mutual covenants hereinafter set forth and other valuable considerations, the parties hereto agree as follows:

1. **Description of Work.** The Artist describes the Work as follows:

   Title _____

   Medium _____

   Size _____

   Framing or mounting _____

   Year of creation _____

   Signed by Artist ❏ Yes   ❏ No

   If the Work is part of a limited edition, indicate the method of production _____; the size of the edition_____; how many multiples are signed_____; how many are unsigned_____; how many are numbered_____; how many are unnumbered_____; how many proofs exist_____; the quantity of any prior editions_____; and whether the master image has been cancelled or destroyed ❏ yes ❏ no.

2. **Sale.** The Artist hereby agrees to sell the Work to the Collector. Title shall pass to the Collector at such time as full payment is received by the Artist pursuant to Paragraph 4 hereof.

3. **Price.** The Collector agrees to purchase the Work for the agreed upon price of $_____, and shall also pay any applicable sales or transfer taxes.

4. **Payment.** Payment shall be made in full upon the signing of this Agreement.

5. **Delivery.** The ❏ Artist ❏ Collector shall arrange for delivery to the following location: _____ _____ no later than _____, 19 _____. The expenses of delivery (including, but not limited to, insurance and transportation) shall be paid by _____.

6. **Risk of Loss and Insurance.** The risk of loss or damage to the Work and the provision of any insurance to cover such loss or damage shall be the responsibility of the Collector from the time of _____.

7. **Copyright and Reproduction.** The Artist reserves all reproduction rights, including the right to claim statutory copyright, in the Work. The Work may not be photographed, sketched, painted, or reproduced in any manner whatsoever without the express, written consent of the Artist. All approved reproductions shall bear the following copyright notice: © by (Artist's name) 19____.

8. **Miscellany.** This Agreement shall be binding upon the parties hereto, their heirs, successors, assigns, and personal representatives. This Agreement constitutes the entire understanding between the parties. Its terms can be modified only by an instrument in writing signed by both parties. A waiver of any breach of any of the provisions of this Agreement shall not be construed as a continuing waiver of other breaches of the same or other provisions hereof. This Agreement shall be governed by the laws of the State of _____.

IN WITNESS WHEREOF, the parties hereto have signed this Agreement as of the date first set forth above.

Artist _____   Collector _____

Basic Contract of Sale

Artist's Letterhead

Purchaser_____   Date_____

Address_____   Account Number_____

_____   Sales Rep_____

Ship to_____   Order Number_____

Address_____   Ship via_____

_____   Date shipped_____

All customers must pay in full at the time of purchase, except for credit-verified trade accounts. If purchaser is such a trade account, payment in full is due within ___ days of receipt of merchandise.

Item Number	Description	Quantity Ordered	Quantity Shipped	Back Ordered	Retail Price	Discount	Unit Price	Amount

Subtotal	
Shipping & Handling	
Sales tax	
Payment received	
Balance due	

Authorization if paying by credit card

Card_____

Number_____

Expiration_____

Purchaser_____   Artist_____

Contract of Sale with Moral Rights and Resale Royalty Rights

AGREEMENT made as of the ____ day of _____, 19____, between _____ (hereinafter referred to as the "Artist"), located at _____ _____, and _____ (hereinafter referred to as the "Collector"), located at _____, with respect to the sale of an artwork (hereinafter referred to as the "Work").

WHEREAS, the Artist has created the Work and has full right, title, and interest therein; and

WHEREAS, the Artist wishes to sell the Work; and

WHEREAS, the Collector has viewed the Work and wishes to purchase it; and

WHEREAS, the Artist wishes to have a continuing relationship with the Work after its sale, including the right to borrow the Work periodically for exhibition, restore the Work if necessary, receive a residual payment if the Work is resold at a profit, and be acknowledged as the creator of the Work; and

WHEREAS, both parties wish to maintain the integrity of the Work and prevent its destruction;

NOW, THEREFORE, in consideration of the foregoing premises and the mutual convenants hereinafter set forth and other valuable considerations, the parties hereto agree as follows:

1. **Description of Work.** The Artist describes the Work as follows:

    Title _____

    Medium _____

    Size _____

    Framing or mounting _____

    Year of creation _____

    Signed by Artist ❑ Yes   ❑ No

    If the Work is part of a limited edition, indicate the method of production _____; the size of the edition_____; how many multiples are signed_____; how many are unsigned_____; how many are numbered_____; how many are unnumbered_____; how many proofs exist_____; the quantity of any prior editions_____; and whether the master image has been cancelled or destroyed ❑ yes ❑ no.

2. **Sale.** The Artist hereby agrees to sell the Work to the Collector. Title shall pass to the Collector at such time as full payment is received by the Artist pursuant to Paragraph 4 hereof.

3. **Price.** The Collector agrees to purchase the Work for the agreed upon price of $_____, and shall also pay any applicable sales or transfer taxes.

4. **Payment.** Payment shall be made in full upon the signing of this Agreement.

5. **Delivery.** The ❑ Artist ❑ Collector shall arrange for delivery to the following location: _____ no later than_____,19_____. The expenses of delivery (including, but not limited to, insurance and transportation) shall be paid by _____.

6. **Risk of Loss and Insurance.** The risk of loss or damage to the Work and the provision of any insurance to cover such loss or damage shall be the responsibility of the Collector from the time of_____ _____.

7. **Copyright and Reproduction.** The Artist reserves all reproduction rights, including the right to claim statutory copyright, in the Work. The Work may not be photographed, sketched, painted, or reproduced in any manner whatsoever without the express, written consent of the Artist. All approved reproductions shall bear the following copyright notice: © by (Artist's name) 19____.

8. **Nondestruction.** The Collector shall not destroy the Work or permit the Work to be destroyed without first offering to return ownership of the Work to the Artist or his or her successors in interest.

9. **Integrity.** The Collector shall not distort, mutilate, or otherwise alter the Work. In the event such distortion, mutilation, or other alteration occurs, whether by action of the Collector or otherwise, the Artist shall, in addition to any other rights and remedies, have the right to have his or her name removed from the Work and no longer have it attributed to him or her as its creator.

10. **Attribution.** The Artist shall, at all times, have the right to have his or her name appear with the Work and to be acknowledged as its creator.

11. **Right to Exhibit.** The Artist may borrow the Work for up to ___ days once every ___ years for exhibition at a nonprofit institution. The Artist shall give the Collector written notice no later than ___ days before the opening and shall provide satisfactory proof of insurance and prepaid transportation. All expenses of the loan to the Artist shall be paid for by the Artist.

12. **Restoration.** In the event of damage to the Work requiring restoration or repair, the Collector shall, if practicable, offer the Artist the first opportunity to restore or repair the Work and, in any case, shall consult with the Artist with respect to the restoration or repairs.

13. **Resale Proceeds.** On resale or other transfer of the Work for a price or value in excess of that paid in Paragraph 3, the Collector agrees to pay the Artist ____ percent of the gross sale price received or, if the Work is transferred other than by sale, to pay ____ percent of the fair market value of the Work as of the date of transfer.

14. **Miscellany.** This Agreement shall be binding upon the parties hereto, their heirs, successors, assigns, and personal representatives. This Agreement constitutes the entire understanding between the parties. Its terms can be modified only by an instrument in writing signed by both parties. A waiver of any breach of any of the provisions of this Agreement shall not be construed as a continuing waiver of other breaches of the same or other provisions hereof. This Agreement shall be governed by the laws of the State of _____.

IN WITNESS WHEREOF, the parties hereto have signed this Agreement as of the date first set forth above.

Artist _____   Collector _____

Invoice

Artist's name _____ Date_____

Artist's address _____

_____

Artist's telephone _____

Purchaser's name _____

Purchaser's address _____

_____

Purchaser's telephone _____

This invoice is for the following Artwork created by the Artist and sold to the Purchaser:

Title _____

Medium _____

Size _____

Framing or mounting _____

Year of creation _____

Signed by Artist   ❏ Yes   ❏ No

If the Work is part of a limited edition, indicate the method of production _____;

the size of the edition_____; how many multiples are signed_____; how many are

unsigned_____; how many are numbered_____; how many are unnumbered_____;

how many proofs exist_____; the quantity of any prior editions_____; and whether the

master image has been cancelled or destroyed ❏ yes ❏ no.

Price..................................... $_____

Delivery................................. $_____

Other charges....................... $_____

Sales or Transfer tax (if any)............... $_____

Total..................................... $_____

❏ Please remit the balance due.   ❏ Paid in full. Thank you.

Artist _____

Basic Invoice

Artist's Letterhead

Purchaser_____ Date_____

Address_____ Account Number_____

_____ Sales Rep_____

Ship to_____ Order Number_____

Address_____ Ship via_____

_____ Date shipped_____

Payment in full is due within _____ days of receipt of merchandise.

Item Number	Description	Quantity Ordered	Quantity Shipped	Back Ordered	Retail Price	Discount	Unit Price	Amount

Subtotal	
Shipping & Handling	
Sales tax	
Payment received	
Balance due	

Commission Contract

AGREEMENT made as of the _____ day of _____, 19 _____, between _____ (hereinafter referred to as the "Artist"), located at _____and _____ (hereinafter referred to as the "Purchaser"), located at _____.

WHEREAS, the Artist is a recognized professional artist; and

WHEREAS, the Purchaser admires the work of the Artist and wishes to commission the Artist to create a work of art ("the Work") in the Artist's own unique style; and

WHEREAS, the parties wish to have the creation of this work of art governed by the mutual obligations, covenants, and conditions herein;

NOW, THEREFORE, in consideration of the foregoing premises and the mutual covenants hereinafter set forth and other valuable considerations, the parties hereto agree as follows:

1. **Preliminary Design.** The Artist hereby agrees to create the preliminary design for the Work in the form of studies, sketches, drawings, or maquettes described as follows: _____ in return for which the Purchaser agrees to pay a fee of $_____ upon the signing of this Agreement. The Artist agrees to develop the preliminary design according to the following description of the Work as interpreted by the Artist:

   Title_____   Medium_____

   Size_____   Price_____

   Description_____
   _____

   The Artist shall deliver the preliminary design to the Purchaser within _____ days of the date hereof. The Purchaser may, within two weeks of receipt of the preliminary design, demand changes, and the Artist shall make such changes for a fee of _____ per hour; provided, however, that the Artist shall not be obligated to work more than _____ hours making changes.

2. **Progress Payments.** Upon the Purchaser's giving written approval of the preliminary design, the Artist agrees to proceed with construction of the Work, and the Purchaser agrees to pay the price of $_____ for the Work as follows:_____% upon the giving of written approval of the preliminary design, _____% upon the completion of _____% of the construction of the Work, and _____% upon the completion of the Work. The Purchaser shall also promptly pay the following expenses to be incurred by the Artist in the course of creating the Work _____
   _____. The Purchaser shall pay the applicable sales tax, if any, with the final progress payment. Completion of the Work is to be determined by the Artist, who shall use the Artist's professional judgment to deviate from the preliminary design as the Artist in good faith believes necessary to create the Work. If, upon the Artist presenting the Purchaser with written notice of any payment being due, the Purchaser fails to make said payment within two weeks of receipt of notice, interest at the rate of _____% shall accrue upon the balance due. The Purchaser shall have a right to inspect the Work in progress upon reasonable notice to the Artist.

3. **Date of Delivery.** The Artist agrees to complete the Work within _____ days of receiving the Purchaser's written approval of the preliminary design. This completion date shall be extended for such period of time as the Artist may be disabled by illness preventing progress of the Work. The completion date shall also be extended in the event of delays caused by events beyond the control of the Artist, including but not limited to fire, theft, strikes, shortages of materials, and acts of God. Time shall not be considered of the essence with respect to the completion of the Work.

4. Insurance, Shipping, and Installation. The Artist agrees to keep the Work fully insured against fire and theft and bear any other risk of loss until delivery to the Purchaser. In the event of loss caused by fire or theft, the Artist shall use the insurance proceeds to recommence the making of the Work. Upon completion of the Work, it shall be shipped at the expense of _____ to the following address specified by the Purchaser: _____. If any special installation is necessary, the Artist shall assist in said installation as follows:_____.

5. Termination. This Agreement may be terminated on the following conditions:

(A) If the Purchaser does not approve the preliminary design pursuant to Paragraph 1, the Artist shall keep all payments made and this Agreement shall terminate.

(B) The Purchaser may, upon payment of any progress payment due pursuant to Paragraph 2 or upon payment of an amount agreed in writing by the Artist to represent the pro rata portion of the price in relation to the degree of completion of Work, terminate this Agreement. The Artist hereby agrees to give promptly a good faith estimate of the degree of completion of the Work if requested by the Purchaser to do so.

(C) The Artist shall have the right to terminate this Agreement in the event the Purchaser is more than sixty days late in making any payment due pursuant to Paragraph 2, provided, however, nothing herein shall prevent the Artist bringing suit based on the Purchaser's breach of contract.

(D) The Purchaser shall have the right to terminate this Agreement if the Artist fails without cause to complete the Work within ninety days of the completion date in Paragraph 3. In the event of termination pursuant to this subparagraph, the Artist shall return to the Purchaser all payments made pursuant to Paragraph 2, but shall not be liable for any additional expenses, damages, or claims of any kind based on the failure to complete the Work.

(E) The Purchaser shall have a right to terminate this Agreement if, pursuant to Paragraph 3, the illness of the Artist causes a delay of more than six months in the completion date or if events beyond the Artist's control cause a delay of more than one year in the completion date, provided, however, that the Artist shall retain all payments made pursuant to Paragraphs 1 and 2.

(F) This Agreement shall automatically terminate on the death of the Artist, provided, however, that the Artist's estate shall retain all payments made pursuant to Paragraphs 1 and 2.

(G) The exercise of a right of termination under this Paragraph shall be written and set forth the grounds for termination.

6. Ownership. Title to the Work shall remain in the Artist until the Artist is paid in full. In the event of termination of this Agreement pursuant to Subparagraphs (A), (B), (C), or (D) of Paragraph 5, the Artist shall retain all rights of ownership in the Work and shall have the right to complete, exhibit, and sell the Work if the Artist so chooses. In the event of termination of this Agreement pursuant to Paragraph 5 (E) or (F), the Purchaser shall own the Work in whatever degree of completion and shall have the right to complete, exhibit, and sell the Work if the Purchaser so chooses. Notwithstanding anything to the contrary herein, the Artist shall retain all rights of ownership and have returned to the Artist the preliminary design, all incidental works made in the creation of the Work, and all copies and reproductions thereof and of the Work itself, provided, however, that in the event of termination pursuant to Paragraph 5 (E) or (F) the Purchaser shall have a right to keep copies of the preliminary design for the sole purpose of completing the Work.

7. Copyright and Reproduction. The Artist reserves all rights of reproduction and all copyrights in the Work, the preliminary design, and any incidental works made in the creation of the Work. Copyright notice in the name of the Artist shall appear on the Work, and the Artist shall also receive authorship credit in connection with the Work or any reproductions of the Work.

8. **Privacy**. The Purchaser gives to the Artist permission to use the Purchaser's name, picture, portrait, and photograph, in all forms and media and in all manners, including but not limited to exhibition, display, advertising, trade, and editorial uses, without violation of the Purchaser's rights of privacy or any other personal or proprietary rights the Purchaser may possess in connection with reproduction and sale of the Work, the preliminary design, or any incidental works made in the creation of the Work.

9. **Nondestruction, Alteration, and Maintenance.** The Purchaser agrees that the Purchaser will not intentionally destroy, damage, alter, modify, or change the Work in any way whatsoever. If any alteration of any kind occurs after receipt by the Purchaser, whether intentional or accidental and whether done by the Purchaser or others, the Work shall no longer be represented to be the Work of the Artist without the Artist's written consent. The Purchaser agrees to see that the Work is properly maintained.

10. **Repairs.** All repairs and restorations which are made during the lifetime of the Artist shall have the Artist's approval. To the extent practical, the Artist shall be given the opportunity to accomplish said repairs and restorations at a reasonable fee.

11. **Possession.** The Purchaser agrees that the Artist shall have the right to possession of the Work for up to _____ days every _____ years for the purpose of exhibition of the Work to the public, at no expense to the Purchaser. The Artist shall give the Purchaser written notice at least _____ days prior to the opening and provide proof of sufficient insurance and prepaid transportation.

12. **Nonassignability.** Neither party hereto shall have the right to assign this Agreement without the prior written consent of the other party. The Artist shall, however, retain the right to assign monies due to him or her under the terms of this Agreement.

13. **Heirs and Assigns.** This Agreement shall be binding upon the parties hereto, their heirs, successors, assigns, and personal representatives, and references to the Artist and the Purchaser shall include their heirs, successors, assigns, and personal representatives.

14. **Integration.** This Agreement constitutes the entire understanding between the parties. Its terms can be modified only by an instrument in writing signed by both parties.

15. **Waivers.** A waiver of any breach of any of the provisions of this Agreement shall not be construed as a continuing waiver of other breaches of the same or other provisions hereof.

16. **Notices and Changes of Address.** All notices shall be sent by registered or certified mail, return receipt requested, postage prepaid, to the Artist and Exhibitor at the address first given above unless indicated to the contrary here _____. Each party shall give written notification of any change of address prior to the date of said change.

17. **Governing Law.** This Agreement shall be governed by the laws of the State of _____.

IN WITNESS WHEREOF, the parties hereto have signed this Agreement as of the date first set forth above.

Artist_____   Purchaser_____

Contract to Create a Limited Edition

AGREEMENT made as of the _____ day of _____, 19____, between _____ (hereinafter referred to as the "Artist"), located at _____ and _____ (hereinafter referred to as the "Distributor"), located at _____.

WHEREAS, the Artist is a professional artist who creates art, including limited editions, for sale and exhibition; and

WHEREAS, the Distributor is in the business of publishing, promoting, distributing, and marketing limited editions; and

WHEREAS, the Artist and Distributor wish to work together with respect to the Artist's creation of a limited edition which shall be published by the Distributor pursuant to the terms and conditions of this Agreement.

NOW, THEREFORE, in consideration of the foregoing premises and the mutual covenants hereinafter set forth, and other valuable considerations, the parties hereto agree as follows:

1. **Creation and Title.** The Artist hereby agrees to create a limited edition (hereinafter referred to as the "edition") and warrants that the Artist shall be the sole creator of the edition, that the Artist is and shall be the owner of unencumbered title in the copyrights for the edition, and that no copies shall exist other than those specified in Paragraph 2.

2. **Description of the Edition and Artist's Certification.** The edition shall conform to the following description:

   Title _____

   Medium _____

   Colors _____

   Size _____

   Materials _____

   Number of copies _____

   Year fabricated _____

   At the conclusion of the creation of the edition, the Artist shall date, sign, and number the copies. The Artist shall certify to the Distributor that the edition conforms to the descriptive information in this Paragraph 2, and shall also certify the year fabricated; the authorized maximum number of copies to be signed or numbered; the authorized maximum number of unsigned or unnumbered copies; the number of proofs or samples created (including trial proofs, Artist's proofs, right to fabricate proof, other fabricator's proofs, Distributor's proofs, and any other proofs); the total size of the edition; whether or not the plates, stones, blocks, or other master image have been cancelled or altered (or, if not cancelled or altered, the restrictions and safeguarding of any master image); any prior or subsequent editions created from such master image; in the event of other editions, the size of all other editions and the series number of the present edition; and the name of the workshop, if any, where the edition was created.

3. **Copyright and Reproduction.** The Artist reserves all reproduction rights, including the right to claim statutory copyright, in the edition and any work created by the Artist during the process of creating the limited edition. The edition may not be photographed, sketched, painted, or reproduced in any manner whatsoever without the express, written consent of the Artist. The Artist shall have the right to control any further use of the fabricator's materials and the making of any derivative work based on the edition. The Artist does grant to the Distributor the nonexclusive right to include images of the edition in its catalog and other promotional materials, provided

such catalog and promotional materials are not offered for sale. The edition and all approved reproductions shall bear the following copyright notice: © by (Artist's name) 19____. The Distributor shall register the copyright with the Copyright Office within three months of publication.

4. **Artistic Control.** The Artist shall have artistic control over the creation of the edition. All artistic decisions shall be made solely by the Artist. The Artist shall have no obligation to sign the edition until the Artist is satisfied with its quality and deems it to be finished. If the fabricator is to be selected by the Distributor, the Artist shall in the exercise of his or her sole discretion have a right of approval over this selection.

5. **Costs of Creating the Edition.** The Distributor shall be solely responsible for and pay all costs of creating the edition. The Distributor shall contract directly with the fabricator or other party responsible for the mechanical processes of creating the edition. The Distributor shall pay any additional costs deriving from the Artist's exercise of artistic control pursuant to Paragraph 4.

6. **Advances to Artist.** The Artist shall receive nonrefundable advances of $_____, payable one-third on signing of this Agreement, one-third on approval of the fabrication of the edition based on an acceptable sample, and one-third on signing of the edition. In addition, the Artist shall at the time of signing receive ____ Artist's proofs from the edition which the Artist shall be free to sell at any time and in any territory at the price specified in Paragraph 7 and shall not share the proceeds of such sales with the Distributor.

7. **Territory, Term, and Termination.** The Distributor shall have the right to sell the edition in the following territory: _____ for a period of _____ years from the date first set forth above. The term shall automatically renew for additional one-year periods unless notice of termination is given by either party thirty days in advance of the renewal commencement. The Distributor's right shall be exclusive only with respect to the sale of the edition described in Paragraph 2, and the Artist shall remain free to create and sell art work of any kind.

8. **Pricing and Commissions.** The price for each copy shall be $____, which may be reduced up to 10 percent for normal trade discounts. Net receipts, which are monies actually received by the Distributor from the sale of the edition, shall be divided ____ percent to the Artist and ____ percent to the Distributor.

9. **Payments to the Artist and Accountings.** All monies payable to the Artist, after the subtraction of advances, shall be paid to the Artist on the last day of the month following the month of sale with an accounting showing the sale price, the name and address of the purchaser, the number of copies sold, and the inventory of copies remaining.

10. **Distributor's Proofs.** The Distributor shall receive ____ Distributor's proofs from the edition, which the Distributor agrees not to sell until after the date of termination determined pursuant to Paragraph 7. All other proofs shall be the property of the Artist.

11. **Title to Copies** Title in each copy sold shall remain in the Artist until such time as Artist has been paid in full pursuant to Paragraph 9 and title shall then pass directly to the purchaser. In the event of termination pursuant to Paragraph 7, title in ____ percent of the edition shall pass to the Distributor and the balance of the edition shall remain the property of and be returned to the Artist.

12. **Loss or Damage and Insurance.** The Distributor shall be responsible for loss of or damage to the edition from the date of delivery to the Distributor until the date of delivery to any purchaser or, if this Agreement is terminated pursuant to Paragraph 7, until the return of the Artist's portion of the edition to the Artist. Distributor shall maintain insurance for each copy at ____ percent of the sale price agreed to in Paragraph 8 and shall divide any insurance proceeds as if these proceeds were net receipts pursuant to Paragraph 8.

13. Promotion. The Distributor agrees to promote the edition in its catalog, by press releases, by direct mail, and by advertising for which the sum of $ _____ shall be spent. The Distributor agrees that all promotion shall be dignified and in keeping with the Artist's reputation as a respected professional. The Artist consents to the use of Artist's name and Artist's portrait, picture, or photograph in such promotion, provided that Artist shall have the right to review any such promotion and Distributor shall change such promotion if Artist objects on the ground that it is harmful to the Artist's reputation.

14. Nonassignability. Neither party hereto shall have the right to assign this Agreement without the prior written consent of the other party. The Artist shall, however, have the right to assign monies due to him or her under the terms of this Agreement.

15. Heirs and Assigns. This Agreement shall be binding upon the parties hereto, their heirs, successors, assigns, and personal representatives, and references to the Artist and the Distributor shall include their heirs, successors, assigns, and personal representatives.

16. Integration. This Agreement constitutes the entire understanding between the parties. Its terms can be modified only by an instrument in writing signed by both parties.

17. Waivers. A waiver of any breach of any of the provisions of this Agreement shall not be construed as a continuing waiver of other breaches of the same or other provisions hereof.

18. Governing Law. This Agreement shall be governed by the laws of the State of_____.

IN WITNESS WHEREOF, the parties hereto have signed this Agreement as of the date first set forth above.

Artist _____   Distributor _____

                                                              Company Name

                                         By _____

                                                  Authorized Signatory, Title

Contract for Receipt and Holding of Work

AGREEMENT made as of the _____ day of _____, 19_____, between _____ (hereinafter referred to as the "Artist"), located at _____, and _____ (hereinafter referred to as the "Recipient"), located at_____.

WHEREAS, the Artist is a professional artist of good standing; and

WHEREAS, the Artist wishes to leave certain works with the Recipient for a limited period of time; and

WHEREAS, the Recipient in the course of its business receives and holds works;

NOW, THEREFORE, in consideration of the foregoing premises and the mutual covenants hereinafter set forth and other valuable considerations, the parties hereto agree as follows:

1. **Purpose.** Artist hereby agrees to entrust the works listed on the Schedule of Works to the Recipient for the purpose of: _____.

2. **Acceptance.** Recipient accepts the listing and values on the Schedule of Works as accurate if not objected to in writing by return mail immediately after receipt of the artworks. If Recipient has not signed this form, any terms on this form not objected to in writing within ten days shall be deemed accepted.

3. **Ownership and Copyright.** Copyright and all reproduction rights in the works, as well as the ownership of the physical works themselves, are the property of and reserved to the Artist. Recipient acknowledges that the works shall be held in confidence and agrees not to display, copy, or modify directly or indirectly any of the works submitted, nor will Recipient permit any third party to do any of the foregoing. Reproduction, display, sale, or rental shall be allowed only upon Artist's written permission specifying usage and fees.

4. **Loss, Theft, or Damage.** Recipient agrees to assume full responsibility and be strictly liable for loss, theft, or damage to the works from the time of ❏ shipment by the Artist ❏ receipt by the Recipient until the time of ❏ shipment by the Recipient ❏ receipt by the Artist. Recipient further agrees to return all of the works at its own expense by the following method of transportation: _____. Reimbursement for loss, theft, or damage to a work shall be in the amount of the value entered for that artwork on the Schedule of Works. Both Recipient and Artist agree that the specified values represent the value of the work.

5. **Insurance.** Recipient ❏ does ❏ does not agree to insure the works for all risks from the time of shipment from the Artist until the time of delivery to the Artist for the values shown on the Schedule of Works.

6. **Holding Fees.** The artworks are to be returned to the Artist within _____ days after delivery to the Recipient. Each work held beyond _____ days from delivery shall incur the following daily holding fee: $_____ which shall be paid to the Artist on a weekly basis.

7. **Arbitration.** Recipient and Artist agree to submit all disputes hereunder in excess of $_____ to arbitration before _____ at the following location _____ under the rules of the American Arbitration Association. The arbitrator's award shall be final and judgment may be entered on it in any court having jurisdiction thereof.

8. **Miscellany.** This Agreement contains the full understanding between the parties hereto and may only be modified by a written instrument signed by both parties. It shall be governed by the laws of the state of _____.

IN WITNESS WHEREOF, the parties hereto have signed this Agreement as of the date first set forth above.

Artist_____   Recipient_____
                                                                                        Company Name

                                             By_____
                                                                         Authorized Signatory, Title

Schedule of Works

	Title	Medium	Description	Size	Value
1.	_____	_____	_____	____	_____
	_____	_____	_____	____	_____
2.	_____	_____	_____	____	_____
	_____	_____	_____	____	_____
3.	_____	_____	_____	____	_____
	_____	_____	_____	____	_____
4.	_____	_____	_____	____	_____
	_____	_____	_____	____	_____
5.	_____	_____	_____	____	_____
	_____	_____	_____	____	_____
6.	_____	_____	_____	____	_____
	_____	_____	_____	____	_____
7.	_____	_____	_____	____	_____
	_____	_____	_____	____	_____
8.	_____	_____	_____	____	_____
	_____	_____	_____	____	_____
9.	_____	_____	_____	____	_____
	_____	_____	_____	____	_____
10.	_____	_____	_____	____	_____
	_____	_____	_____	____	_____
11.	_____	_____	_____	____	_____
	_____	_____	_____	____	_____
12.	_____	_____	_____	____	_____
	_____	_____	_____	____	_____
13.	_____	_____	_____	____	_____
	_____	_____	_____	____	_____
14.	_____	_____	_____	____	_____
	_____	_____	_____	____	_____
15.	_____	_____	_____	____	_____
	_____	_____	_____	____	_____

Consignment Contract
with Record of Consignment and Statement of Account

AGREEMENT made as of the _____ day of _____, 19_____, between_____ (hereinafter referred to as the "Artist"), located at _____, and _____ (hereinafter referred to as the "Gallery"), located at _____.

WHEREAS, the Artist is a professional artist of good standing; and

WHEREAS, the Artist wishes to have certain works represented by the Gallery, and

WHEREAS, the Gallery wishes to represent the Artist under the terms and conditions of this Agreement,

NOW, THEREFORE, in consideration of the foregoing premises and the mutual covenants hereinafter set forth and other valuable considerations, the parties hereto agree as follows:

1. **Scope of Agency.** The Artist appoints the Gallery to act as Artist's ❑ exclusive ❑ nonexclusive agent in the following geographic area:_____ for the exhibition and sale of works in the following media: _____. This agency shall cover only work completed by the Artist while this Agreement is in force. The Gallery shall document receipt of all works consigned hereunder by signing and returning to the Artist a Record of Consignment in the form annexed to this contract as Appendix A.

2. **Term and Termination.** This Agreement shall have a term of _____ years and may be terminated by either party giving sixty days written notice to the other party. The Agreement shall automatically terminate with the death of the Artist, the death or termination of employment of _____ with the Gallery, if the Gallery moves outside of the area of _____, or if the Gallery becomes bankrupt or insolvent. On termination, all works consigned hereunder shall immediately be returned to the Artist at the expense of the Gallery.

3. **Exhibitions.** The Gallery shall provide a solo exhibition for the Artist of _____ days between _____ and _____ in the exhibition space located at _____ which shall be exclusively devoted to the Artist's exhibition for the specified time period. The Artist shall have artistic control over the exhibition of his or her work and the quality of reproduction of such work for promotional or advertising purposes. The expenses of the exhibition shall be paid for in the respective percentages shown below:

Exhibition Expenses	Artist	Gallery
Transporting work to Gallery (including insurance and packing)...........	_____	_____
Advertising...	_____	_____
Catalogs..	_____	_____
Announcements...	_____	_____
Frames..	_____	_____
Special installations..	_____	_____
Photographing work...	_____	_____
Party for opening..	_____	_____
Shipping to purchasers...	_____	_____
Transporting work back to artist (including insurance and packing)........	_____	_____
All other expenses arising from the exhibition............................	_____	_____

No expense which is to be shared shall be incurred by either party without the prior written consent of the other party as to the amount of the expense. After the exhibition, the frames, photographs, negatives, and any other tangible property created in the course of the exhibition shall be the property of _____.

4. **Commissions.** The Gallery shall receive a commission of ____ percent of the retail price of each work sold. In the case of discount sales, the discount shall be deducted from the Gallery's commission. If the Gallery's agency is exclusive, then the Gallery shall receive a commission of _____ percent of the retail price for each studio sale by the Artist that falls within the scope of the Gallery's exclusivity. Works done on a commissioned basis by the Artist ❑ shall ❑ shall not be considered studio sales on which the Gallery may be entitled to a commission.

5. **Prices.** The Gallery shall sell the works at the retail prices shown on the Record of Consignment, subject to the Gallery's right to make customary trade discounts to such purchasers as museums and designers.

6. **Payments.** The Gallery shall pay the Artist all proceeds due to the Artist within thirty days of sale. No sales on approval or credit shall be made without the written consent of the Artist and, in such cases, the first proceeds received by the Gallery shall be paid to the Artist until the Artist has been paid all proceeds due.

7. **Accounting.** The Gallery shall furnish the Artist with an accounting every _____ months in the form attached hereto as Appendix B, the first such accounting to be given on the first day of _____, 19____. Each accounting shall state for each work sold during the accounting period the following information: the title of the work, the date of sale, the sale price, the name and address of the purchaser, the amounts due the Gallery and the Artist, and the location of all works consigned to the Gallery that have not been sold. An accounting shall be provided in the event of termination of this Agreement.

8. **Inspection of Books.** The Gallery shall maintain accurate books and documentation with respect to all transactions entered into for the Artist. On the Artist's written request, the Gallery will permit the Artist or the Artist's authorized representative to examine these books and documentation during normal business hours of the Gallery.

9. **Loss or Damage.** The Gallery shall be responsible for the safekeeping of all consigned artworks. The Gallery shall be strictly liable for loss or damage to any consigned artwork from the date of delivery to the Gallery until the work is returned to the Artist or delivered to a purchaser. In the event of loss or damage that cannot be restored, the Artist shall receive the same amount as if the work had been sold at the retail price listed in the Record of Consignment. If restoration is undertaken, the Artist shall have a veto power over the choice of the restorer.

10. **Insurance.** The Gallery shall insure the work for ____ percent of the retail price shown in the Record of Consignment.

11. **Copyright.** The Gallery shall take all steps necessary to insure that the Artist's copyright in the consigned works is protected, including but not limited to requiring copyright notices on all reproductions of the works used for any purpose whatsoever.

12. **Security Interest.** Title to and a security interest in any works consigned or proceeds of sale under this Agreement are reserved to the Artist. In the event of any default by the Gallery, the Artist shall have all the rights of a secured party under the Uniform Commercial Code and the works shall not be subject to claims by the Gallery's creditors. The Gallery agrees to execute and deliver to the Artist, in the form requested by the Artist, a financing statement and such other documents which the Artist may require to perfect its security interest in the works. In the event of the purchase of any work by a party other than the Gallery, title shall pass directly from the Artist to the other party. In the event of the purchase of any work by the Gallery, title shall pass only upon full payment to the Artist of all sums due hereunder. The Gallery agrees not to pledge or encumber any works in its possession, nor to incur any charge or obligation in connection therewith for which the Artist may be liable.

13. Assignment. This Agreement shall not be assignable by either party hereto, provided, however, that the Artist shall have the right to assign money due to him or her hereunder.

14. Arbitration. All disputes arising under this Agreement shall be submitted to binding arbitration before _____ in the following location _____ and the arbitration award may be entered for judgment in any court having jurisdiction thereof. Notwithstanding the foregoing, either party may refuse to arbitrate when the dispute is for a sum of less than $_____.

15. Modifications. All modifications of this Agreement must be in writing and signed by both parties. This Agreement constitutes the entire understanding between the parties hereto.

16. Governing Law. This Agreement shall be governed by the laws of the State of _____.

IN WITNESS WHEREOF, the parties hereto have signed this Agreement as of the date first set forth above.

Artist _____   Gallery _____
Company Name

By_____
Authorized Signatory, Title

APPENDIX A: Record of Consignment

This is to acknowledge receipt of the following works on consignment:

Title	Medium	Description	Retail Price
1. _____	_____	_____	_____
2. _____	_____	_____	_____
3. _____	_____	_____	_____
4. _____	_____	_____	_____
5. _____	_____	_____	_____
6. _____	_____	_____	_____
7. _____	_____	_____	_____
8. _____	_____	_____	_____
9. _____	_____	_____	_____

Gallery _____
Company Name

By_____
Authorized Signatory, Title

APPENDIX B: Statement of Account

Date: _____, 19_____

Acounting for period from _____, 19_____, through _____, 19_____.

The following works were sold during this period:

Title	Date Sold	Purchaser's Name and Address	Sale Price	Gallery's Commission	Due Artist
1. _____	___	_____	_____	_____	_____
_____	___	_____	_____	_____	_____
2. _____	___	_____	_____	_____	_____
_____	___	_____	_____	_____	_____
3. _____	___	_____	_____	_____	_____
_____	___	_____	_____	_____	_____
4. _____	___	_____	_____	_____	_____
_____	___	_____	_____	_____	_____

The total due you of $_____ is enclosed with this Statement of Account.

The following works remain on consignment with the Gallery:

Title	Location
1. _____	_____
2. _____	_____
3. _____	_____
4. _____	_____
5. _____	_____
6. _____	_____
7. _____	_____
8. _____	_____
9. _____	_____

Gallery _____
                    Company Name

By_____
            Authorized Signatory, Title

Distribution Contract

AGREEMENT made as of the _____ day of _____, 19____, between _____ (hereinafter referred to as the "Artist"), located at _____, and _____ (hereinafter referred to as the "Distributor"), located at _____.

WHEREAS, Artist has developed and created inventory of a product or products and seeks distribution; and

WHEREAS, Distributor is in the business of distribution and wishes to distribute products of the Artist;

NOW, THEREFORE, in consideration of the foregoing premises and the mutual covenants hereinafter set forth and other valuable considerations, the parties hereto agree as follows:

1. **Duties of the Parties and Products Covered.** This Agreement shall provide the terms under which Distributor and Artist shall henceforth do business. The Artist shall perform at its sole expense and be solely responsible for the development and manufacture of products. The Distributor shall perform at its sole expense and be solely responsible for soliciting orders pursuant to the grant of rights in Paragraph 2, order processing and billing, maintaining and collecting accounts receivable, shipping and warehousing of products and processing of returns, and listing Artist's products in its catalog. The expense of and responsibility for promotion shall be determined pursuant to Paragraph 13 hereof. For each product to be distributed a Distribution Memorandum in the form attached hereto as Schedule A shall be completed and signed by the parties.

2. **Grant of Rights.** For each product, Artist grants to Distributor the ❑ exclusive ❑ nonexclusive rights to distribute and sell the products in the following markets:_____ and in the following territories: _____. All rights not granted to Distributor are reserved by Artist.

3. **Term.** For each product, this Agreement shall have a term ending one year after the distribution date, after which it is automatically renewed for periods of one year.

4. **Sale.** ❑ Artist agrees to sell products to Distributor at a discount of _____ percent off the suggested retail price. All products are purchased on a nonreturnable basis.

5. **Consignment.** ❑ Artist agrees to consign products to Distributor which agrees to pay Artist _____ percent of Distributor's net receipts for each product sold. Net receipts are defined as all proceeds received by the Distributor from sales of the product, except for proceeds received to cover shipping costs or sales tax. In no event shall Distributor sell products at a discount of more than _____ percent from retail price without obtaining the prior written consent of the Artist.

6. **Delivery.** Artist agrees to deliver the products by the delivery date set forth in each Distribution Memorandum. Freight and insurance charges for the delivery shall be paid by Distributor.

7. **Payment.** If products are sold pursuant to Paragraph 4, any payment to be made to the Artist at the time of signing for each product shall be specified in the Distribution Memorandum for that product and the remaining balance shall be payable _____ days after receipt of the inventory in Distributor's warehouse. If products are consigned pursuant to Paragraph 5, payment shall be due _____ days after the last day of the month in which the inventory was sold by the Distributor. Any advance for consigned inventory shall be specified in the Distribution Memorandum for each product, paid at the time of signing that Memorandum, and recouped from first proceeds due Artist hereunder. Time is of the essence with respect to payment. Consigned inventory shall be deemed sold in the accounting period in which the order is received. The Distributor shall bear the risk of any accounts which have purchased inventory consigned hereunder and prove to be uncollectible. Without limitation on any other rights or remedies available to Artist, if Distributor does not pay on time Artist may add a late payment charge of _____ percent per month on the unpaid balance.

8. **Statements of Account.** Distributor shall provide Artist with a monthly statement of account including, for each product, sales for the month and sales to date. If the products are consigned pursuant to Paragraph 5, the statement of account shall also show for each product the net receipts for the month and the amount due Artist.

Each statement of account shall be provided within _____ days after the last day of the month for which the accounting is given.

9. **Inspection of Books.** The Distributor shall maintain accurate books and documentation with respect to all transactions entered into for the Artist. Within two weeks of receipt of the Artist's written request, the Distributor shall permit the Artist or the Artist's authorized representative to examine these books and documentation during the normal business hours of the Distributor. If such inspection causes errors to be found which are to the Artist's disadvantage and represent more than 5 percent of the payment due the Artist pursuant to a statement of account, the cost of that inspection shall be paid for by the Distributor.

10. **Title and Security Interest.** Until such time that Distributor shall fully pay for any inventory pursuant to Paragraph 7, Artist retains and is vested with full title and interest to the inventory not paid for. For any inventory not paid for under this Agreement, a security interest in such inventory or any proceeds of sale therefrom is reserved to the Artist. In the event of any default by the Distributor, the Artist shall have the rights of a secured party under the Uniform Commercial Code and the inventory shall not be subject to claims by the Distributor's creditors. The Distributor agrees to execute and deliver to the Artist, in the form requested by the Artist, a financing statement and such other documents which the Artist may require to perfect its security interest in the inventory. Distributor agrees not to pledge or encumber any inventory to which Artist retains title, nor to incur any charge or obligation in connection therewith for which the Artist may be liable.

11. **Termination.** Either party may terminate this Agreement as to any product by giving the other party sixty days written notice prior to the renewal date. In the event the Distributor is in default of any of its obligations hereunder, the Artist may terminate this Agreement at any time by giving written notice to the Distributor. This Agreement shall automatically terminate in the event of the insolvency or bankruptcy of the Distributor. In the event of termination, Distributor shall at its own expense immediately return to the Artist all inventory consigned pursuant to Paragraph 5 and shall have the right to sell off books purchased pursuant to Paragraph 4 for a period of _____ months only. The rights and obligations of the Distributor pursuant to Paragraphs 7, 8, 9, 11, 12, and 14 shall survive termination hereunder.

12. **Risk of Loss or Damage and Insurance.** In the event the inventory is consigned pursuant to Paragraph 5, Distributor agrees that such inventory is the property of the Artist and shall keep it insured in the name of the Artist against all risks for _____ percent of retail value until it is sold or returned to the Artist. Distributor shall be liable to Artist for any damages to the consigned inventory arising from any cause whatsoever from the time Distributor receives possession through the time the inventory is sold or returned to the Artist. Distributor shall keep the consigned inventory in a warehouse area separate from any area containing products owned by the Distributor, and shall mark said area as containing products which are the property of the Artist.

13. **Promotion.** Distributor agrees to use best efforts to sell the products. Distributor shall include all products in its catalog and, in addition, promote each product as follows: _____

_____

Artist shall cooperate in promotional matters, providing samples, photos, and other material whenever possible, including advance information for Distributor's catalogs. Artist agrees to list information regarding the Distributor as follows:_____

_____

_____

14. **Sell-off Rights.** Commencing _____ months after the date of delivery, Distributor shall have the right to sell off inventory purchased pursuant to Paragraph 4 at whatever price Distributor shall determine, except that prior to any such sell off Distributor shall offer to sell the inventory to Artist at either the sell-off price or Distributor's purchase price, whichever is less. Artist shall accept or reject such offer within thirty days of receipt.

15. **Force Majeure.** If either party is unable to perform any of its obligations hereunder by reason of fire or other casualty, strike, act or order of a public authority, act of God, or other cause beyond the control of the party, then such party shall be excused from such performance during the pendency of such cause.

16. **Assignment.** This Agreement shall not be assignable by either party hereto, provided, however, that the Artist shall have the right to assign monies due to him or her hereunder, and the Distributor shall have the right to employ at its own cost and expense subdistributors or sales representatives to work for the Distributor in the sale and distribution of the Artist's products.

17. **Relationship of Parties.** The parties hereto are independent entities and nothing contained in this Agreement shall be construed to constitute a partnership, joint venture, or similar relationship between them.

18. **Arbitration.** All disputes arising under this Agreement shall be submitted to binding arbitration before _____ in the following location _____ and the arbitration award may be entered for judgment in any court having jurisdiction thereof.

19. **Notices and Changes of Address.** All notices shall be sent by registered or certified mail, return receipt requested, postage prepaid, to the Artist and Distributor at the addresses first given above unless indicated to the contrary here: _____. Each party shall give written notification of any change of address prior to the date of said change.

20. **Miscellany.** This Agreement shall be binding upon the parties and their respective heirs, successors, assigns, and personal representatives. This Agreement constitutes the entire understanding between the parties hereto and may not be modified, amended, or changed except by an instrument in writing signed by both parties. A waiver of any breach of any of the provisions of this Agreement shall not be construed as a continuing waiver of other breaches of the same or other provisions hereof. This Agreement shall be governed by the laws of the State of _____.

IN WITNESS WHEREOF, the parties hereto have signed this Agreement as of the date first set forth above.

Distributor_____
            Company Name

Artist_____
            Company Name

By_____
      Authorized Signatory, Title

By_____
      Authorized Signatory, Title

Schedule A: Distribution Memorandum

This Memorandum is to confirm that the product listed below is to be distributed pursuant to the contract between the parties dated as of the _____ day of _____, 19____.

Description _____

_____

Size _____

Additional specifications _____

_____

_____

_____

_____

Quantity _____

Retail price _____

Delivery date _____

Distribution date _____

If this product is consigned to Distributor, an advance of $_____ shall be paid on signing this Memorandum.

If this product is sold to Distributor, a partial payment of $_____ shall be paid on signing this Memorandum.

AGREED TO:

Distributor_____   Artist_____
            Company Name   Company Name

By_____   By_____
        Authorized Signatory, Title   Authorized Signatory, Title

Basic Distribution Contract

Artist's Letterhead

Distributor_____ Date_____

Address_____ Account Number_____

_____ Sales Rep_____

Ship to_____ Order Number_____

Address_____ Ship via_____

_____ Date shipped_____

Item Number	Description	Quantity Ordered	Quantity Shipped	Back Ordered	Retail Price	Commission	Unit Price	Amount Due on Sale

The merchandise shown above is consigned to the Distributor. Shipping costs to Distributor shall be paid by _____. At the end of each month, the Distributor shall render full payment with a statement of account detailing for each item the number sold, the amount due to the Artist after deduction of the Distributor's commission, and the remaining items still on consignment. In the event of loss or damage to any items, such items shall be treated as if sold during the month in which the loss or damage is discovered. Upon Artist's written request, Artist shall have the right to inspect the books of the Distributor during regular business hours. The Distributor shall not pledge or encumber any of the items consigned by the Artist. The Artist reserves a security interest in the consigned items pursuant to the Uniform Commercial Code, and the Distributor shall cooperate in the execution and signing of any documents which Artist may require to perfect the security interest. Neither party may assign its interest hereunder, although the Artist may assign monies due. All disputes in excess of $_____ arising under this Agreement shall be submitted to binding arbitration before _____ in the following location _____ and the arbitration award may be entered for judgement in any court having jurisdiction thereof. This agreement may only be modified in writing and shall be governed by the laws of the State of _____.

Other provisions: _____

_____.

IN WITNESS WHEREOF, the parties hereto have signed this Agreement as of the date shown above.

Artist_____ Distributor_____
                                                         Company Name

                                 By_____
                                              Authorized Signatory, Title

Contract with a Sales Representative

AGREEMENT made as of the _____ day of _____, 19_____, between _____ (hereinafter referred to as the "Artist"), located at _____, and _____ (hereinafter referred to as the "Sales Representative"), located at _____.

WHEREAS, Artist has created a crafts line for which he or she seeks sales representation; and

WHEREAS, Sales Representative is in the business of representing such lines;

NOW, THEREFORE, in consideration of the foregoing premises and the mutual covenants hereinafter set forth and other valuable considerations, the parties hereto agree as follows:

1. **Scope of Representation.** The Artist appoints the Sales Representative to act as Artist's ❏ exclusive ❏ nonexclusive sales representative in selling the following crafts lines_____ created by the Artist to ❏ retail ❏ wholesale crafts accounts in the following sales territory: _____ _____. House accounts, which are listed in Schedule A, are excluded from this Agreement and no commissions shall be payable on such accounts. Other accounts excluded from this Agreement include but are not limited to direct mail sales or other sales to individual buyers and_____.

2. **Term.** This Agreement shall have a term of _____ months, which shall be automatically renewed until the date of termination.

3. **Duties of the Parties.** The Sales Representative agrees to use his or her best efforts to promote and sell the Artist's products in the sales territory. The Artist shall use best efforts to have inventory sufficient to meet market demand in the territory handled by the Sales Representative, and shall make deliveries of all products sold by the Sales Representative, but shall have no liability for commissions with respect to orders which are not fulfilled for causes including but not limited to products which were not created, products which are out of stock, or products which are discontinued.

4. **Commissions.** For the services of the Sales Representative, the Artist agrees to pay Sales Representative a commission of ____ percent of the net receipts from all sales made by the Sales Representative to retail accounts and ____ percent of the net receipts from all sales made by the Sales Representative to wholesale accounts. Net receipts shall be all payments due the Artist for the products sold, less any deductions specified here:_____ _____. Commissions paid on sales which result in returns or bad debts shall be deducted from commissions due for the month in which the returns or bad debts are recorded.

5. **Payment.** Commissions shall be paid to the Sales Representative on a monthly basis at the time of rendering the Statement of Account for the month.

6. **Statements of Account.** Statements of account shall be given by the Artist to the Sales Representative on a monthly basis _____ days after the last day of the month accounted for. Each statement shall show for the month the net receipts from sales made by the Sales Representative to eligible accounts, the appropriate commission rates, the commissions due, and any deductions from commissions.

7. **Relationship of the Parties.** The parties hereto are independent entities and nothing contained in this Agreement shall be construed to constitute the Sales Representative an agent, employee, partner, joint venturer, or any similar relationship with or of the Artist. Further, the Sales Representative hereby indemnifies the Artist against any claim by the Sales Representative or others accompanying him or her with respect to injuries or damages sustained or caused while traveling, including but not limited to those caused while traveling by automobile or any other form of transportation.

8. **Assignment.** This Agreement shall not be assignable by either party hereto, provided, however, that the Sales Representative shall have the right to employ or commission at its own cost and expense other sales representatives to sell the Artist's works in the territory of the Sales Representative.

9. **Inspection of Books.** Each party shall maintain accurate books and documentation with respect to all transactions

entered into pursuant to this Agreement. Within two weeks of receipt of a written request by either party, the other party shall permit the requesting party or its authorized representative to examine these books and documentation during normal business hours.

10. **Termination.** Either party may terminate this Agreement by giving the other party sixty days written notice. In the event either party is in default of any of its obligations hereunder, the other party may terminate this Agreement at any time by giving written notice of termination. This Agreement shall automatically terminate in the event of the insolvency or bankruptcy of either party. The rights and obligations of the parties pursuant to Paragraphs 4, 5, and 7 shall survive termination hereunder.

11. **Arbitration.** All disputes arising under this Agreement shall be submitted to binding arbitration before _____ in the following location _____ and the arbitration award may be entered for judgment in any court having jurisdiction thereof.

12. **Notices and Changes of Address.** All notices shall be sent by registered or certified mail, return receipt requested, postage prepaid, to the Artist and Sales Representative at the addresses first given above unless indicated to the contrary here: _____

_____. Each party shall give written notification of any change of address prior to the date of said change.

13. **Miscellany.** This Agreement shall be binding upon the parties and their respective heirs, successors, assigns, and personal representatives. This Agreement constitutes the entire understanding between the parties hereto and may not be modified, amended, or changed except by an instrument in writing signed by both parties. A waiver of any breach of any of the provisions of this Agreement shall not be construed as a continuing waiver of other breaches of the same or other provisions hereof. This Agreement shall be governed by the laws of the State of _____.

IN WITNESS WHEREOF, the parties hereto have signed this Agreement as of the date first set forth above.

Sales Representative_____   Artist_____
Company Name   Company Name

By_____   By_____
Authorized Signatory, Title   Authorized Signatory, Title

Schedule A: House Accounts

Account Name	Address
1._____	_____
2._____	_____
3._____	_____
4._____	_____
5._____	_____
6._____	_____
7._____	_____
8._____	_____
9._____	_____

Contract with an Independent Contractor

AGREEMENT entered into as of the_____day of _____, 19____, between _____ (hereinafter referred to as the "Artist"), located at _____, and _____(hereinafter referred to as the "Contractor"), located at

_____.

The parties hereto agree as follows:

1. **Services to be Rendered.** The Contractor agrees to perform the following services for the Artist

_____
_____
_____
_____
_____
_____.

If needed, a list of procedures, diagram, or plan for the services shall be attached to and made part of this Agreement.

2. **Schedule**. The Contractor shall complete the services pursuant to the following schedule_____
_____
_____.

3. **Fee and Expenses.** The Artist shall pay the Contractor as follows:
   - ❏ Project rate $_____
   - ❏ Day rate $_____/ day
   - ❏ Hourly rate $_____/ hour
   - ❏ Other _____ $_____

The Artist shall reimburse the Contractor only for the expenses listed here _____
_____.

Expenses shall not exceed $_____. The Contractor shall provide full documentation for any expenses to be reimbursed, including receipts and invoices. An advance of $_____ against expenses shall be paid to the Contractor and recouped when payment is made pursuant to Paragraph 4.

4. **Payment.** Payment shall be made: ❏ at the end of each day ❏ upon completion of the project ❏ within thirty days of Artist's receipt of Contractor's invoice.

5. **Cancellation.** In the event of cancellation, Artist shall pay a cancellation fee under the following circumstances and in the amount specified _____
_____.

6. **Warranties**. The Contractor warrants as follows:

   (A) Contractor is fully able to enter into and perform its obligations pursuant to this Agreement.
   (B) All services shall be performed in a professional manner.
   (C) If employees or subcontractors are to be hired by Contractor they shall be competent professionals.
   (D) Contractor shall pay all necessary local, state, or federal taxes, including but not limited to withholding taxes, workers' compensation, F.I.C.A., and unemployment taxes for Contractor and its employees.

(E) Any other criteria for performance are as follows:

_____
_____.

7. Insurance. The Contractor shall maintain in force the following insurance _____

_____
_____.

8. Relationship of Parties. Both parties agree that the Contractor is an independent contractor. This Agreement is not an employment agreement, nor does it constitute a joint venture or partnership between the Artist and Contractor. Nothing contained herein shall be construed to be inconsistent with this independent contractor relationship.

9. Assignment. This Agreement may not be assigned by either party without the written consent of the other party hereto.

10. Arbitration. All disputes shall be submitted to binding arbitration before _____ in the following location _____ and settled in accordance with the rules of the American Arbitration Association. Judgment upon the arbitration award may be entered in any court having jurisdiction thereof. Disputes in which the amount at issue is less than $_____ shall not be subject to this arbitration provision.

11. Miscellany. This Agreement constitutes the entire agreement between the parties. Its terms can be modified only by an instrument in writing signed by both parties, except that oral authorizations of additional fees and expenses shall be permitted if necessary to speed the progress of work. This Agreement shall be binding on the parties, their heirs, successors, assigns, and personal representatives. A waiver of a breach of any of the provisions of this Agreement shall not be construed as a continuing waiver of other breaches of the same or other provisions hereof. This Agreement shall be governed by the laws of the State of _____.

IN WITNESS WHEREOF, the parties hereto have signed this as of the date first set forth above.

Artist_____   Contractor_____
                                                                Company Name

                                                  By_____
                                                                Authorized Signatory, Title

Rental Contract

AGREEMENT made as of the _____ day of _____, 19 _____, between _____ (hereinafter referred to as the "Artist"), located at _____ , and _____ (hereinafter referred to as the "Renter"), located at _____.

WHEREAS, the Artist is a recognized professional artist who creates work for rental and sale; and

WHEREAS, the Renter wishes to rent and have the option to purchase certain works by the Artist; and

WHEREAS, the parties wish to have the rentals and any purchases governed by the mutual obligations, covenants, and conditions herein;

NOW, THEREFORE, in consideration of the foregoing premises and the mutual covenants hereinafter set forth and other valuable considerations, the parties hereto agree as follows:

1. **Creation and Title.** The Artist hereby warrants that the Artist created and possesses unencumbered title to the works of art listed and described on the attached Schedule of Works ("the Schedule").

2. **Rental and Payments.** The Artist hereby agrees to rent the works listed on the Schedule at the rental fees shown thereon and the Renter agrees to pay said rental fees as follows: $_____ per_____.

3. **Delivery and Condition.** The Artist shall be responsible for delivery of the works listed on the Schedule to the Renter by the following date: _____. All costs of delivery (including transportation and insurance) shall be paid by _____. The Renter agrees to make an immediate written objection if the works upon delivery are not in good condition or appear in any way in need of repair. Further, the Renter agrees to return the works in the same good condition as received, subject to the provisions of Paragraph 4.

4. **Loss or Damage and Insurance.** The Renter shall be responsible for loss of or damage to the rented works from the date of delivery to the Renter until the date of delivery back to the Artist. The Renter shall insure each work against all risks for the benefit of the Artist up to _____ percent of the sale price shown in the Schedule and shall provide Artist with a Certificate of Insurance showing the Artist as the named beneficiary.

5. **Term.** The term of this Agreement shall be for a period of _____ months, commencing as of the date of the signing of the Agreement.

6. **Use of Work.** The Renter hereby agrees that the rental under this Agreement is solely for personal use and that no other uses shall be made of the work, such other uses including but not being limited to public exhibition, entry into contests, and commercial exploitation.

7. **Framing, Cleaning, Repairs.** The Artist agrees to deliver each work ready for display. The Renter agrees not to remove any work from its frame or other mounting or in any way alter the framing or mounting. The Renter agrees that the Artist shall have sole authority to determine when cleaning or repairs are necessary and to choose who shall perform such cleaning or repairs.

8. **Location and Access.** The Renter hereby agrees to keep the works listed on the Schedule at the following address: _____, which may be changed only with the Artist's written consent, and to permit the Artist to have reasonable access to said works for the purpose of taking photographs of same.

9. **Copyright and Reproduction.** The Artist reserves all reproduction rights, including the right to claim statutory copyright, on all works listed on the Schedule. No work may be photographed, sketched, painted, or reproduced in any manner whatsoever without the express, written consent of the Artist. All approved reproductions shall bear a copyright notice composed of the following elements: the word Copyright or © by (Artist's name) 19____.

10. Termination. Either party may terminate this Agreement upon fifteen days written notice to the other party. This Agreement shall automatically terminate in the event of the Renter's insolvency or bankruptcy. Upon termination, the Artist shall refund to the Renter a pro rata portion of any prepaid rental fees allocable to the unexpired rental term, said refund to be made after the works have been returned to the Artist in good condition.

11. Return of Works. The Renter shall be responsible for the return of all works upon termination of this Agreement. All costs of return (including transportation and insurance) shall be paid by _____.

12. Option to Purchase. The Artist hereby agrees not to sell any works listed on the Schedule during the term of this Agreement. During the term the Renter shall have the option to purchase any work listed on the Schedule at the sale price shown thereon. This option to purchase shall be deemed waived by Renter if he or she fails to make timely payments pursuant to Paragraph 2. If the Renter chooses to purchase any work, all rental fees paid to rent that work ❏ shall ❏shall not be applied to reduce the sale price. Any purchase under this paragraph shall be subject to the following restrictions:

(A) The Artist shall have the right to borrow any work purchased for up to sixty days once every five years for exhibition at a nonprofit institution at no expense to the Renter-Purchaser, provided that the Artist gives 120 days advance notice in writing prior to the opening and offers satisfactory proof of insurance and prepaid transportation.

(B) The Renter-Purchaser agrees not to permit any intentional destruction, damage, or modification of any work.

(C) If any work is damaged, the Renter-Purchaser agrees to consult with the Artist before restoration is undertaken and must give the Artist the first opportunity to restore the work, if practicable.

(D) The Renter-Purchaser agrees to pay the Artist any sales or other transfer tax due on the full sale price.

(E) The Renter agrees to make full payments of all sums due on account of the purchase within fifteen days after notifying the Artist of the Renter's intention to purchase.

13. Security Interest. Title to and a security interest in any works rented or sold under this Agreement is reserved in the Artist. In the event of any default by the Renter, the Artist shall have all the rights of a secured party under the Uniform Commercial Code and the works shall not be subject to claims by the Renter's creditors. Renter agrees to execute and deliver to the Artist, in the form requested by the Artist, a financing statement and such other documents which the Artist may require to perfect its security interest in the works. In the event of purchase of any work pursuant to Paragraph 12, title shall pass to the Renter only upon full payment to the Artist of all sums due hereunder. The Renter agrees not to pledge or encumber any works in his or her possession, nor to incur any charge or obligation in connection therewith for which the Artist may be liable.

14. Attorney's Fees. In any proceeding to enforce any part of this Agreement, the aggrieved party shall be entitled to reasonable attorney's fees in addition to any available remedy.

15. Nonassignability. Neither party hereto shall have the right to assign this Agreement without the prior written consent of the other party. The Artist shall, however, retain the right to assign monies due to him or her under the terms of this Agreement.

16. Heirs and Assigns. This Agreement shall be binding upon the parties hereto, their heirs, successors, assigns, and personal representatives, and references to the Artist and the Renter shall include their heirs, successors, assigns, and personal representatives.

17. Integration. This Agreement constitutes the entire understanding between the parties. Its terms can be modified only by an instrument in writing signed by both parties.

18. Waivers. A waiver of any breach of any of the provisions of this Agreement shall not be construed as a continuing waiver of other breaches of the same or other provisions hereof.

19. Notices and Changes of Address. All notices shall be sent to the Artist at the following address: _____ and to the Renter at the following address: _____ Each party shall give written notification of any change of address prior to the date of said change.

20. Governing Law. This Agreement shall be governed by the laws of the State of _____.

IN WITNESS WHEREOF, the parties have signed this Agreement as of the date first set forth above.

Artist _____   Renter _____

Schedule of Works

	Title	Medium	Size	Rental Fee	Sale Price
1.					
2.					
3.					
4.					
5.					
6.					
7.					
8.					
9.					
10.					
11.					
12.					
13.					
14.					
15.					

Contract for an Exhibition Loan

AGREEMENT made as of the _____ day of _____, 19 ____, between _____ (hereinafter referred to as the "Artist"), located at_____ and _____ (hereinafter referred to as the "Exhibitor"), located at _____.

WHEREAS, the Artist is a recognized professional artist who creates work for sale and exhibition; and

WHEREAS, the Exhibitor admires and wishes to exhibit the work of the Artist; and

WHEREAS, the parties wish to have the exhibition governed by the mutual obligations, covenants, and conditions herein,

NOW THEREFORE, in consideration of the foregoing premises and the mutual covenants hereinafter set forth and other valuable considerations, the parties hereto agree as follows:

1. **Creation and Title.** The Artist hereby warrants that the Artist created and possesses unencumbered title to the works of art listed and described on the attached Schedule of Works ("the Schedule") and has the right to loan these works for purposes of exhibition.

2. **Duration of Loan, Manner of Exhibition, and Fee.** The Artist hereby agrees to loan to the Exhibitor the works listed on the Schedule for the time period commencing _____, 19____, and concluding _____, 19____. The Exhibitor agrees to exhibit these works for no less than ____ days during this time period as part of the exhibition titled: _____. These works ❑ shall ❑ shall not be exhibited with the works of other artists. Other restrictions on the treatment of the works include:_____ _____. Upon signing of this Agreement, the Exhibitor shall pay the Artist a fee of $_____ for the right to exhibit the works.

3. **Delivery, Condition, and Care.** The Exhibitor shall be responsible for arranging to have the works listed on the Schedule shipped from the Artist's studio to the Exhibitor by the following method of transport: _____. All costs of delivery (including transportation and insurance) shall be paid by the Exhibitor. The Exhibitor agrees to transmit a written report to the Artist within five working days of the delivery of the works, specifying their condition and whether they appear in any way in need of repair. Further, the Exhibitor agrees to use the same standard of care for the works as it uses for comparable works in its own collection. The Exhibitor agrees to return the works in the same condition as received, subject to the provisions of Paragraph 4. The Exhibitor shall return the works by the date specified in Paragraph 2 for the conclusion of the loan and shall use the following method of transport: _____. The Exhibitor shall pay for the costs of delivery (including transportation and insurance) of the works back to the Artist.

4. **Loss or Damage and Insurance.** The Exhibitor shall be responsible for loss of or damage to the works from the time of shipment from the Artist through the time of delivery back to the Artist. The Exhibitor shall insure each work for the benefit of the Artist for the full value listed on the Schedule. This insurance shall be pursuant to a policy providing wall-to-wall all-risks coverage maintained in force by the Exhibitor. The Exhibitor shall provide a Certificate of Insurance for the works if the Artist so requests.

5. **Use of Work.** The Exhibitor hereby agrees that the loan of the works under this Agreement is solely for purposes of exhibition and that no other uses shall be made of the work, such other uses including but not being limited to commercial exploitation, broadcasts, or other reproduction. The Exhibitor further agrees that the works shall be kept at the following location: _____, and shall not be moved or displayed elsewhere without the express, written consent of the Artist.

6. **Framing, Installation, Cleaning, Repairs.** The Artist agrees to deliver each work ready for display unless framing, mounting, or a special installation is required. The Exhibitor agrees not to remove any work from its frame

or other mounting or in any way alter the framing or mounting. In the event framing, mounting, or a special installation is required for the display of any work, it shall be described on the Schedule of Works and paid for by _____. Exhibitor agrees that the Artist shall have sole authority to determine when cleaning or repairs are necessary and to choose who shall perform such cleaning or repairs.

7. Copyright and Reproduction. The Artist reserves all reproduction rights, including the right to claim statutory copyright, on all works listed on the Schedule. No work may be photographed, sketched, painted, or reproduced in any manner whatsoever without the express, written consent of the Artist. The Exhibitor may reproduce the works for its catalog of the exhibition and promotion related thereto for a fee of $_____. All approved reproductions shall bear the following copyright notice: © by (Artist's name) 19____.

8. Collection of the Artist. When displayed, each work shall be accompanied by a label or plaque identifying the work as a loan from the collection of the Artist. This label or plaque shall also include the following copyright notice: © by (Artist's name) 19____.

9. Termination of Right to Exhibit. The right to exhibit pursuant to this Agreement shall terminate as of the date specified in Paragraph 2. In the event of the failure of the Exhibitor to exhibit the works or in the event of an exhibition or other act in violation of the terms of this Agreement, the Artist shall have the right to terminate the right to exhibit under this Agreement by written notice to the Exhibitor. The right to exhibit pursuant to this Agreement shall automatically terminate in the event of the Exhibitor's insolvency or bankruptcy. In the event of termination of the right to exhibit pursuant to this Paragraph 9, the works shall be returned forthwith to the Artist pursuant to the provisions of Paragraph 4.

10. Nonassignability. Neither party hereto shall have the right to assign this Agreement without the prior written consent of the other party. The Artist shall, however, retain the right to assign monies due to him or her under the terms of this Agreement.

11. Heirs and Assigns. This Agreement shall be binding upon the parties hereto, their heirs, successors, assigns, and personal representatives, and references to the Artist and the Exhibitor shall include their heirs, successors, assigns, and personal representatives.

12. Integration. This Agreement constitutes the entire understanding between the parties. Its terms can be modified only by an instrument in writing signed by both parties.

13. Waivers. A waiver of any breach of any of the provisions of this Agreement shall not be construed as a continuing waiver of other breaches of the same or other provisions hereof.

14. Notices and Changes of Address. All notices shall be sent by registered or certified mail, return receipt requested, postage prepaid, to the Artist and Exhibitor at the addresses first given above unless indicated to the contrary here:_____ . Each party shall give written notification of any change of address prior to the date of said change.

15. Governing Law. This Agreement shall be governed by the laws of the State of _____.

IN WITNESS WHEREOF, the parties have signed this Agreement as of the date first set forth above.

Artist_____   Exhibitor_____
                                                                          Company Name

                                                     By_____
                                                                        Authorized Signatory, Title

Schedule of Works

	Title	Date Created	Medium	Size	Insurance Value	Framing, Mounting, or Installation	Condition
1.							
2.							
3.							
4.							
5.							
6.							
7.							
8.							
9.							
10.							
11.							
12.							
13.							
14.							
15.							
16.							
17.							
18.							
19.							
20.							
21.							
22.							
23.							
24.							
25.							
26.							
27.							
28.							
29.							

Lecture Contract

AGREEMENT made as of the _____ day of _____, 19 ____, between_____ (hereinafter referred to as the "Artist"), located at _____and _____(hereinafter referred to as the "Sponsor"), located at _____.

WHEREAS, the Sponsor is familiar with and admires the work of the Artist; and

WHEREAS, the Sponsor wishes the Artist to visit the Sponsor to enhance the opportunities for its students to have contact with working professional artists; and

WHEREAS, the Artist wishes to lecture with respect to his or her work and perform such other services as this contract may call for;

NOW, THEREFORE, in consideration of the foregoing premises and the mutual covenants hereinafter set forth and other valuable considerations, the parties hereto agree as follows:

1. **Artist to Lecture.** The Artist hereby agrees to come to the Sponsor on the following date(s): _____ and perform the following services: _____. The Artist shall use best efforts to make his or her services as productive as possible to the Sponsor. The Artist further agrees to bring examples of his or her own work in the form of _____.

2. **Payment.** The Sponsor agrees to pay as full compensation for the Artist's services rendered under Paragraph 1 the sum of \$_____. This sum shall be payable to the Artist on completion of the _____ day of the Artist's residence with the Sponsor.

3. **Expenses.** In addition to the payments provided under Paragraph 2, the Sponsor agrees to reimburse the Artist for the following expenses:

   (A) Travel expenses in the amount of \$_____.

   (B) Food and lodging expenses in the amount of \$_____.

   (C) Other expenses listed here:_____in the amount of \$_____.

   The reimbursement for travel expenses shall be made fourteen days prior to the earliest date specified in Paragraph 1. The reimbursement for food, lodging, and other expenses shall be made at the date of payment specified in Paragraph 2, unless a contrary date is specified here:_____.

   In addition, the Sponsor shall provide the Artist with the following:

   (A) Tickets for travel, rental car, or other modes of transportation as follows: _____ _____

   (B) Food and lodging as follows: _____ _____

   (C) Other hospitality as follows: _____ _____

4. **Inability to Perform.** If the Artist is unable to appear on the dates scheduled in Paragraph 1 due to illness, the Sponsor shall have no obligation to make any payments under Paragraphs 2 and 3, but shall attempt to re-schedule the Artist's appearance at a mutually acceptable future date. If the Sponsor is prevented from having the Artist appear by acts of God, hurricane, flood, governmental order, or other cause beyond its control,

the Sponsor shall be responsible only for the payment of such expenses under Paragraph 3 as the Artist shall have actually incurred. The Sponsor agrees in such a case to attempt to reschedule the Artist's appearance at a mutually acceptable future date.

5. **Late Payment.** The Sponsor agrees that, in the event it is late in making payment of amounts due to the Artist under Paragraphs 2, 3, or 8, it will pay as additional liquidated damages _____ percent in interest on the amounts it is owing to the Artist, and said interest is to run from the date stipulated for payment in Paragraphs 2, 3, or 8 until such time as payment is made.

6. **Copyrights and Recordings.** Both parties agree that the Artist shall retain all rights, including copyrights, in relation to recordings of any kind made of the appearance or any works shown in the course thereof. The term "recording" as used herein shall include any recording made by electrical transcription, tape recording, wire recording, film, videotape, or other similar or dissimilar method of recording, whether now known or hereinafter developed. No use of any such recording shall be made by the Sponsor without the written consent of the Artist and, if stipulated therein, additional compensation for such use.

7. **Insurance and Loss or Damage.** The Sponsor agrees that it shall provide wall-to-wall insurance for the works listed on the Schedule of Works for the values specified therein. The Sponsor agrees that it shall be fully responsible and have strict liability for any loss or damage to the works from the time said works leave the Artist's residence or studio until they are returned.

8. **Packing and Shipping.** The Sponsor agrees that it shall fully bear any costs of packing and shipping necessary to deliver the works specified in Paragraph 7 to the Sponsor and return them to the Artist's residence or studio.

9. **Modification.** This Agreement constitutes the entire understanding between the parties. Its terms can be modified only by an instrument in writing signed by both parties.

10. **Governing Law.** This contract shall be governed by the laws of the State of _____.

IN WITNESS WHEREOF, the parties hereto have signed this Agreement as of the date first set forth above.

Artist _____   Sponsor _____
                                                                                          Company Name

                                                              By _____
                                                                            Authorized Signatory, Title

Schedule of Works

	Title	Medium	Size	Value
1.				
2.				
3.				
4.				
5.				
6.				
7.				
8.				

Licensing Contract

AGREEMENT made as of the _____ day of _____, 19_____, between _____ (hereinafter referred to as the "Artist"), located at _____ and _____ (hereinafter referred to as the "Licensee"), located at _____.

with respect to the use of a certain image or design created by the Artist (hereinafter referred to as the "Image") for manufactured products (hereinafter referred to as the "Licensed Products").

WHEREAS, the Artist is a professional artist of good standing; and

WHEREAS, the Artist has created the Image which the Artist wishes to license for purposes of manufacture and sale; and

WHEREAS, the Licensee wishes to use the Image to create a certain product or products for manufacture and sale; and

WHEREAS, both parties want to achieve the best possible quality to generate maximum sales;

NOW, THEREFORE, in consideration of the foregoing premises and the mutual covenants hereinafter set forth and other valuable considerations, the parties hereto agree as follows:

1. **Grant of Merchandising Rights.** The Artist grants to the Licensee the ❏ exclusive ❏ nonexclusive right to use the Image, titled _____ and described as _____ _____, which was created and is owned by the Artist, as or as part of the following type(s) of merchandise: _____ _____ for manufacture, distribution, and sale by the Licensee in the following geographical area: _____ and for the following period of time: _____.

2. **Ownership of Copyright.** The Artist shall retain all copyrights in and to the Image. The Licensee shall identify the Artist as the creator of the Image on the Licensed Products and shall reproduce thereon a copyright notice for the Artist which shall include the word "Copyright" or the © by (Artist's name) 19____.

3. **Advance and Royalties.** Licensee agrees to pay Artist a nonrefundable advance in the amount of $_____ upon signing this Agreement, which advance shall be recouped from first royalties due here-under. Licensee further agrees to pay Artist a royalty of _____ percent of the net sales of the Licensed Products. "Net Sales" as used herein shall mean sales to customers less prepaid freight and credits for lawful and customary volume rebates, actual returns, and allowances. Royalties shall be deemed to accrue when the Licensed Products are sold, shipped, or invoiced, whichever first occurs.

4. **Payments and Statements of Account.** Royalty payments shall be paid monthly on the first day of each month commencing _____, 19 _____, and Licensee shall with each payment furnish Artist with a monthly statement of account showing the kinds and quantities of all Licensed Products sold, the prices received therefor, and all deductions for freight, volume rebates, returns, and allowances. The Artist shall have the right to terminate this Agreement upon thirty days notice if Licensee fails to make any payment required of it and does not cure this default within said thirty days, whereupon all rights granted herein shall revert immediately to the Artist.

5. **Inspection of Books and Records.** Artist shall have the right to inspect Licensee's books and records concerning sales of the Licensed Products upon prior written notice.

6. **Samples.** Licensee shall give the Artist _____ samples of the Licensed Products for the Artist's personal use. The Artist shall have the right to purchase additional samples of the Licensed Products at the Licensee's manufacturing cost.

7. **Quality of Reproductions.** The Artist shall have the right to approve the quality of the reproduction of the Image for the Licensed Products, and the Artist agrees not to withhold approval unreasonably.

8. **Promotion.** Licensee shall use its best efforts to promote, distribute, and sell the Licensed Products.

9. **Trademarks and Other Rights.** The Licensee's use of the Image shall inure to the benefit of the Artist if the Licensee acquires any trademarks, trade rights, equities, titles, or other rights in and to the Image whether by operation of law, usage, or otherwise during the term of this Agreement or any extension thereof. Upon the expiration of this Agreement or any extension thereof or sooner termination, Licensee shall assign and transfer the said trademarks, trade rights, equities, titles, or other rights to the Artist without any consideration other than the consideration of this Agreement.

10. **Reservation of Rights.** All rights not specifically transferred by this Agreement are reserved to the Artist.

11. **Indemnification.** The Licensee shall hold the Artist harmless from and against any loss, expense, or damage occasioned by any claim, demand, suit, or recovery against the Artist arising out of the use of the Image for the Licensed Products.

12. **Assignment.** Neither party shall assign rights or obligations under this Agreement, except that the Artist may assign the right to receive money due hereunder.

13. **Nature of Contract.** Nothing herein shall be construed to constitute the parties hereto joint venturers, nor shall any similar relationship be deemed to exist between them.

14. **Governing Law.** This Agreement shall be construed in accordance with the laws of _____; Licensee consents to the jurisdiction of the courts of _____.

15. **Addresses.** All notices, demands, payments, royalty payments, and statements shall be sent to the Artist at the following address: _____ and to the Licensee at: _____.

16. **Modifications in Writing.** This Agreement constitutes the entire agreement between the parties hereto and shall not be modified, amended, or changed in any way except by a written agreement signed by both parties hereto.

IN WITNESS WHEREOF, the parties have signed this Agreement as of the date first set forth above.

Artist_____   Licensee_____
                                                                  Company Name

                                             By_____
                                                        Authorized Signatory, Title

Release Form for Models

In consideration of _____ dollars ($_____), receipt of which is acknowledged, I, _____ , do hereby give _____ , his or her assigns, licensees, and legal representatives the irrevocable right to use my name (or any fictional name), picture, portrait, or photograph in all forms and media and in all manners, including composite or distorted representations, for advertising, trade, or any other lawful purposes, and I waive any right to inspect or approve the finished version(s), including written copy that may be created in connection therewith. I am of full age.* I have read this release and am fully familiar with its contents.

Witness_____   Model_____

Address_____   Address_____

Date _____, 19 ___

━━━━━━━━━━━━━━━━━━━ **Consent (if applicable)** ━━━━━━━━━━━━━━━━━━━

I am the parent or guardian of the minor named above and have the legal authority to execute the above release. I approve the foregoing and waive any rights in the premises.

Witness_____   Parent or Guardian_____

Address_____   Address_____

Date _____, 19 ___

* Delete this sentence if the subject is a minor. The parent or guardian must then sign the consent.

Property Release

In consideration of the sum of _____dollars ($_____),

receipt of which is hereby acknowledged, I, _____,

located at _____, do irrevocably authorize

_____, his or her assigns, licensees, heirs and legal representatives, to copyright, publish, and use in all forms and media and in all manners for advertising, trade, or any other lawful purpose, images of the following property which I own and have full and sole authority to license for such uses: _____ , regardless of whether said use is composite or distorted in character or form, whether said use is made in conjunction with my own name or with a fictitious name, or whether said use is made in color or otherwise or other derivative works are made through any medium.

I waive any right that I may have to inspect or approve the finished version(s), including written copy that may be used in connection therewith.

I am of full age and have every right to contract in my own name with respect to the foregoing matters. I have read the above authorization and release prior to its execution and I am fully cognizant of its contents.

Witness_____   Owner_____

Address_____   Date _____, 19_____

FORM VA
For a Work of the Visual Arts
UNITED STATES COPYRIGHT OFFICE

REGISTRATION NUMBER

_____

VA   VAU

EFFECTIVE DATE OF REGISTRATION

_____

Month   Day   Year

DO NOT WRITE ABOVE THIS LINE. IF YOU NEED MORE SPACE, USE A SEPARATE CONTINUATION SHEET.

1

TITLE OF THIS WORK ▼

NATURE OF THIS WORK ▼ See instructions

PREVIOUS OR ALTERNATIVE TITLES ▼

PUBLICATION AS A CONTRIBUTION If this work was published as a contribution to a periodical, serial, or collection, give information about the collective work in which the contribution appeared.   **Title of Collective Work ▼**

If published in a periodical or serial give: **Volume ▼**   **Number ▼**   **Issue Date ▼**   **On Pages ▼**

2

a

NAME OF AUTHOR ▼

DATES OF BIRTH AND DEATH
Year Born ▼   Year Died ▼

Was this contribution to the work a "work made for hire"?
☐ Yes
☐ No

AUTHOR'S NATIONALITY OR DOMICILE
Name of Country
OR { Citizen of ▶ _____
Domiciled in ▶ _____

WAS THIS AUTHOR'S CONTRIBUTION TO THE WORK
Anonymous? ☐ Yes ☐ No
Pseudonymous? ☐ Yes ☐ No

If the answer to either of these questions is "Yes," see detailed instructions.

NATURE OF AUTHORSHIP Check appropriate box(es). **See instructions**
☐ 3-Dimensional sculpture   ☐ Map   ☐ Technical drawing
☐ 2-Dimensional artwork   ☐ Photograph   ☐ Text
☐ Reproduction of work of art   ☐ Jewelry design   ☐ Architectural work
☐ Design on sheetlike material

NOTE

Under the law, the "author" of a "work made for hire" is generally the employer, not the employee (see instructions). For any part of this work that was "made for hire" check "Yes" in the space provided, give the employer (or other person for whom the work was prepared) as "Author" of that part, and leave the space for dates of birth and death blank.

b

NAME OF AUTHOR ▼

DATES OF BIRTH AND DEATH
Year Born ▼   Year Died ▼

Was this contribution to the work a "work made for hire"?
☐ Yes
☐ No

AUTHOR'S NATIONALITY OR DOMICILE
Name of Country
OR { Citizen of ▶ _____
Domiciled in ▶ _____

WAS THIS AUTHOR'S CONTRIBUTION TO THE WORK
Anonymous? ☐ Yes ☐ No
Pseudonymous? ☐ Yes ☐ No

If the answer to either of these questions is "Yes," see detailed instructions.

NATURE OF AUTHORSHIP Check appropriate box(es). **See instructions**
☐ 3-Dimensional sculpture   ☐ Map   ☐ Technical drawing
☐ 2-Dimensional artwork   ☐ Photograph   ☐ Text
☐ Reproduction of work of art   ☐ Jewelry design   ☐ Architectural work
☐ Design on sheetlike material

3

a
YEAR IN WHICH CREATION OF THIS WORK WAS COMPLETED This information must be given ◀ Year in all cases.

b
DATE AND NATION OF FIRST PUBLICATION OF THIS PARTICULAR WORK
Complete this information ONLY if this work has been published.
Month ▶ _____ Day ▶ _____ Year ▶ _____
◀ Nation

4

See instructions before completing this space.

COPYRIGHT CLAIMANT(S) Name and address must be given even if the claimant is the same as the author given in space 2. ▼

TRANSFER If the claimant(s) named here in space 4 is (are) different from the author(s) named in space 2, give a brief statement of how the claimant(s) obtained ownership of the copyright. ▼

MORE ON BACK ▶   • Complete all applicable spaces (numbers 5-9) on the reverse side of this page.
   • See detailed instructions.   • Sign the form at line 8.

DO NOT WRITE HERE

Page 1 of _____ pages

DO NOT WRITE ABOVE THIS LINE. IF YOU NEED MORE SPACE, USE A SEPARATE CONTINUATION SHEET.

5 **PREVIOUS REGISTRATION** Has registration for this work, or for an earlier version of this work, already been made in the Copyright Office?

☐ **Yes** ☐ **No** If your answer is "Yes," why is another registration being sought? (Check appropriate box) ▼

a. ☐ This is the first published edition of a work previously registered in unpublished form.

b. ☐ This is the first application submitted by this author as copyright claimant.

c. ☐ This is a changed version of the work, as shown by space 6 on this application.

If your answer is "Yes," give: **Previous Registration Number** ▼   **Year of Registration** ▼

6 **DERIVATIVE WORK OR COMPILATION** Complete both space 6a and 6b for a derivative work; complete only 6b for a compilation.

a. **Preexisting Material** Identify any preexisting work or works that this work is based on or incorporates. ▼

b. **Material Added to This Work** Give a brief, general statement of the material that has been added to this work and in which copyright is claimed. ▼

See instructions before completing this space.

7 **DEPOSIT ACCOUNT** If the registration fee is to be charged to a Deposit Account established in the Copyright Office, give name and number of Account.

Name ▼   **Account Number** ▼

CORRESPONDENCE Give name and address to which correspondence about this application should be sent.   Name/Address/Apt/City/State/ZIP ▼

Area Code and Telephone Number ►

Be sure to give your daytime phone ◄ number

8 **CERTIFICATION*** I, the undersigned, hereby certify that I am the

check only one ▼

☐ author

☐ other copyright claimant

☐ owner of exclusive right(s)

☐ authorized agent of _____

Name of author or other copyright claimant, or owner of exclusive right(s) ▲

of the work identified in this application and that the statements made
by me in this application are correct to the best of my knowledge.

Typed or printed name and date ▼ If this application gives a date of publication in space 3, do not sign and submit it before that date.

_____ **Date**► _____

☞ **Handwritten signature (X)** ▼

9 **Mail certificate to:**

Certificate will be mailed in window envelope

Name ▼

Number/Street/Apt ▼

City/State/ZIP ▼

⊚INSTRUCTIONS FOR SHORT FORM VA

For pictorial, graphic, and sculptural works

USE THIS FORM IF—
1. you are the **only** author and copyright owner of this work; *and*
2. the work was **not** made for hire, *and*
3. the work is completely new (does not contain a substantial amount of material that has been previously published or registered or is in the public domain).

If any of the above does not apply, you must use standard Form VA.
NOTE: Short Form VA is not appropriate for an anonymous author who does not wish to reveal his or her identity.

HOW TO COMPLETE SHORT FORM VA

■ Type or print in black ink.

■ Be clear and legible. (Your certificate of registration will be copied from your form.)

■ Give only the information requested.

■ Do **not** use continuation sheets or any other attachments.

1 Title of This Work

You must give a title. If there is no title, state "UNTITLED." If you are registering an unpublished collection, give the collection title you want to appear in our records (for example: "Jewelry by Josephine, 1995 Volume"). Alternative title: If the work is known by two titles, you also may give the second title. If the work has been published as part of a larger work (including a periodical), give the title of that larger work instead of an alternative title.

2 Name and Address of Author/Owner of the Copyright

Give your name and mailing address. (You may include your pseudonym followed by "pseud.") Also, give the nation of which you are a citizen or where you have your domicile (i.e., permanent residence).
Please give daytime phone and fax numbers, if available.

3 Year of Creation

Give the year in which you completed the work you are registering at this time. (A work is "created" when it is "fixed" in a tangible form. Examples: drawn on paper, molded in clay, stored in a computer.)

4 Publication

If the work has been published (i.e., if copies have been distributed to the public), give the complete date of publication (month, day, and year) and the nation where the publication first took place.

5 Type of Authorship in This Work

Check the box or boxes that describe the kind of material you are registering. Check *only* the authorship included in the copy you are sending with the application. For example, if you are registering illustrations but have not written the story yet, check only the box for "2-dimensional artwork".

6 Signature of Author

Sign the application in black ink.

7 Person to Contact for Rights and Permissions

This space is optional. You may give the name and address of the person or organization to contact for permission to use the work. You may also provide phone, fax, or e-mail information.

8 Mail Certificate to

This space must be completed. Your certificate of registration will be mailed in a window envelope to this address. Also, if the Copyright Office needs to contact you, we will write to this address.

9 Deposit Account

Complete this space only if you currently maintain a deposit account in the Copyright Office.

PRIVACY ACT ADVISORY STATEMENT Required by the Privacy Act of 1974 (P.L. 93-579)
The authority for requesting this information is title 17 U.S.C., secs.409 and 410. Furnishing the requested information is voluntary. But if the information is not furnished, it may be necessary to delay or refuse registration and you may not be entitled to certain relief, remedies, and benefits provided in chapters 4 and 5 of title 17 U.S.C.
The principal uses of the requested information are the establishment and maintenance of a public record and the examination of the application for compliance with legal requirements.
Other routine uses include public inspection and copying, preparation of public indexes, preparation of public catalogs of copyright registrations, and preparation of search reports upon request.
NOTE: No other advisory statement will be given in connection with this application. Please keep this statement and refer to it if we communicate with you regarding this application.

MAIL WITH THE FORM—-
• a $20.00 filing fee in the form of a check or money order (*no cash*) payable to "Register of Copyrights," **and**
• one or two copies of the work or identifying material consisting of photographs or drawings showing the work. See table below for the requirements for most works. **Note:** Inquire about the requirements for other works or for any work first published before 1978. Copies submitted become the property of the U.S. Government.

If you are registering	And the work is *unpublished*, send	And the work is *published*, send
2-dimensional artwork in a book, map, poster, or print	one complete copy or identifying material	two copies of the best published edition
3-dimensional sculpture, T-shirt design	identifying material	identifying material
a greeting card, pattern, commercial print or label, fabric, wallpaper	one complete copy or identifying material	one copy of the best published edition

Mail everything **(application form, copy or copies, and fee)** *in one package* to: Register of Copyrights
Library of Congress
Washington, D.C. 20559-6000

Questions? Call (202) 707-3000 between 8:30 a.m. and 5:00 p.m. Eastern Time, Monday through Friday. For forms, call (202) 707-9100 24 hours a day, 7 days a week.

SHORT FORM VA ■

For a Work of the Visual Arts
UNITED STATES COPYRIGHT OFFICE

REGISTRATION NUMBER

	VA	VAU

Effective Date of Registration

Month	Day	Year

Application Received

Examined By

Deposit Received	
One	Two

Correspondence ☐

Fee Received

TYPE OR PRINT IN BLACK INK. DO NOT WRITE ABOVE THIS LINE.

Title of This Work: **1**

Alternative title or title of larger work in which this work was published:

Name and Address of Author/Owner of the Copyright: **2**

Nationality or domicile:

Phone and Fax numbers: Phone ( )   Fax ( )

Year of Creation: **3**

If work has been published, Date and Nation of Publication: **4**

a. Date _____ _____ _____ (Month, day, and year all required)
   (Month)   (Day)   (Year)

b. Nation

Type of Authorship in This Work: (Check all that apply. **5**

☐ 3-Dimensional sculpture   ☐ Photograph   ☐ Map
☐ 2-Dimensional artwork   ☐ Jewelry design   ☐ Text
☐ Technical drawing   ☐ Architectural work

Signature of Author: **6**

*I certify that the statements made by me in this application are correct to the best of my knowledge.**

OPTIONAL

Name and Address of Person to Contact for Rights and Permissions: **7**

☐ Check here if same as #2 above

Phone and Fax numbers: Phone ( )   Fax ( )
E-mail address: E-mail

8

MAIL CERTIFICATE TO

Certificate will be mailed in window envelope

Name ▼

Number/Street/Apartment Number ▼

City/State/ZIP ▼

9

Deposit Account #_____

Name _____

_____

_____

_____

Permission Form

The Undersigned hereby grants permission to _____ (hereinafter referred to as the "Artist"), located at _____, and to the Artist's successors and assigns, to use the material specified in this Permission Form for the following artwork, design, book or other project _____

This permission is for the following material:

Nature of material _____

Source _____

Exact description of material, including page numbers_____

If published, date of publication _____

Publisher _____

Author(s) _____

This material may be used for the artwork, book, design, or other project named above and in any future revisions, derivations, editions, or electronic versions thereof, including nonexclusive world rights in all languages.

It is understood that the grant of this permission shall in no way restrict republication of the material by the Undersigned or others authorized by the Undersigned.

If specified here, the material shall be accompanied on publication by a copyright notice as follows_____
_____

and a credit line as follows _____.

Other provisions, if any: _____

If specified here, the requested rights are not controlled in their entirety by the Undersigned and the following owners must be contacted: _____
_____

One copy of this Permission Form shall be returned to the Artist and one copy shall be retained by the Undersigned.

_____   _____
Authorized Signatory   Date

_____   _____
Authorized Signatory   Date

<table>
<tr><td>**TRADEMARK/SERVICE MARK APPLICATION, PRINCIPAL REGISTER, WITH DECLARATION**</td><td>MARK (Word(s) and/or Design)</td><td>CLASS NO. (If known)</td></tr>
</table>

TO THE ASSISTANT COMMISSIONER FOR TRADEMARKS:

APPLICANT'S NAME:

APPLICANT'S MAILING ADDRESS:

(Display address exactly as it should appear on registration)

_____

_____

_____

APPLICANT'S ENTITY TYPE: (**Check one** and supply requested information)

Individual - Citizen of (Country):

Partnership - State where organized (Country, if appropriate): _____
Names and Citizenship (Country) of General Partners: _____

_____

_____

Corporation - State (Country, if appropriate) of Incorporation: _____

Other (Specify Nature of Entity and Domicile): _____

GOODS AND/OR SERVICES:

Applicant requests registration of the trademark/service mark shown in the accompanying drawing in the United States Patent and Trademark Office on the Principal Register established by the Act of July 5, 1946 (15 U.S.C. 1051 et. seq., as amended) for the following goods/services **(SPECIFIC GOODS AND/OR SERVICES MUST BE INSERTED HERE)**:

_____

_____

_____

_____

_____

BASIS FOR APPLICATION: (Check boxes which apply, **but never both the first AND second boxes**, and supply requested information related to each box checked.)

[ ] Applicant is using the mark in commerce on or in connection with the above identified goods/services. (15 U.S.C. 1051(a), as amended.) Three specimens showing the mark as used in commerce are submitted with this application.
- Date of first use of the mark in commerce which the U.S. Congress may regulate (for example, interstate or between the U.S. and a foreign country): _____
- Specify the type of commerce: _____
  (for example, interstate or between the U.S. and a specified foreign country)
- Date of first use anywhere (the same as or before use in commerce date): _____
- Specify intended manner or mode of use of mark on or in connection with the goods/services: _____
  (for example, trademark is applied to labels, service mark is used in advertisements)

[ ] Applicant has a bona fide intention to use the mark in commerce on or in connection with the above identified goods/services. (15 U.S.C. 1051(b), as amended.)
- Specify manner or mode of use of mark on or in connection with the goods/services: _____
  (for example, trademark will be applied to labels, service mark will be used in advertisements)

[ ] Applicant has a bona fide intention to use the mark in commerce on or in connection with the above identified goods/services, and asserts a claim of priority based upon a foreign application in accordance with 15 U.S.C. 1126(d), as amended.
- Country of foreign filing: _____   - Date of foreign filing: _____

[ ] Applicant has a bona fide intention to use the mark in commerce on or in connection with the above identified goods/services and, accompanying this application, submits a certification or certified copy of a foreign registration in accordance with 15 U.S.C 1126(e), as amended.
- Country of registration: _____   - Registration number: _____

NOTE: Declaration, on Reverse Side, MUST be Signed

DECLARATION

The undersigned being hereby warned that willful false statements and the like so made are punishable by fine or imprisonment, or both, under 18 U.S.C. 1001, and that such willful false statements may jeopardize the validity of the application or any resulting registration, declares that he/she is properly authorized to execute this application on behalf of the applicant; he/she believes the applicant to be the owner of the trademark/service mark sought to be registered, or if the application is being filed under 15 U.S.C. 1051(b), he/she believes the applicant to be entitled to use such mark in commerce; to the best of his/her knowledge and belief no other person, firm, corporation, or association has the right to use the above identified mark in commerce, either in the identical form thereof or in such near resemblance thereto as to be likely, when used on or in connection with the goods/services of such other person, to cause confusion, or to cause mistake, or to deceive; and that all statements made of his/her own knowledge are true and that all statements made on information and belief are believed to be true.

_____
DATE

_____
SIGNATURE

_____
TELEPHONE NUMBER

_____
PRINT OR TYPE NAME AND POSITION

INSTRUCTIONS AND INFORMATION FOR APPLICANT

TO RECEIVE A FILING DATE, THE APPLICATION <u>MUST</u> BE COMPLETED AND SIGNED BY THE APPLICANT AND SUBMITTED ALONG WITH:

1. The prescribed **FEE ($245.00)** for each class of goods/services listed in the application;
2. A **DRAWING PAGE** displaying the mark in conformance with 37 CFR 2.52;
3. If the application is based on use of the mark in commerce, **THREE (3) SPECIMENS** (evidence) of the mark as used in commerce for each class of goods/services listed in the application. All three specimens may be the same. Examples of good specimens include: (a) labels showing the mark which are placed on the goods; (b) photographs of the mark as it appears on the goods, (c) brochures or advertisements showing the mark as used in connection with the services.
4. An **APPLICATION WITH DECLARATION** (this form) - The application must be signed in order for the application to receive a filing date. Only the following persons may sign the declaration, depending on the applicant's legal entity: (a) the individual applicant; (b) an officer of the corporate applicant; (c) one general partner of a partnership applicant; (d) all joint applicants.

SEND APPLICATION FORM, DRAWING PAGE, FEE, AND SPECIMENS (IF APPROPRIATE) TO:

Assistant Commissioner for Trademarks
Box New App/Fee
2900 Crystal Drive
Arlington, VA 22202-3513

Additional information concerning the requirements for filing an application is available in a booklet entitled **Basic Facts About Registering a Trademark,** which may be obtained by writing to the above address or by calling: (703) 308-HELP.

INDEX

Books from Allworth Press

The Artist-Gallery Partnership: A Practical Guide to Consigning Art, Revised Edition
by Tad Crawford and Susan Mellon (softcover, 6 x 9, 128 pages, $16.95)

How to Start and Succeed as an Artist
by Daniel Grant (softcover, 6 x 9, 240 pages, $18.95)

The Artist's Resource Handbook, Second Edition
by Daniel Grant (softcover, 6 x 9, 248 pages, $18.95)

The Business of Being an Artist, Revised Edition
by Daniel Grant (softcover, 6 x 9, 272 pages, $18.95)

Artists Communities by the Alliance of Artists' Communities
(softcover, 6 3/4 x 10, 224 pages, $16.95)

The Fine Artist's Guide to Marketing and Self-Promotion
by Julius Vitali (softcover, 6 x 9, 224 pages, $18.95)

Arts and the Internet by V. A. Shiva
(softcover, 6 x 9, 208 pages, $18.95)

Caring for Your Art, Revised Edition
by Jill Snyder (softcover, 6 x 9, 192 pages, $16.95)

Fine Art Publicity: The Complete Guide for Galleries and Artists
by Susan Abbott and Barbara Webb (softcover, 8 1/2 x 11, 190 pages, $22.95)

Legal Guide for the Visual Artist, Third Edition
by Tad Crawford (softcover, 8 1/2 x 11, 256 pages, $19.95)

Business and Legal Forms for Fine Artists, Revised Edition
by Tad Crawford (softcover, 8 1/2 x 11, 144 pages, $16.95)

Licensing Art and Design, Revised Edition
by Caryn Leland (softcover, 6 x 9, 128 pages, $16.95)

The Artist's Complete Health and Safety Guide, Second Edition
by Monona Rossol (softcover, 6 x 9, 344 pages, $19.95)

The Copyright Guide by Lee Wilson
(softcover, 6 x 9, 192 pages, $18.95)

Uncontrollable Beauty: Toward a New Aesthetics
edited by Bill Beckley with David Shapiro (hardcover, 6 x 9, 448 pages, $24.95)

Lectures on Art, by John Ruskin, introduction by Bill Beckley
(softcover, 6 x 9, 264 pages, $18.95)

Please write to request our free catalog. To order by credit card, call 1-800-491-2808 or send a check or money order to Allworth Press, 10 East 23rd Street, Suite 210, New York, NY 10010. Include $5 for shipping and handling for the first book ordered and $1 for each additional book. Ten dollars plus $1 for each additional book if ordering from Canada. New York State residents must add sales tax.

To see our online catalog, visit the Allworth Press Web site at **www.allworth.com**